CW01083336

Cambridge English

Objective Proficiency

Teacher's Book

Online resources

Go to **www.cambridge.org/objectiveproficiency/teacher**
to access the additional resources available online.

Resources include:
- complete practice test with audio
- answer keys
- sample answers.

Annette Capel   Wendy Sharp

Second Edition

CAMBRIDGE
UNIVERSITY PRESS

University Printing House, Cambridge CB2 8BS, United Kingdom

Cambridge University Press is part of the University of Cambridge.

It furthers the University's mission by disseminating knowledge in the pursuit of education, learning and research at the highest international levels of excellence.

www.cambridge.org
Information on this title: www.cambridge.org/9781107670563

First published 2002
Second Edition 2013
3rd printing 2013

A catalogue record for this publication is available from the British Library

ISBN 978-1-107-64637-7 Student's Book with answers with Downloadable Software
ISBN 978-1-107-61116-0 Student's Book without answers with Downloadable Software
ISBN 978-1-107-67056-3 Teacher's Book
ISBN 978-1-107-67634-3 Class Audio CDs (2)
ISBN 978-1-107-61920-3 Workbook with answers with Audio CD
ISBN 978-1-107-62156-5 Workbook without answers with Audio CD
ISBN 978-1-107-63368-1 Student's Book Pack (Student's Book with answers with Downloadable Software and Class Audio CDs (2))

Contents

Acknowledgements

The authors would like to thank Graham Burton for his meticulous editorial work at manuscript stage, Alyson Maskell for her constructive comments and careful management of proof stages, and Una Yeung of Cambridge University Press for her help and support throughout the project.

This product is informed by the English Vocabulary Profile, built as part of English Profile, a collaborative programme designed to enhance the learning, teaching and assessment of English worldwide. Its main funding partners are Cambridge University Press and Cambridge ESOL and its aim is to create a 'profile' for English linked to the Common European Framework of Reference for Languages (CEFR). English Profile outcomes, such as the English Vocabulary Profile, will provide detailed information about the language that learners can be expected to demonstrate at each CEFR level, offering a clear benchmark for learners' proficiency. For more information, please visit www.englishprofile.org

Development of this publication has made use of the Cambridge English Corpus (CEC). The CEC is a computer database of contemporary spoken and written English, which currently stands at over one billion words. It includes British English, American English and other varieties of English. It also includes the Cambridge Learner Corpus, developed in collaboration with the University of Cambridge ESOL Examinations. Cambridge University Press has built up the CEC to provide evidence about language use that helps to produce better language teaching materials.

The authors and publishers acknowledge the following sources of copyright material and are grateful for the permissions granted. While every effort has been made, it has not always been possible to identify the sources of all the material used, or to trace all copyright holders. If any omissions are brought to our notice, we will be happy to include the appropriate acknowledgements on reprinting.

Cambridge ESOL for the table on p. 24 and the sample answer sheets on pages 153–157. Reproduced with permission of Cambridge ESOL © 2013

The Guardian 26/2/2001, for the listening exercise on p. 121 adapted from 'Why I dumped the City job with the six-figure salary' by Bruce Robinson, *The Guardian* 3/4/2001;

BBC Radio 3 for the listening exercise on p. 48 from *Music Machine* originally broadcast 26 January 1999;

The Times 24/11/1999, for the listening exercise on p. 91 (Extract 3) adapted from 'Glad to be a Gaia' by Anjana Ahuja *The Times* 15/5/2000. Copyright © The Times 2000, 1999;

Mark Wilbur for the listening exercise on p. 74 (Extract 3) adapted from Doubting to shuo www.toshuo.com. Reproduced with permission;

BBC Wildlife Magazine for the listening exercise on p. 91 (Extract 1) from *My Kind of Life* by Sue Beenstock, January 2001.

Map of Objective Proficiency Student's Book

TOPIC	LESSON FOCUS	EXAM SKILLS	GRAMMAR	VOCABULARY
Unit 1 **Ring the changes** 8–13 Talking about change	1.1 Listening and Vocabulary 1.2 Grammar 1.3 Reading into Writing	Paper 1 Reading and Use of English: 1 Paper 2 Writing: 1 Summarising ideas Paper 3 Listening: 4	Perfect tenses	Introduction to idioms Phrasal verbs Word formation – suffix endings
Exam folder 1 14–15		Paper 1 Reading and Use of English: 3 Word formation		
Unit 2 **Expectation** 16–21 Expectations	2.1 Reading and Vocabulary 2.2 Grammar and Vocabulary 2.3 Listening and Speaking	Paper 1 Reading and Use of English: 7 Paper 3 Listening: 1 Paper 4 Speaking: 1	Aspects of the future Pronunciation: homophones	Collocations with *traveller* Prepositional phrases *Have no* + noun Phrases – nouns with related verbs
Writing folder 1 22–23		Paper 2 Writing: 1 Essay		
Unit 3 **Strange behaviour** 24–29 Human and animal behaviour	3.1 Listening and Vocabulary 3.2 Grammar 3.3 Reading into Writing	Paper 1 Reading and Use of English: 2 Paper 2 Writing: 1 Reformulation	Conditional clauses	Phrases – fixed pairs of words Modifiers – *quite, rather, fairly* Word formation – negative adjectives
Exam folder 2 30–31		Paper 1 Reading and Use of English: 2 and 4 Open cloze Key word transformations		
Unit 4 **Sweet rituals** 32–37 Food and ritual	4.1 Reading and Vocabulary 4.2 Grammar and Vocabulary 4.3 Listening and Speaking	Paper 1 Reading and Use of English: 5 Paper 4 Speaking: 2	Past tenses	Collocations Compound adjectives Adjectives and idioms to do with food
Writing folder 2 38–39		Paper 2 Writing: 2 Review		
Revision Units 1–4 40–41				
Unit 5 **The consumer society** 42–47 Advertising, shopping	5.1 Listening and Vocabulary 5.2 Grammar and Vocabulary 5.3 Reading into Writing	Paper 1 Reading and Use of English: 1 Paper 2 Writing: 1 Working with two texts Paper 3 Listening: 2	Countable/ uncountable nouns Possession Spelling	Phrasal verbs Phrases with *right* Prepositions Abstract nouns
Exam folder 3 48–49		Paper 1 Reading and Use of English: 1 Multiple-choice cloze		
Unit 6 **The sound of music** 50–55 Music	6.1 Reading and Vocabulary 6.2 Grammar 6.3 Listening and Speaking	Paper 1 Reading and Use of English: 2, 4 and 6 Paper 3 Listening: 2 Paper 4 Speaking: 2	Degrees of likelihood Pronunciation: contrastive stress	Phrases with *take* Collocations with adjectives and adverbs Idioms with music words
Writing folder 3 56–57		Paper 2 Writing: 1 Essay		
Unit 7 **Before your very eyes** 58–63 Art and sight	7.1 Listening and Vocabulary 7.2 Grammar 7.3 Reading into Writing	Paper 1 Reading and Use of English: 3 Paper 2 Writing: 1 Exemplifying your ideas Paper 3 Listening: 1	Participle clauses	Idioms with *eye* Extended noun phrases Adjectives showing disapproval
Exam folder 4 64–65		Paper 1 Reading and Use of English: 7 Multiple matching		

TOPIC	LESSON FOCUS	EXAM SKILLS	GRAMMAR	VOCABULARY
Unit 8 **Urban jungle** 66–71 City living	8.1 Reading and Vocabulary 8.2 Grammar and Vocabulary 8.3 Listening, Speaking and Vocabulary	Paper 1 Reading and Use of English: 4 and 7 Paper 4 Speaking: 3	Inversion	Compound adjectives Phrases with *place*
Writing folder 4 72–73		Paper 2 Writing: 2 Set text question: Film tie-in		
Revision Units 5–8 74–75				
Unit 9 **Fitting in** 76–81 Attitudes	9.1 Listening and Vocabulary 9.2 Grammar and Vocabulary 9.3 Reading into Writing	Paper 1 Reading and Use of English: 2 and 4 Paper 2 Writing: 1 Linking Paper 3 Listening: 4	Gerunds and infinitives	Phrases with *come* Prefixes Linking words and phrases Personal appearance, personality
Exam folder 5 82–83		Paper 1 Reading and Use of English: 6 Gapped text		
Unit 10 **Globalisation** 84–89 Language and culture	10.1 Reading and Vocabulary 10.2 Grammar and Vocabulary 10.3 Listening and Speaking	Paper 1 Reading and Use of English: 1, 3 and 4 Paper 3 Listening: 1 Paper 4 Speaking: 2	Reference devices Expressing wishes and preferences Pronunciation: word stress	Expressions with *turn*
Writing folder 5 90–91		Paper 2 Writing: 2 Article		
Unit 11 **For better, for worse** 92–97 Relationships	11.1 Listening and Vocabulary 11.2 Grammar 11.3 Reading into Writing	Paper 1 Reading and Use of English: 2 and 3 Paper 2 Writing: 1 Reformulation 2 Paper 3 Listening: 3	Gradability	Phrasal verbs Idioms to do with relationships
Exam folder 6 98–99		Paper 3 Listening: 4 Multiple matching		
Unit 12 **At the cutting edge** 100–105 Scientific advances	12.1 Reading and Vocabulary 12.2 Grammar 12.3 Listening and Speaking	Paper 1 Reading and Use of English: 1, 4 and 6 Paper 4 Speaking: 3	Passive structures Pronunciation: stress and emphasis	Idioms with technical words Phrases with *set*
Writing folder 6 106–107		Paper 2 Writing: 2 Report		
Revision Units 9–12 108–109				
Unit 13 **Save the planet** 110–115 The environment	13.1 Listening and Vocabulary 13.2 Grammar 13.3 Reading into Writing	Paper 1 Reading and Use of English: 1 and 2 Paper 2 Writing: 1 Giving opinions Paper 3 Listening: 1	Reported speech	Vocabulary – the environment Register Synonyms
Exam folder 7 116–117		Paper 1 Reading and Use of English: 5 Multiple-choice text		
Unit 14 **Get fit, live longer!** 118–123 Sport and health	14.1 Reading and Vocabulary 14.2 Grammar and Vocabulary 14.3 Listening and Speaking	Paper 1 Reading and Use of English: 4 and 7 Paper 3 Listening: 3 Paper 4 Speaking: 2	Articles review Pronunciation: noun/verb/adjective stress	Register Phrases with *live* Phrases with nouns and no article Prepositions Word formation
Writing folder 7 124–125		Paper 2 Writing: 2 Letter		

Content of Cambridge English: Proficiency (CPE)

Cambridge English: Proficiency, also known as *Certificate of Proficiency in English (CPE)* consists of four papers. The Reading and Use of English paper carries 40% of the marks while the Writing, Listening and Speaking papers each carry 20% of the marks. It is not necessary to pass all four papers in order to pass the examination. If you achieve a grade A, B or C in the examination, you will receive the *Cambridge English: Proficiency* certificate at Level C2. If your performance is below Level C2, but falls within Level C1, then you will receive a *Cambridge English* certificate stating that you have demonstrated ability at C1 level.

As well as being told your grade, you will also be given a Statement of Results – a graphical profile of your performance, i.e. it will show whether you have done especially well or badly on some of the papers.

Paper 1 Reading and Use of English 1 hour 30 minutes

There are seven parts to this paper and they are always in the same order. For Parts 1 to 4, the test contains texts with accompanying grammar and vocabulary tasks, and separate items with a grammar and vocabulary focus. For Parts 5 to 7, the test contains a range of texts and accompanying reading comprehension tasks. The texts are from books (fiction and non-fiction), non-specialist articles from magazines, newspapers and the internet.

Part	Task Type	Number of Questions	Task Format	Objective Exam Folder
1	Multiple-choice cloze	8	You must choose which word from four answers completes each of the gaps in a text.	**3** (48–49)
2	Open cloze	8	You must complete a text with eight gaps using only one word in each gap.	**2** (30–31)
3	Word formation	8	You need to use the right form of a given word to fill each of eight gaps in a text.	**1** (14–15)
4	Key word transformations	6	You must complete a sentence with a given word, so that it means the same as the first sentence.	**2** (30–31)
5	Multiple-choice text	6	You must read a text and answer the questions by finding the relevant information in the text.	**7** (116–117)
6	Gapped text	7	You must read a text from which paragraphs have been removed and placed in jumbled order, together with an additional paragraph, after the text. You need to decide from where in the text the paragraphs have been removed.	**5** (82–83)
7	Multiple matching	10	You read a text or several short texts, preceded by multiple-matching questions. You must match a prompt to elements in the text.	**4** (64–65)

Paper 2 Writing 1 hour 30 minutes

There are two parts to this paper. Part 1 is compulsory, you have to answer it. In Part 2 there are five questions and you must choose one. Each part carries equal marks and you are expected to write 240–280 words for Part 1 and 280–320 words for Part 2.

Part	Task Type	Number of Tasks	Task Format	Objective Writing Folder or Unit
1	Question 1 An essay with a discursive focus	1 compulsory	You are given two short texts and you must write an essay summarising and evaluating the key ideas contained in the texts.	WF 1 (22–23); U1 (12–13); U3 (28–29); U5 (46–47); U7 (62–63); U9 (80–81); U11 (96–97); U13 (114–115); U15 (130–131); U17 (148–149); U19 (164–165)
2	Questions 2–4 • an article • a letter • a report • a review Question 5 Choice of two questions – one on each of the specified set texts: article, essay, letter, review, report	5 choose one	You are given a choice of topics which you have to respond to in the way specified.	Essay WF 3 (56–57) Article WF 5, 9 and 10 (90–91; 158–159; 174–175) Letter WF 7 and 10 (124–125; 174–175) Review WF 2 (38–39) Report WF 6 (106–107) Set text: Film tie-in WF 4 (72–73) Set text: Review WF 8 (140–141)

Paper 3 Listening about 40 minutes

There are four parts to this paper. Each part is heard twice. The texts are a variety of types either with one speaker or more than one.

Part	Task Type	Number of Questions	Task Format	Objective Exam Folder
1	Multiple-choice questions	6	You hear three short, unrelated extracts, with either one or two speakers. You must answer two questions on each extract, choosing from A, B or C.	9 (150–151)
2	Sentence completion	9	You must complete spaces in sentences with information given by one speaker.	8 (132–133)
3	Multiple-choice questions	5	You will hear two or more speakers interacting. You must choose your answer from A, B, C or D.	9 (150–151)
4	Multiple matching	10	There are two tasks, each task containing five questions. You must select five correct options from a list of eight.	6 (98–99)

Paper 4 Speaking about 16 minutes

There are three parts to this paper. There are usually two of you taking the examination and two examiners. This paper tests your accuracy, vocabulary, pronunciation and ability to communicate and manage the tasks.

Part	Task Type	Time	Task Format	Objective Exam Folder
1	The interviewer asks each candidate some questions	2 minutes	You will be asked some questions about yourself and asked to express personal opinions.	10 (166–167)
2	Two-way conversation between candidates	4 minutes	You will be given visual and written prompts which are used in a decision-making task.	10 (166–167)
3	A long turn for each candidate followed by a discussion on related topics	10 minutes in total	You will be given a written question to respond to. You will then be asked to engage in a discussion on related topics.	10 (166–167)

Introduction to the Second Edition

What is new about this second edition?

Although the basic structure and approach of *Objective Proficiency* remains the same, you will find a lot that is new. The second edition has addressed all the changes in specification to the *Cambridge English: Proficiency* (*CPE*) examination (2013) and the material has also been informed by the English Vocabulary Profile – see below.

Student's Book with Downloadable Practice Material

In the Student's Book, the unit topics are unchanged but many of the texts are new, together with new illustrations and photos, additional exercises and new audio recordings. Special attention has been paid to the compulsory task on Paper 2 Writing. Ten new Reading into Writing lessons offer systematic training for this exam task and also develop relevant sub-skills for academic writing.

A set of online interactive exercises provides extra practice in reading, listening, writing, grammar and vocabulary. The software includes full answer keys and recording scripts and is available to download for free from www.cambridge.org/objectiveproficiency/student

Workbook with Audio CD

The Workbook has been revised and extended to provide more practice in grammar, vocabulary, reading, writing and listening, with a new audio CD component.

Teacher's Book with Downloadable Teacher's Resources

The Teacher's Book provides lesson plans, detailed unit notes, answer keys and sample answers for all writing tasks, recording scripts, extension activities and background information. There are also photocopiable recording scripts for certain activities.

Additional Teacher's Resources, including a photocopiable complete practice test for *Cambridge English: Proficiency* with audio, answer keys and sample answers, are available to download for free from www.cambridge.org/objectiveproficiency/teacher

What is English Profile?

English Profile is a long-term research programme that is seeking to describe what learners know and can do in English at each level of the Common European Framework of Reference (CEFR). The CEFR is 'language-neutral', as it is designed to work for all languages. A number of English Profile projects, initially targeting grammar, functions, and vocabulary, will illustrate in detail what the CEFR means for English.

English Profile researchers make extensive use of various corpora of language data, including the largest analysed corpus of learner data in the world: the Cambridge Learner Corpus. This contains learner writing at all levels of the CEFR from more than 200 countries.

What is the English Vocabulary Profile?

Over four years in research and development, the English Vocabulary Profile is an interactive web resource that provides detailed information on the words, phrases, phrasal verbs and idioms that are known by learners at each level of the CEFR. There are around 7,000 headword entries included up to C2 level.

Each entry presents the individual meanings and uses of a word in CEFR order, to suggest learning priorities. For example, the entry for the word *line* includes the core meaning of the noun LONG MARK – as in *write on the line* – at A2, RAILWAY – a railway track – at B1, PRODUCT – a type of product that a company sells – at C1, and a number of idioms featuring the noun at C2: *toe the line, the bottom line, (put yourself) on the line*, etc. The verb *line* and two related phrasal verbs are also included within the entry.

The English Vocabulary Profile lists many common phrases within its entries too: the entry for the noun *way* includes 22 phrases across the CEFR levels, such as *by the way* at A2, *one way or another* at B2, and *go out of your way (to do something)* at C2. Phrasal verbs are included at the end of an entry, and it is possible to search for words, phrases, phrasal verbs and idioms as separate categories by level.

How has this new edition of *Objective Proficiency* been informed by the English Vocabulary Profile?

The authors have made use of the online resource to add to the breadth and reliability of the course content, providing additional level-appropriate words, phrases, phrasal verbs and idioms for individual units. The *Idiom spot* and *Phrase spot* sections have been revised in this way to ensure they continue to represent current usage.

Successful candidates at *Cambridge English: Proficiency* must demonstrate 'exceptional English ability' and this mastery of the language presupposes a very wide command of vocabulary. To this end, *Objective Proficiency* also features words and phrases that lie outside the scope of the English Vocabulary Profile.

How to get involved in English Profile

The English Profile Programme is developing a new corpus of learner English – the Cambridge English Profile Corpus – which will include both spoken and written data. You and your students can get involved! Joining the data contributor network is straightforward and has many benefits. Visit the English Profile website to find out more at www.englishprofile.org, where you will also be able to sign up to the English Vocabulary Profile for free.

1 Ring the changes

1.1	
Exam skills	Listening Paper 3 Part 4
	Reading and Use of English Paper 1
	Part 1
Vocabulary	Introduction to idioms
	Phrasal verbs
1.2	
Grammar	Perfect tenses
1.3	
Exam skills	Reading into Writing: Summarising
	ideas – Paper 2 Part 1
Vocabulary	Word formation – suffix endings:
	-al, -ful, -less, -able, -ive, -ous
Workbook contents	
1, 2, 3, 4	Reading
5	Grammar – tenses
6, 7, 8, 9	Vocabulary

1.1 SB pages 8–9

Throughout the unit notes, approximate timings are given for guidance. These relate to two lengths of lesson: SV (short version), corresponding to a lesson of 60–70 minutes, and LV (long version), for a lesson of 90–100 minutes. Below these timings in the *Lesson plan*, there is always an indication of what can be cut out of the lesson (and set for homework) for the short version or, conversely, how the material can be extended in the long version. In these Lesson plans we have used *Introduction* for warm-up activities, which are usually spoken.

Lesson plan	
Introduction	15–20 minutes
Idiom spot	10–10 minutes
Listening	20–30 minutes
Vocabulary	10–20 minutes
Use of English	5–20 minutes
SV	Set 5 and 6 for homework (but see notes for 6).
LV	See Extension activity for 1 and Photocopiable recording script activity for 3.

Speaking

Elicit the two idioms: *a change for the better* and *a change of heart*. *Ring the changes*, the unit title, is also an idiom. Point out that you can also say *a change for the worse*.

1   Encourage students to talk at length in this first lesson, so that, if the class is new to you, you can gauge their language ability. The discussion can take place in pairs or small groups, with a class round-up at the end. Write any useful vocabulary that comes up on the board.

Possible answers

When my family moved to a new house, it was definitely a change for the better. That is also the earliest change I can remember. I had my own large bedroom for the first time, instead of having to share with my sister, and there was a much bigger garden too.

When I left home and went to university, I moved to the opposite side of the country, which was very different from where I had grown up.

I used to have a stressful job in investment banking, but two months ago I resigned and went off travelling. This new experience made me think seriously about my future and when I came back, I decided to retrain as a teacher.

I found some old letters the other day, which I had kept for more than twenty years – but I had a sudden change of heart and burnt the lot!

 Extension activity

Suggest that some of the life changes described by students are written up as brief texts, to be displayed on the classroom wall or posted on a class website. Each group or pair could be responsible for producing one finished text. Encourage the use of the idioms and phrasal verbs given on pages 8 and 9.

Idiom spot

Idioms are an important area of vocabulary at Proficiency level, so encourage students to record new idioms in a vocabulary notebook and use them occasionally in their writing. The Idiom spot sections in this second edition have been informed by the English Vocabulary Profile (see page 10), to ensure that students learn current idioms that will be useful to them.

Answers
1 b 2 a 3 b 4 b

Listening

2 **1** 🔲02 Explain to students that this is a 'non-exam' listening task, which trains them to listen both for gist and detailed meaning. The texts are of a similar length to those in Paper 3 Part 4. Before playing the recording, check that students understand the wording of the 'life-changing moments' and elicit predictions about what they might hear.

The relevant parts of the recording script are always underlined in the *Objective Proficiency Teacher's Book*.

Answers
1 gaining media attention
2 stepping in for someone
3 heading the wrong way
4 being made redundant
5 meeting 'Mr Right'

Recording script

Speaker 1

I've had a really fantastic year. It all started last November, when I was dragged along to a party by a friend. I was in a terrible mood, I remember, and nearly didn't go. Anyway, I was wearing an outfit I'd made myself – in soft black leather and antique lace, quite an unusual combination! Kelly Johns, the presenter of a big daytime TV show, was there and my little number caught her eye. We got chatting and she asked whether I could come up with something original for her to wear on the show. I jumped at the opportunity. That was a real turning point for me and I was soon able to quit my day job and concentrate on the clothes side full time. Through Kelly's show, I've had lots of orders. I've just finished an exclusive range for a top designer and I've even taken on an assistant to help me. Just think if I'd stayed at home that night!

Speaker 2

People often ask me how I got to be where I am today, with sell-out concerts in big stadiums around the world, thinking that I've spent years playing in local clubs, but the truth is, I'm literally an overnight sensation! I don't mean that arrogantly. It was just one lucky break, all down to being in the right place at the right time. There I was, an absolute nobody, hanging around backstage with Arrowhead, when their lead guitarist tripped over a pile of speakers and broke his arm, five minutes before they were due on. I'd been telling them about my awesome guitar style, so naturally, they all turned to me and said 'Kid, help us out here ...' and I did. The place was packed and I can still feel my hands shaking as I played that very first solo. It went OK though, and the rest is ... history.

Speaker 3

I was in Milan visiting friends, trying to cheer myself up after a dismal few months – my long-term boyfriend and I had broken up, plus I'd left a job without another to go to. My money was running out and I was planning to leave a few days later. Anyway, my friends suggested that I should take a look at Verona before going back home and told me what time train I could get from Milan. Well, for some reason, I ended up on a slow train going south, without realising my mistake – both trains had left at the same time. I fell asleep in the compartment and woke just as the train arrived in Bologna! I had a wander round and fell in love with the place, and knew it was where I wanted to be. Everything just fell into place – I found a teaching job, took a room in a beautiful flat and settled in immediately. I lived there for six years and I go back regularly.

Speaker 4

It's funny how you can hit a run of bad luck: one moment, things are moving along quite normally in your life and then, bam, something comes out of the blue and knocks you sideways and then, wham, something else. I'm OK now, but I've had a difficult couple of years. My problem was quite simply that I'd been living beyond my means for a long time and some debts finally caught up with me. Even then, I thought I'd be OK; I arranged to pay them off little by little from my salary, monthly, you know. But then, the place where I was working cut back on its workforce, and they let me go. Well, that was it, I suppose I panicked, I wasn't thinking straight, you know. So I just packed a bag, got on a coach and left town for London, where my life went downhill fast. I got in with a bad crowd, and one thing led to another. It's a miracle my brother ever tracked me down, but he's got me back and sorted, with a roof over my head and a new job on the cards.

Speaker 5

It could be a story in *True Romance*, but it really happened just like this. Almost twenty years ago to the day, I was waiting for a bus after another mind-numbingly awful day at work, no bus in sight, of course. I was in a rut, my job was going nowhere. Anyway, there I was, staring gloomily at my reflection in a puddle, feeling utterly sorry for myself and thinking: is this really all there is to life? Then I saw two things in that puddle, one imperceptibly after the other. The first was no surprise, huge splashes of rain, as the heavens opened yet again, but then, this enormous red umbrella, appearing behind my head as if by magic! A gorgeous gravelly voice to my left said did I mind, it was big enough for two and he didn't want my hair to get wet. Very fortunately, it was another fifteen minutes before the bus finally turned up and hooray, it didn't stop raining! His name was Terence, though he's been Terry to me ever since – and Dad to our three wonderful children.

3 ♪**1** **02** Play the recording again to allow students to check their answers. Then elicit brief descriptions about each speaker, building up relevant language on the board. If necessary, ask questions about each speaker, for example:

Speaker 1: *What does she do for a living? How long has she been doing this? What happened at the party she went to? Who did she meet there?*

Photocopiable recording script activity **P→page 140**

Hand out copies of the recording script and ask students to underline examples of informal language. Then ask students to work in groups, each group choosing one of the five extracts and preparing a paragraph of around 100 words about the speaker, in a neutral style.

> **Suggested answer**
> *Speaker 1*
> The speaker recalls a party she went to, almost against her will, last November. She describes in detail what she was wearing that night, which was important as it attracted the attention of a famous TV presenter. The presenter commissioned her to design an outfit for her to wear on the show, which gave the speaker useful exposure in the media and led to a number of orders for her unusual clothes. She is now a successful clothes designer and her business is growing in size.

Vocabulary

4 Refer students to the Exam spot. Remind students to be careful with word order when using phrasal verbs. The verb and particle cannot be separated:

- when it is a three-part phrasal verb
  I caught up with Jack further down the road.
- if the phrasal verb is used intransitively (without an object)
  All my hard work paid off.
- when the particle is a preposition
  Sally jumped at the chance of visiting Rome.

> **Answers**
> break up (Speaker 3) jump at (Speaker 1)
> catch up with (Speaker 4) pay off (debts) (Speaker 4)
> cheer sb up (Speaker 3) run out (Speaker 3)
> come up with (Speaker 1) settle in (Speaker 3)
> cut back on (Speaker 4) take on (staff) (Speaker 1)
> end up (Speaker 3) track (somebody) down
> get in with (Speaker 4) (Speaker 4)
> hang around (Speaker 2) turn up (Speaker 5)
> help out (Speaker 2)

5

> **Answers**
> a was / had been paid off   e broke up
> b tracked (me) down   f getting in with
> c jumped at   g turned up
> d cut back on; were / have   h help (me) out
>   been taken on

6 Refer students to the Exam spot and explain that this text is an example of the type of text that appears in Paper 1 Part 1, the multiple-choice cloze. Phrasal verbs are commonly tested in this part of the paper.

> **Answers**
> 1 A 2 D 3 C 4 B 5 A 6 B 7 C 8 D

1.2 SB pages 10–11

Grammar clinic

> **Lesson plan**
> Introduction   5–15 minutes
> Grammar   55–75 minutes
>
> **SV** Set 5 for homework; reduce discussion time in 4.
> **LV** See Extension activity for 2.

1 Give students time to read both texts and check understanding. The texts relate to the unit theme of change – knitting items to cover objects in cities and changing career to become a busker.

Ask students to identify the areas of grammar highlighted in the texts. They illustrate areas that C2 level students still have problems with.

> **Answers**
> Yellow = Perfect tenses
> Blue = Passive forms
> Pink = Relative clauses
> Green = Reported speech

2 Explain to students that although they may 'know' these areas of grammar, learner evidence suggests that they are areas that students at this level still commonly make mistakes in. Suggest that students refer to the Grammar folder on pages 178–188 if they are unsure of a point covered in any unit.

Here is a checklist of things students should watch out for:

- subject–verb agreement
- choice of modal verb
- tense in conditional structures
- choice of past/present/future tense

- choice of preposition
- punctuation in relative clauses
- structure with reporting verbs, e.g. *insist on doing*, *urge someone to.*

Elicit other problem areas that students may have.

 Extension activity

Extend the 'grammar clinic' idea by asking students to review the contents pages of a suitable advanced grammar practice book, such as *Advanced Grammar in Use* by Martin Hewings. Discuss other ways in which they could practise 'weak' grammar areas independently.

 Corpus spot

These sentences come from the *Cambridge Learner Corpus*, a large collection of candidates' scripts from past sessions of various exams, including *Cambridge English: Proficiency*. While writing this course, we have made extensive use of both this and the *Cambridge English Corpus*. Reference to the scripts in the *Cambridge Learner Corpus* has given us a much fuller picture of what Proficiency-level students can and cannot do.

Answers
a went to **b** has been used **c** had never seen
d were measured **e** I've been practising, (I've been) trying / I've tried **f** you have bought **g** they had got married **h** people care

3 Allow students a few minutes to discuss their views in pairs, before eliciting answers.

Answers
a *has gone* = he is still there
   went = he is no longer there
b *has been suffering* = ongoing situation, i.e. unemployment is still high
   was suffering = continuous situation at unspecified time in the past
c *were given* = one specific instance in the past
   have been given = task is ongoing
d *have been dealing* = continuous action that is not yet completed
   have dealt = action completed, i.e. problem successfully handled
e No difference in meaning
f *I've thought* = focus is on the result, implies that a decision has been taken
   I've been thinking = focus is on the activity, implies that person is still thinking
g *could have done* = past speculation
   will have done = future forecast, e.g. 'I'm writing up our annual report – is there anything else we will have done (by the end of the year)?'
h No difference in meaning, though the future perfect continuous tense is more common, as 'living here' is continuous and ongoing.

4 Encourage students to answer in complete sentences, using the perfect tenses featured in the questions. Refer students to the section in the Grammar folder if they still seem unsure about these.

Possible answers
a I've been learning English for ten years.
b I've never done a course in deep-sea diving, though I would really like to.
c One particular street in the centre has been closed to private cars, which has made traffic in other parts of the town much worse.
d My quality of life would be improved by the purchase of a dishwasher because then I wouldn't have to wash everything up by hand.
e I may have moved to another city for work.

5 Ask students to complete the text on their own and then compare answers. Elicit their views on the final paragraph of the text – what may happen by 2025.

Answers
1 have been continually transformed
2 being improved / improving / having improved / having been improved
3 was further stimulated / was stimulated further
4 would have been able to
5 even have thought / have even thought
6 be being used constantly / constantly be being used
7 have embraced / be embracing
8 have been depleted / be depleted

1.3 SB pages 12–13
Reading into Writing: Summarising ideas

Lesson plan	
Introduction	5–10 minutes
Vocabulary	15–30 minutes
Summarising ideas	40–60 minutes
SV	Keep discussion in 1 brief.
LV	See Extension activities for 2 and 6.

Explain that Paper 2 Part 1 of *Cambridge English: Proficiency* requires candidates to summarise and evaluate two short texts. As this is a compulsory task, *Objective Proficiency (Second Edition)* contains ten lessons that develop the relevant skills and language for Part 1. These are 1.3, 3.3, 5.3, 7.3, 9.3, 11.3, 13.3, 15.3, 17.3 and 19.3. This Reading into Writing lesson looks at summarising ideas, which is a particularly important area for students who are studying an academic subject through English.

1 The pictures on the left show the same location in New Orleans during and after Hurricane Katrina in 2005 and the ones on the right show school children working in an IT suite and school children using tablets in a class.

Background information
Hurricane Katrina is the costliest natural disaster to take place in the USA to date. New Orleans suffered huge devastation and most of its major roads were damaged. A 2007 report found design flaws in its flood protection levees.

Suggested answers
The pictures on the left show a natural disaster that has caused a change in the environment. The road is flooded in one picture and people are using small boats to get around, so they may have lost their homes. In the other picture, things are back to normal although the road is still wet so the weather conditions must be bad. Other environmental changes include the effects of global warming – flooding again, or dry river valleys – and the results of deforestation, although that could also come under the commercial category?

The pictures on the right show technological change, in the space of only a few years I suspect? The children in the computer room are working with clunky big machines, whereas the kids using tablets are working in their normal classroom. There are countless other recent technological changes in the world around us, for example wind turbines and solar panels for generating electricity would not have been prevalent twenty years ago.

Vocabulary

 English Profile

Using the English Vocabulary Profile (see Introduction to the Second Edition on page 10), you can run an advanced search for words containing individual prefixes and suffixes at each level of the Common European Framework. The Word family panels within English Vocabulary Profile entries also indicate the level at which members of a word family are likely to be known – anything in italics is probably restricted to learners at C1 and C2 level.

2 Elicit the formation rules.

Answers
commerce – ial (drop the 'e' and add 'ial')
technology – ical (drop the 'y' and add 'ical')
create – ive (drop the 'e' and add 'ive')
vary – iable (change 'y' to 'i' and add 'able')

Examples of -ous: ambitious, luxurious, monotonous, nutritious, rebellious, suspicious
Examples of -ful: doubtful, eventful, fruitful, pitiful, resourceful, thoughtful
Examples of -less: countless, faultless, helpless, priceless, tactless, tasteless

 Extension activity

This would be an ideal opportunity to brainstorm further adjectives within the suffix groups, perhaps by using an English–English dictionary.

Further examples you could elicit from the relevant nouns or verbs are:

-al: accident, continent, geography, president, season
-able: adore, compare, manage, recognise
-ive: compete, imagine, offend, protect
-ful: grace, thought, waste
-less: air, brain, end, heart, seed, spine, tact

Students should list these adjectives in a notebook under each suffix, including any negative prefixes, for example:

-able
(in)advisable
(un)comfortable
impressionable

3 Suggest that students complete a–j in pairs, each doing alternate sentences if time is short.

Answers
a predictable b alternative c hopeful
d philosophical e experimental f speechless
g noticeable h flawless i disposable j disastrous
Adjectives formed from the four remaining words:
adventurous, identifiable, massive, understandable

4 Refer students to the Exam spot and stress the importance of summarising ideas from the texts in the exam task. Explain that underlining important information is a vital first step in planning any kind of summary, as it pinpoints which ideas must be included.

Answers
Extract 3
Rather than burgers and fries being a <u>product</u> of the <u>social changes</u> seen over the <u>last fifty years in America</u>, the author suggests that <u>fast food brands</u> were to a large extent <u>responsible for these changes</u>, as they profoundly <u>affected both lifestyle and diet</u>.

Extract 4
<u>Tiny holes</u> found <u>in human teeth</u> estimated to be <u>over 8,000 years old</u> are now believed to be the <u>earliest evidence of dentistry</u>, for when these holes were examined with an electron microscope, researchers found their <u>sides were too perfectly rounded</u> to be caused by bacteria and have therefore proposed that they were <u>drilled by prehistoric dentists</u>.

1 The sentence summarises the general idea that people pick up on things through facial features, but it omits any reference to health and social status, which means it is less clear than the original text.
2 The word *judge* could be replaced with *assess* or *evaluate*.

3 The underlined words in text 2 that could be replaced are: *produced* (developed, concocted, made); *chance* (accident); *revolutionised* (changed, updated, modernised); *innovations* (new techniques/inventions); *significantly* (notably, importantly). A word like *mauve* or *aspirin* cannot be paraphrased, as it is something very specific.

5 Allow students to work through the sentences on their own or in pairs, then elicit their views on the most successful sentence.

Answers
c is the best choice, as it captures all the important information, uses new words not in the text where possible, is written in a suitably neutral register and is concise (13 words).
Comments on the other sentences:
a Omits reference to Perkin and does not highlight the fact that aspirin was the most significant innovation.
b Unduly informal, with use of phrasal verbs; quite wordy.
d Unnecessary reformulation of *mauve* leads to lack of clarity and wordiness; other words are lifted from the text, e.g. *revolutionary*, *innovation*; too long a sentence.
e Wrong focus of information (aspirin); incomplete.
f Good attempt at reformulating, but lacks precision due to omission of *mauve*; register slightly too informal – better if sentence started 'Commercially' rather than 'Commercially-speaking'.

6 Suggest that students compare their draft sentences in pairs and then produce a final version together, stating the number of words used.

Suggested answers
3 According to the author, fast food has caused social change recently, by influencing how Americans live and changing their diet. (20 words)
4 Research has uncovered evidence of prehistoric dentistry, as minute, round holes in 8,000-year-old teeth cannot have been caused by bacteria. (20 words)

Extension activity

Do similar work at sentence level with other factual texts on subjects of interest to the class. Students may also like to surf the Internet for suitable texts: research papers often have short abstracts accompanying them, which are clear examples of concise writing.

Exam folder 1

SB pages 14–15

Paper 1 Part 3
Word formation

Refer students to the information box.

1 This exercise is to give practice in the range of different affixes that are commonly tested. Ask students to work through a–o. They should take particular care to take note of plurals.

Answers
a extracurricular **b** beneficial **c** opinionated
d kingdom **e** compulsive **f** apparent
g innovators **h** constraints **i** consumption
j Domesticity **k** strengthened **l** misfortune
m irreplaceable **n** disapproval **o** occupants

2 Compounds are also tested in this part of the paper. For exercise 2, there is sometimes more than one answer.

Answers
framework; update/upturn; outfall/outbreak; windfall/windbreak/windproof; rainfall/rainproof; creditworthy; downfall/downturn

3 Refer students to the Exam advice. For this part of Paper 1, students will need to write their answers in CAPITAL LETTERS on their answer sheet in the examination. American spelling is accepted.

The photos are of:
- a young woman with tattoos and piercings
- a man with traditional designs on his face and body.

Answers
1 antiquity **2** dominant **3** customising/izing
4 kinship **5** apparently **6** underline **7** Arguably
8 infinitely

2 Expectation

2.1

| Exam skills | Reading and Use of English Paper 1 Part 7 |
| Vocabulary | Collocations with *traveller* |

2.2

| Grammar | Aspects of the future |
| Vocabulary | Prepositional phrases *have no* + noun |

2.3

Exam skills	Listening for detail Speaking Paper 4 Part 1
Pronunciation	Homophones
Vocabulary	Phrases – nouns with related verbs

Workbook contents

1, 2, 3	Listening
4	Grammar – future tenses
5	Punctuation
6, 7	Vocabulary
8	Use of English Paper 1 Part 3
9	Use of English Paper 1 Part 2

2.1 SB pages 16–17

Lesson plan

Introduction	10–15 minutes
Reading	30–30 minutes
Vocabulary	15–45 minutes

SV   Keep discussion in 1 brief.
LV   See Extension activities for 4.

Speaking

1   Elicit reactions to the photographs and ask students to discuss the questions in pairs or groups.

The photos are of:
- a campsite
- an expensive hotel
- Barbados – Bottom Bay
- Machu Picchu

Background information
Barbados is an island in the Caribbean.

Machu Picchu is a 15th-century Inca site located in a mountainous region in Peru, South America. It is often referred to as the 'Lost City of the Incas'.

Possible answers
Beach scene: be able to chill out; end up spending a fortune; be in the lap of luxury
Machu Picchu: possibly have to rough it; get by on a shoestring budget; enjoy being a culture vulture; get back to nature
Campsite: get off the beaten track; possibly have to rough it; get by on a shoestring budget; get back to nature
Expensive hotel: end up spending a fortune; be in the lap of luxury

Reading

2   Refer students to the advice in the Exam spot. If they are not familiar with multiple-matching questions, more advice and a sample of this part of the exam is in the Exam folder on pages 64–65.

Ask students to read through the article to get an idea of what it is about. Tell them to ignore the highlighting for now. They should focus on the question: What does the writer think about holidays?

Answer
The writer thinks that holidays away from home are overrated and that thinking about them is probably better than actually going on one.

3   Ask students to do the example question and read the guidance that goes with it. Students should read the questions and then try to find the paragraphs that contain the information. Ask them to underline the word or phrase that contains the information.

Answers
1 B   2 D   3 B   4 C   5 A   6 D   7 B   8 A

Vocabulary

4   Collocations are frequently tested at Proficiency level. Ask students to decide which of the two options collocates with *traveller/travellers*.

> **Answers**
> a frequent   b independent   c Seasoned
> d intrepid   e weary   f discerning
> g an armchair   h inveterate   i unwary

Extension activity 1

Explain what a simile is – a figurative device in language where something is referred to explicitly to make writing more descriptive or interesting. There are many in English which are fixed expressions. However, writers often make up their own similes to suit their own purposes. In his article the writer says that his worries and regrets acted 'like panes of distorting glass between myself and the world'. This simile is the writer's own. He has used it to make his writing more interesting. Ask students to make up similes to describe the following:

EXAMPLE: *The setting sun was like a drop of blood in the sky.*

- the setting sun   • a lake
- snow   • a full moon
- a child   • a storm
- a club night   • a burning house

There are also some similes in English which are fixed expressions. Ask students to use one of the similes from the box below to describe a person, object or event. Check that they understand the vocabulary and allow them to use an English–English dictionary.

EXAMPLE: *The child's behaviour was perfect all weekend.*

The child was as good as gold *all weekend.*

> as good as gold
> as thin as a rake
> fits like a glove
> as light as a feather
> like chalk and cheese
> as white as a sheet
> as red as a beetroot
> as stubborn as a mule
> as cool as a cucumber
> as fit as a fiddle
> as flat as a pancake
> like water off a duck's back

You can then ask students to discuss whether they have similar expressions in their own language and to discuss them with a partner.

Extension activity 2

Ask students to choose a famous landmark in their country and write a paragraph about it. They should try to see it as if through the eyes of a first time visitor. Would the visitor be impressed or would they feel let down? Is the building as beautiful or interesting as it is said to be? Ask them to use at least one simile of their own in the description.

5   Ask students to discuss the questions.

2.2 SB pages 18–19

Aspects of the future

> **Lesson plan**
> Grammar   50–60 minutes
> Vocabulary   10–30 minutes
>
> SV   Set 6 for homework.
> LV   See Extension activity for 4.

1   Go through the information about the future. Explain what is meant by 'aspects of the future' – that in English the future is not just about using the *will/shall* tense. Refer students to the Grammar folder on pages 178–179 of the Student's Book if they are unsure about which tense is used to express a particular aspect.

> **Possible answers**
> a   To talk about arranged plans for this evening; things you have already organised or booked, e.g. a cinema or theatre visit or friends for dinner.
> b   To talk about plans which are not organised and maybe are just ideas or spur of the moment plans. These could include plans which might change depending on circumstances, e.g. If it rains, I'll watch TV instead of playing tennis.
> c   To talk about your intentions this evening; something which you are thinking of doing but haven't quite got around to booking/planning in detail.
> d   Usually used to talk about a specific time in the future, e.g. What will you be doing at 8.00 this evening? I'll be washing my hair.
> e   To talk about what will have happened by a certain time in the future. You are looking into the future and saying 'this will have happened', e.g. I will have finished all my homework by 10 tonight.
> f   To talk about plans which have been abandoned for one reason or another, e.g. I was going to play tennis tonight, but now I have to stay in to babysit my little sister.

2 Ask students to do the exercise in pairs. Only one answer is correct.

Answers
a he's going to get   b will be   c leaves
d is going to get   e I'll go   f I'm not going
g will you be doing   h will have travelled
i is not allowing   j will do   k will have been painting
l will have finished   m he'll feel   n will you do   o is
p am having   q arrive   r will be arriving   s Shall

3 Ask students to continue working with a partner and to decide which tense they would use for situations a–g. Sometimes more than one answer may be correct, depending on what exactly is meant.

Possible answers
a I'm going to clean my car tomorrow.
b It's going to rain.
c It will rain next week.
d I'm having salmon and salad for dinner tonight.
e My government will have found a solution to pollution by the year 2050.
f I'll be a doctor in 10 years' time. / I'm going to be a doctor in 10 years' time. Note that you can't say *I'll be being a doctor in 10 years' time*.
g The flight to Singapore leaves at 6.00 on Fridays.

4 Ask students to discuss statements a–c using the expressions given. Explain that *to be bound to* expresses a strong feeling of certainty. Students should make a note of this as it is often tested at Proficiency level.

Possible answers
a I expect that we will be able to travel to the USA in less than a couple of hours and to the other side of the world in a maximum of four hours. Travel within a country will be very rapid, which will mean that you will be able to live quite a distance away from your work.
b I am unlikely to have become a millionaire by the middle of the century, but I hope I will be reasonably comfortable. I am bound to have been to university and trained to become a doctor. I am also likely to have married and had three children.
c I think you can expect to have a good time in my town. There's quite a bit to see and there are many cafés and restaurants to have a coffee or a snack in. The people will be quite friendly, especially if the sun is shining. There's a good bus service and lots of taxis but they are quite expensive. In the afternoon, you'll be able to walk alongside the river or even go out on a boat.

 Extension activity

Students can go on to talk about the following before doing a small piece of writing.

What changes do you expect to happen in your country in the next thirty years? Think about social/educational/cultural/governmental changes.

Write a short paragraph on the types of changes you expect to happen in your country in the next 30 to 40 years.

5 Explain how to use the expressions *to be about to* and *to be on the brink/point/verge of*. Ask students to write sentences using these expressions and including the words/phrases given.

Possible answers
Lack of rain will leave parts of Africa on the verge/brink of a disaster.
I'm about to go to bed.
Some animals are on the verge/brink of extinction.
The country is on the brink of revolution.
She was on the verge of leaving home when she received the news.
I am about to leave home to get the bus.
I'm about to get married.
Scientists are on the brink/verge of a scientific breakthrough.

Vocabulary

6 Explain the meaning of any of the phrases that students are not familiar with.

in the region of – about

on the brink of – to say when something good or bad is about to happen

to some extent – partly

in conjunction with – together with

on behalf of – instead of

in vain – without success

on the verge of – to say when something good or bad is about to happen

on the grounds (that) – because

with the exception of – not including

Now ask students to complete the exercise.

Answers
a on the grounds   b on behalf of   c to some extent
d on the verge of   e on the brink of   f in the region of
g in vain   h in conjunction with   i with the exception of

7   Students should learn the construction *have no* + noun as it is often used and frequently appears in Paper 1 Reading and Use of English.

Answers
a   I have no interest in going somewhere like Las Vegas. ...
b   I have no regrets about spending too much money on my last holiday. ...
c   I have no recollection/memory of childhood holidays. ...
d   I would have no hesitation in booking a cruise. ...
e   I have no alternative/choice/option but to stay at home this year rather than go away. ...
f   I have no intention of ever going to Disneyland. ...
g   I have no time to look at lots of travel brochures. ...

Refer students to the Exam spot and encourage them to keep a vocabulary notebook.

2.3 SB pages 20–21

Listening and Speaking

Lesson plan	
Listening	20–20 minutes
Phrase spot	10–30 minutes
Speaking	20–20 minutes
Pronunciation	10–20 minutes

SV   Set sentences in Pronunciation for homework.
LV   See Extension activity for Phrase spot.

1   This is a pre-listening activity to help students with possibly unfamiliar vocabulary. Ask students to work in pairs to decide what the meaning of the words and phrases in italics is.

Suggested answers
a   annoy me   b   overexcited   c   pay   d   large
e   limited   f   be unrestrained / go unchecked
g   determined to   h   similar to

2   **1 03** The extracts each only have one question, unlike in Paper 3 Listening, where there are three short extracts, each with two questions. Ask students to read through the questions and then play the recording twice.

Answers
Extract One B   Extract Two C   Extract Three B

Recording Script
Extract One
There was a mad excitement about standing in front of a world map and tracing a circumnavigation with my fingertip. Everything seemed possible and my family's nagging doubts really got my goat. I'd say you can't really go *wrong* when choosing the stops on a round-the-world trip, but I found that some routes worked out better than others. You need a good variety of destinations. You might love the beach, but a trip that stops in California, Australia and Thailand, all for the sun and sand, does get a bit repetitive. At the same time, I didn't want to get carried away trying to see the whole world.

Next, I knew I would have to fork out a pretty hefty sum for the plane ticket as I didn't intend to be thumbing lifts. My budget was tight so I had to play around with my route to get the best value for money. I also had to research my destinations to see what the average daily costs would be and figure out a budget (adding a good 10 or 20 per cent buffer to be on the safe side). I decided to spend longer in cheaper countries and have a relatively short stay in more expensive places, which was sometimes quite a difficult decision as there were so many things I wanted to see. In fact, planning the trip was just as much fun as the actual travelling. I really let my imagination run wild and the trip itself was everything I'd expected.

Extract Two
I really hope to make it as an entrepreneur and I guess the person who's influenced me most has been a well-known British businessman. I was given a copy of his autobiography for my fourteenth birthday and it really made a huge impression on me. He had an amazing childhood. Apparently, when he was just four years old his mother stopped the car a few kilometres from their house and made him find his own way home. Then when he was eleven or twelve his mum decided that he should cycle seventy kilometres to another town to teach him the importance of stamina and to learn a sense of direction! He said he felt great when he'd done it but his mum wasn't worried or relieved or anything – just acted calm as you like and told him to go and help someone in the village chop some logs. His family seemed to thrive on challenges – physical ones rather than educational, which I think's quite unusual. I know my family are dead set on my getting a degree but quite a few entrepreneurs start out without one and look at them!

Anyway, there was another occasion he mentions when his aunt had promised him some money if he learnt to swim. He spent a holiday trying desperately, but just couldn't do it. Then, on the way home in the car, he spotted a river. He made his father stop the car and just dived into the river in his underpants. The river was quite fast-flowing and it seemed like he was going to drown, but then he pushed really hard and actually managed to swim. <u>My childhood was nothing like that, but I guess what I read has made me realise I need to take on challenges and try to fulfil my hopes and aspirations.</u>

Extract Three

According to the latest survey, commissioned by one of our leading banks, over three-quarters of 12- to 19-year-olds said they kept track of their money, up from twelve months ago. Half of young people said they were content that they had enough money, something only 46 per cent said a year earlier, while the amount that those who were unhappy said they would need to be happy has fallen. However, the 9,000 young people questioned continued to have unrealistic salary expectations. The average teenager said they thought they would be earning double what is actually the current average salary for a 35-year-old. Not only this, but nearly three-quarters of those interviewed thought they would have a car by the time they were 21, while more than half hoped to own their own home by the age of 25. <u>Overall, the bank calculates that the average expectation gap between where people thought they would be financially, and where they would actually be, was around £72,133, a small drop compared with last year's figure.</u> Interestingly, although the figures differ somewhat, the findings are very much in line with previous surveys done over the past twenty years.

 Phrase spot

Explain that many nouns for parts of the body also have a related verb, as in the example *thumb*. Sometimes the verb takes on a figurative or idiomatic meaning, as in *toe the line*, *foot the bill*. Students match the verbs with the words or phrases, using an English–English dictionary to help them.

Answers
1 f 2 e/c 3 b 4 a 5 c 6 d

The verb *face* combines with many nouns, including *fact, idea, problem, thought*.

a shoulder the burden b foot the bill
c faced the music d toed the line
e stomach/face the idea f elbowed people aside

Extension activity

Put these nouns on the board and ask students which ones have a related verb (three do not – flaw, ratio and vision).

corner, figure, flaw, house, profile, ratio, staff, stage, table, vision

Students can work with a dictionary or corpus to find phrases using these verbs.

Possible answers
corner someone about something, corner a thief
figure prominently, figure out a problem (phrasal verb)
house asylum seekers, house an exhibition
profile an issue, profile market needs
staff an organisation, staff a call centre
stage a comeback, stage an event
table a proposal, table a bill (for legislation)

3 Refer the class to the Exam spot. Ask them to answer the questions. They should try to use some of the phrases contained in the Exam spot in their answers.

Possible answers
a On the whole, I don't have a great deal of opportunity to get away for a while from my desk. At my level in the company, I get very little holiday. However, given the chance and the choice, I'd go to Tahiti.
b Speaking personally, a round-the-world trip would be incredibly stimulating – just think of all the cultures and landscapes you would be able to sample.
c My main objective in life is to join the police force and become a super sleuth, a detective like my hero Sherlock Holmes. I think the salary is now much higher than it used to be and people generally have more respect for the police in my country than for many other professions.
d Given the problems that abound with recession, in my view your best chance is to get as well qualified as you possibly can.
e It's my belief I'm not cut out to become an entrepreneur but I admire people who are. They seem to have some sort of inner drive which pushes them on to obtain their objectives.
f Personally, I guess my main priority would be to make sure they were safe and happy, but also that they were able to mix socially with people from different backgrounds.

Pronunciation

4 Refer students to the explanation of homophones in their books. Check they understand and then ask them to do the exercise. An English–English dictionary may help.

Writing folder 1

SB pages 22–23

Part 1 Essay

The compulsory task in Paper 2 Part 1 involves reading two short texts in order to summarise and evaluate the ideas they contain. *Objective Proficiency* develops the language and skills needed for this task in the Reading into Writing lessons, which occur in alternate Student's Book units. In this Writing folder, students are given training in exam technique, as well as specific advice on how to answer Part 1.

In Paper 2 Writing, students must write in a register that is suitable for the task set. Most questions will demand an unmarked register and it is vital to produce this *consistently*, as inappropriately informal language would have a negative effect on the reader (examiner).

If timetabling permits, work through all the Writing folder exercises in class, as they raise awareness of the requirements of the exam tasks and allow students to share ideas and best practice. Many *Cambridge English: Proficiency* candidates tend to under-perform on Paper 2, often because they have paid insufficient attention to writing skills. Encourage students to keep all their written homework. It can be very effective for them to work on a second draft following your marking and feedback on their first attempts, as they will learn from earlier mistakes and better understand how to improve their writing.

1   Give students time to read the two texts and elicit their ideas.

Answer
The texts contain opposing points of view with regard to the use of technology: Text 1 sees this as an appropriate way of widening the audience, while Text 2 suggests that it undermines a museum's primary role, that of educating its visitors.

2   In the exam, there will be four main points covered across the two texts. Encourage students to underline the key ideas as this will help them plan their answer.

Answers
Text 1
b   '… museums have become more community-orientated …'; '… museum curators have looked to modern technology to breathe more life into exhibits, …'
e   'Over the last decade in particular, … the majority seek to be inclusive rather than elitist, reaching out to everyone.'

Text 2
c   'The dumbing down of exhibitions is widespread – in short, the medium has become more important than the message'; 'Learning is all too often compromised by technological wizardry, which may impress on a superficial level but essentially trivialises, and provides a content-lite "experience"'.
f   'The purpose of a museum is to stimulate learning and broaden the horizons of its visitors, yet many museums nowadays appear to neglect this responsibility …'; 'Whether this is in response to government cuts or merely reflects a trend among museum directors, it is undoubtedly a change for the worse.'

3 Explain to students that they should vary the beginning of sentences as the sentence openers show – this will help to demonstrate their range of language. This exercise trains them to use their own words where possible – they should avoid 'lifting' the words and phrases in the texts and reusing them in their answers, as they may be penalised for doing this. Certain key words will need to be reused as they cannot be paraphrased and the suggested answers below reflect this. It is also permissible to quote verbatim from a text (see Suggested answer c), but this should always be limited to a short phrase – the examiners need to assess the candidate's own language.

Suggested answers
Text 1
b The first text suggests that the policy of introducing new technology into museum displays has been of benefit to visitors because it is more meaningful and 'hands-on'.
e The writer is of the opinion that in the last ten years in particular, museums have tried to engage a broader cross-section of the public.

Text 2
c The second text raises the issue of 'dumbing down', claiming that insufficient content is conveyed in 'modern' museums, due to the implementation of these creative effects.
f Additionally, it is argued that many museums are ignoring their original function, to educate and inform, which the writer sees as regrettable.

4 Suggest students do this in pairs, discussing their ideas.

Answer
All four points from the texts are summarised.
Only the points in Text 1 are evaluated.
The writer has copied a considerable amount of input from Text 2 rather than using their own words.
The writer has not included any of their own ideas.

5 Ask students to draft a new second sentence for the third paragraph. They should do this on their own. Elicit some sentences and write them on the board. Decide which one is the most effective at reformulating the ideas from the second text.

Suggested answer
Many museum curators seem to have forgotten that their institutions exist in order to promote the transfer of knowledge and the writer sees the introduction of new technology as a bad thing, because the actual subject matter has become subservient to the method of delivery.

6 Point out that in the exam, it will not matter if students go a little beyond the upper word limit – it is much more important to bring a piece of writing to a suitable close. However, they should not exceed 300 words on the Part 1 task – if an answer is substantially longer than this, it is likely to include some repetition or irrelevance.

Suggested answer
These texts present different reactions to what museums are offering in the 21st century. To my mind, their curators have acted appropriately in embracing the new technology at their disposal. The current reality where I live is that many more people are going to museums than before and the majority of them benefit from this experience. Any transfer of knowledge is a positive outcome and museums definitely contribute to a better educated society.
(72 words)

Note on assessment
The Cambridge ESOL C2 assessment criteria operate across five bands of performance and there are four distinct assessment sub-scales. These are Content, Communicative achievement, Organisation and Language. See the table on the next page. Further information about the marking of Paper 2 can be found in the *Cambridge English: Proficiency* Handbook, downloadable from the Cambridge ESOL website. Use some of the wording in the assessment sub-scales when giving feedback to students on their written work, in order to familiarise them with what is expected in the exam.

Cambridge English: Proficiency Writing assessment scale

C2	Content	Communicative achievement	Organisation	Language
5	All content is relevant to the task. Target reader is fully informed.	Demonstrates complete command of the conventions of the communicative task. Communicates complex ideas in an effective and convincing way, holding the target reader's attention with ease, fulfilling all communicative purposes.	Text is organised impressively and coherently using a wide range of cohesive devices and organisational patterns with complete flexibility.	Uses a wide range of vocabulary, including less common lexis, with fluency, precision, sophistication, and style. Use of grammar is sophisticated, fully controlled and completely natural. Any inaccuracies occur only as slips.
4	*Performance shares features of Bands 3 and 5.*			
3	Minor irrelevances and/ or omissions may be present. Target reader is on the whole informed.	Uses the conventions of the communicative task with sufficient flexibility to communicate complex ideas in an effective way, holding the target reader's attention with ease, fulfilling all communicative purposes.	Text is a well-organised, coherent whole, using a variety of cohesive devices and organisational patterns with flexibility.	Uses a range of vocabulary, including less common lexis, effectively and precisely. Uses a wide range of simple and complex grammatical forms with full control, flexibility and sophistication. Errors, if present, are related to less common words and structures, or as slips.
2	*Performance shares features of Bands 1 and 3.*			
1	Irrelevances and misinterpretation of task may be present. Target reader is minimally informed.	Uses the conventions of the communicative task effectively to hold the target reader's attention and communicate straightforward and complex ideas, as appropriate.	Text is well organised and coherent, using a variety of cohesive devices and organisational patterns to generally good effect.	Uses a range of vocabulary, including less common lexis, appropriately. Uses a range of simple and complex grammatical forms with control and flexibility. Occasional errors may be present but do not impede communication.
0	Content is totally irrelevant. Target reader is not informed.	*Performance below Band 1.*		

3 Strange behaviour

Topic Human and animal behaviour

3.1

Listening	Non-exam true/false
Vocabulary	Phrases – fixed pairs of words
	Modifiers – *quite, rather, fairly*
Exam skills	Reading and Use of English Paper 1 Part 2

3.2

Grammar	Conditional clauses

3.3

Vocabulary	Extreme emotions
Exam skills	Reading into Writing: Reformulation 1 – Paper 2 Part 1
Vocabulary	Word formation – negative adjectives

Workbook contents

1	Reading Paper 1 Part 7
2	Grammar – conditional clauses
3, 4, 5, 6	Vocabulary
7	Use of English Paper 1 Part 1

3.1 SB pages 24–25

Lesson plan	
Introduction	5–10 minutes
Listening	20–40 minutes
Phrase spot	10–20 minutes
Vocabulary	10–10 minutes
Use of English	15–15 minutes

SV Set sentences in Phrase spot for homework.
LV See Photocopiable recording script activity and Extension activity for 2.

Speaking

1 The photograph is of a sunset to show 'red sky at night'. Ask students to discuss the questions in pairs or groups.

Possible answer
I think the one about *red sky at night, shepherd's delight* is true. I've often noticed that if there is a red sky at night the weather the following day is good. It's something to do with the refraction of ice crystals in the atmosphere I think.

Listening

2 **1** [04] Ask students to read through the questions and check they understand the vocabulary. A rain goose is a type of bird. Play the recording twice – first so students can get an idea of what it is about, and secondly so they can write their answers.

Answers
a T b F c F d T e F f T g F h T i T j T

Recording script
Sue: Good morning. Now, the huge growth of interest in environmental issues has led to a careful re-examination of all kinds of traditional lore. With me today, I have Peter Watkins. He's written a best-selling book *The History of Weather Folklore*, which explains country sayings and the role of animals and birds in forecasting the weather. Sayings my granny used to come out with, like *Birds flying low, expect rain and a blow*, which I've always felt rather sceptical about.

Peter: Well, Sue, the way in which animals and birds can apparently predict changes in the weather before we can has always fascinated people and, for that matter, still does. If it didn't, the sayings wouldn't still be in current use, and of course, nowadays the weather is anxiously studied because of climate change.

Sue: But is there any truth in these old sayings? Given that there are so many, apparently 500 at the last count, and they've been around a while, presumably they should be fairly accurate?

Peter: Mm, well generally, there's a better chance of their being right for short-term weather forecasting rather than long-term. Of course, the most interesting natural weather forecasters are the birds, which is why there are so many sayings relating to them. Birds depend on the right weather conditions for flying and, in particular, birds that fly very high, like swifts and swallows, stand very little chance of survival if they get caught in a bad storm. They are also insect feeders and when the weather is fine the insects are high and the birds will follow them. Insects have good reason to dive for cover if rain is imminent as they are covered with water-repellent hairs. It actually doesn't take much for them to get completely soaked, so they respond quite rapidly if there's a drop in temperature or a rise in humidity.

Sue: Oh, so there's an element of truth in that one. Now, I used to live off the coast of Scotland and they had a saying on the islands about a bird called the red-throated diver. They used to call this bird the rain goose, and the saying went pretty much like this: *If the rain goose flies to the hill, you can put your boat where you will, but if she flies to the sea, you must draw your boat and flee.* I must say that I used to be rather puzzled by this saying, as I didn't understand why it would fly out to sea when the weather was getting worse. Anyway, one time when I was out in a boat the wind started to get up. We tuned into the radio and it said a gale was due from the north. We saw the geese everywhere flying around and heading out to sea. <u>So despite common sense telling you otherwise</u>, the saying of the local people seemed to be true.

Peter: Yes, and we still don't know the reasons for its strange behaviour. But you know, not all weather lore is about misery. Some birds can predict when things are about to brighten up. Certain geese set off for their breeding grounds in Iceland when the weather is fine – you just have to wait and watch and then plan your harvesting or house painting!

Sue: Not very practical! However, if there is some truth behind these weather sayings, do they ever have any practical use?

Peter: Obviously, weather lore had a very important application in the farmer's world. Farming and weather are intrinsically linked and the ability to predict, or at least think you could predict, was very important to them, <u>although of course, they weren't the only ones with a vested interest in weather forecasting</u>. One of the things about human beings is that we do not like to feel that things are happening with no purpose whatsoever. Weather lore makes a connection between something that is happening and something that is going to happen – <u>we need to feel we're not simply the victims of chance and circumstance</u>. Although it's very difficult to put dates on these sayings, many of them probably go back thousands of years. Some of them work and some of them don't, and some of them don't even make sense. Many actually negate each other.

Sue: <u>Quite.</u> So, how reliable are sayings which predict the year ahead, if we can't even rely on ones predicting the weather the next day?

Peter: Mm, well, I find it very difficult to believe that you can tell the rest of the winter from the way birds are flying or how your cat behaves in the autumn. By putting our own interpretations on how nature works we can get it completely wrong. For our ancestors the weather was a life and death situation – not just an inconvenience – and I think that had they had

anything more reliable, they wouldn't have had to base their predictions on this kind of thing. <u>They were really clutching at straws when they observed animal and bird behaviour and linked it to the weather</u>, but they really had no other choice.

Sue: My thanks to Peter Watkins. Next week we'll ...

Photocopiable recording script activity ⓟ→page 141

Ask students to find the following words and expressions and explain their meaning from the context.

to come out with	*the wind started to get up*
is starting to bite	*are intrinsically linked*
is imminent	*many actually negate each other*
an element of truth	*clutching at straws*

Suggested answers
to come out with – to say
is starting to bite – is starting to take effect
is imminent – is fast approaching
an element of truth – some truth
the wind started to get up – the wind started to get stronger
are intrinsically linked – are essentially/fundamentally linked
many actually negate each other – many contradict each other
clutching at straws – turning to something in desperation

 Extension activity

Students should write out sentences of their own, showing how the vocabulary in the Photocopiable recording script activity, above, is used.

 Phrase spot

Ask students to work in pairs to first of all check the phrases are correct and then to complete the sentences with the correct phrase.

Answers
These were the phrases that needed correcting:
time and again; fame and fortune; flesh and blood; touch and go; life and soul

a thick and thin	**b** fame and fortune
c touch and go	**d** First and foremost
e Time and again	**f** give and take
g life and soul	**h** flesh and blood
i high and dry	**j** black and white

Vocabulary

3 **1 [05]** *Quite, fairly* and *rather* are often confused. Refer students to the Grammar folder on page 184 in the Student's Book if more help is needed.

Refer students to the note about gradable and ungradable adjectives before playing the recording.

Answers
1 a 2 b 3 a 4 b 5 a

> **Recording script**
> 1 You're quite wrong in what you say about her!
> 2 It's quite a nice dress, but I can't make up my mind whether to buy it or not.
> 3 Quite!
> 4 She's quite happy in her new house, but she does still miss her friends.
> 5 This cake is quite delicious.

4 Ask students to work in pairs or small groups and to discuss the sayings using some of the phrases and the adverb of degree specified.

⬤ Extension activity

For homework students should find another saying and write a short paragraph on whether they think this saying has any basis in fact. They should read out their paragraphs to the class who should vote on the saying's usefulness.

5 Refer students to the Exam spot. Point out the importance of reading the text through to the end, before attempting to fill the gaps. In the following exercise the answers are given, but in the examination students have to come up with their own. Further information about this part of the exam can be found in the Exam folder on pages 30–31 of the Student's Book.

Answer
The article is about animal behaviour and how it may be possible to use it to predict major earthquakes.

6

Answers
1 far 2 date 3 given 4 turn
5 make 6 put 7 whatever 8 as

3.2 SB pages 26–27
Review of conditional clauses

Lesson plan	
Grammar	50–70 minutes
Speaking	10–20 minutes
SV	Set 6 for homework.
LV	See Extension activity for 3.

1 Ask students to talk about whether the weather affects their mood and to try to come up with some examples. For example, are people in hot countries temperamental? Are the British reserved because of the rain?

2 Students should read the article and then work with a partner to complete the sentences. The sentences are all conditional.

Suggested answers
a there are 50% more traffic accidents and 20% more industrial injuries.
b the air will make you feel invigorated.
c the number of murders would rise.
d if there hadn't been a Santa Ana blowing.
e you leave Switzerland during a Föhn.
f I would go to California if I wanted to murder my husband.

3 Students should be able to explain what kind of conditional sentence each is. They are all examples of basic forms. Refer them to the Grammar folder on pages 179–180 of the Student's Book if they have any problems with this.

Answers
a Zero conditional used for general truths.
b First conditional used when something is possible.
c Second conditional used to talk about something that is unreal and is improbable.
d Third conditional to talk about something impossible.
e Zero conditional to talk about a general truth.
f Second conditional to talk about something which is unreal or improbable.

Extension activity

If students need more spoken practice in the basic forms of the conditionals then ask them to form groups and discuss the idea that a crime of passion should be treated leniently. They could then go on to discuss capital punishment and whether some crimes deserve the death penalty.

Corpus spot

Refer students to the Corpus spot and ask them to decide what the mistake is in the sentence.

Answer
Making the verb following *unless* negative. It should be: *If someone treats these two things equally, he can easily succeed in both,* **unless he succumbs / if he does not succumb** *to the temptation of laziness.*

4   This exercise gives examples of other forms of conditional sentences.

Answers
a   inverted first conditional to express tentative statements = *If you should happen to ...*
b   polite use of *would* = first conditional
c   parallel conditional – first conditional = *I'll do something if you do something.*
d   disguised conditional – *as long as = if*
e   inverted third conditional = If I had known about the weather conditions ...
f   disguised first conditional – *provided that = if*
g   mixed conditional – second + third using *now* to show past effect on present
h   inverted second conditional to express tentative statements = *If the Prime Minister were to announce ...*
i   zero conditional with *unless = if not*

5   This exercise is also an awareness exercise so that students realise that other words and phrases besides *if* are possible in a conditional sentence.

Answers
a Given that   b Unless   c As long as / Provided that
d But for / Without   e Even if   f on condition that
g Suppose / Supposing

6   This exercise can be given for homework if time is short. Many of the forms, especially the inversions, are quite formal.

Suggested answers
a   Should you see her, could you tell her my address? OR Should you happen to see her, could you tell her my address?
b   Given that people were dependent on farming for their livelihood, it's not surprising that they used animal behaviour to predict the weather.
c   Provided that you take care of it, you can borrow my bike.
d   If you'd (like to) take a seat, I'm sure Mr Johnson won't be long.
e   If I were you, I'd get another job.
f   If I had worked harder to pass my diploma, I would be earning more money now.
g   But for my grandmother leaving me some money, I wouldn't have been able to afford to go to university.

h   Were climatic changes to occur / Were there to be climatic changes, weather lore would be rendered obsolete.

Speaking

7   Ask students to work in groups to talk about the situations.

Possible answers
a   I'll book into a hotel.
b   I'll just have to do it!
c   I'll ring up my service provider.
d   I'll grab my things and rush out.
e   I'd have a year-long holiday.
f   I'd report it to the police.
g   I'd try to keep a low profile.
h   I'd just take off wherever I felt like it.
i   I would / I'd have been delighted and studied hard to make the most of it.
j   I would / I'd have tried to get into one of the Ivy League universities.
k   I would / I'd have done my best to make money.

3.3 SB pages 28–29
Reading into Writing:
Reformulation 1

Lesson plan	
Introduction	20–20 minutes
Reading	30–30 minutes
Vocabulary	10–20 minutes
Writing	0–20 minutes

SV	Set 5 for homework.
LV	See Extension activity for 4.

Refer students to the photos. They are of people showing strong emotions.

• two angry footballers
• stressed commuters
• a child's birthday

Ask students to discuss with a partner how the people are reacting in the situation they are in.

1   This exercise looks at anger. Students should put the situations a–g in order of irritation and then compare answers round the class.

2   Ask students to find the synonyms in the box for the words given in a–f.

3   Ask students to read through the article and then
    answer the questions that follow.

Vocabulary

4   Refer the class to the Exam spot. Students often find
    it difficult to find different ways of saying the same
    thing. Here they are introduced to the use of negative
    prefixes. They will gain marks if they can show they
    can manipulate language, either to make a sentence
    shorter or to show they can paraphrase a sentence.

◯ Extension activity

Divide students into teams. Each team should write a list
of ten or more adjectives or adverbs which can be made
negative with a prefix. They then ask the other team to give
the word with a negative prefix. The team with the most
correct answers wins.

5   Students should try to summarise the text in 3 using
    no more than 18 words.

Exam folder 2

SB pages 30–31

Paper 1 Part 2 Open cloze

1   Refer students to the examples and Exam advice. They
    should then read through the text carefully before
    trying to fill in the gaps.

    The photos are of Henri Cartier-Bresson.

Paper 1 Part 4
Key word transformations

2   Refer students to the information and to the Exam
    advice. They should remember that only between
    three and eight words are required. A contraction
    counts as two words. They mustn't forget to use the
    key word.

4 Sweet rituals

4.1

Exam skills	Reading and Use of English Paper 1 Part 5
Style extra	Narrative description: comparison to animals; colours
Vocabulary	Collocations

4.2

Grammar	Past tenses
Vocabulary	Compound adjectives

4.3

Exam skills	Speaking Paper 4 Part 2
Vocabulary	Adjectives and idioms to do with food

Workbook contents

1	Listening Paper 3 Part 1
2, 3	Listening follow-up
4	Grammar – past tenses
5, 6	Vocabulary
7	Use of English Paper 1 Part 2
8	Use of English Paper 1 Part 4

4.1 SB pages 32–33

Lesson plan

Introduction	5–10 minutes
Listening	10–20 minutes
Reading	40–40 minutes
Style extra	0–10 minutes
Vocabulary	5–10 minutes

SV Set Style extra and 6 for homework. See also notes on final part of 2.

LV Spend more time on 1 and do Photocopiable recording script activity in 2.

1 Elicit examples of ritual behaviour from students, starting from the pictures shown:

- a Japanese Tea Ceremony
- a bride and groom cutting their tiered wedding cake

Another example of ritual behaviour in eating and drinking is making a toast at an official dinner, where everyone raises a glass and drinks to something or someone.

2 🔊**1 06** Explain that students will hear a short extract, which is recorded at natural speed and contains some difficult vocabulary. They should listen out for time phrases and sequence words, which will cue the information needed.

Answers
Before the meal: phone calls to relations, preparation of lots of food
During the meal: eating, praising the food, criticism of family members, family disputes, more general arguments about politics, coffee, senior member leaves, end of event

Recording script

Unlike many modern families, mine still holds to the tradition of large family meals at times of celebration or crisis. I use the word 'large' of both the group and the amount of food on offer. The pattern is always the same: endless phone calls weeks ahead of the occasion to mobilise distant cousins and elderly aunts; on the eve of the event, the preparation of excessive amounts of food by the host family member, which never fails to be stress-inducing for all concerned; and then, on the day itself, we slip into our well-established roles, devouring all that is set before us and expressing the joy and contentment that convention demands. Once the wine has started to flow, the praise of succulent dishes gives way to another, more sinister part of the ritual: snide comments on family members not present, the surfacing of ancient grudges and petty family rivalries. This in turn leads to the more general but equally predictable debates on politics and the world at large. Manners always prevent us from actual bodily assault, but the verbal gloves are certainly off at this late stage in the proceedings. As the insults start to fly, the host hurries away to prepare coffee, hunting out chocolates and jugs of ice-cold water, in a valiant attempt to restore calm. Ritual behaviour dictates that all hostilities cease at this point and so, finally, peace prevails. After his second cup of coffee, handing down a final blessing to the assembled group, the most senior member takes his leave, signalling that it is time for others to do the same. Another memorable family occasion draws to a close.

Photocopiable recording script activity page 142

Hand out the recording script and ask students to underline any words or phrases they are unfamiliar with. Then write these words on the board and elicit guesses on their meaning, suggesting that students look at the surrounding context. Alternatively, treat the activity as dictionary work, where students work in pairs.

Elicit students' experience of similar family events, or set as written homework if time is short.

> **Possible answer**
> In Melbourne last Christmas, I was invited to Christmas lunch with my brother-in-law's Armenian family by marriage. There were over thirty people present, ranging from young children to grandparents. We started off in the garden, eating appetisers and toasting everyone's good health – including the health of the entire Liverpool football team. Eventually we all went inside and sat down together, at the longest table I have ever seen! There were so many succulent things to eat, including huge trays of sliced roast lamb and pork, different types of potato dishes, vegetarian salads and roasted vegetables. The meal was a leisurely affair, punctuated every so often by fresh supplies of warm bread. A tempting selection of desserts was then wheeled out and we were allowed to help ourselves and adjourn once more to the garden, where the sun was shining. Later still we came inside again, for the children to be given their presents. It was a truly splendid day.

Reading

3 The narrator, Triton, is Mister Salgado's cook.

> **Background information**
> Romesh Gunesekera has been favourably compared to Chekhov and Graham Greene. Much of his writing portrays the dilemma of living in Sri Lanka during the long period of civil war (1983–2009), where violence and political unrest were a part of daily life. *Reef*, his first novel, was shortlisted for the Booker prize in 1994 and won the Italian Premio Mondello in 1997. His other books include *Monkfish Moon*, a set of short stories, and other novels, *The Sandglass* and *The Match*.

4 Refer students to the Exam spot. Ask students to work through the questions on their own and then compare answers. Elicit reasons for their choice of answers (see detailed explanation opposite).

Answers
1 B 2 C 3 A 4 D 5 A 6 C

Detailed explanation:

1 The answer, B, can be found in the sentence *He was concerned to make sure there was plenty of time to prepare, even though he acted so nonchalant*. A is ruled out because the narrator says *it had never happened before in his life*. C is wrong as Mr Salgado did give his cook advance warning. D is plausible though the first paragraph shows that Triton has plenty of culinary experience.

2 The answer, C, is supported by the references Triton makes to Miss Nili's manner of eating in the second half of the first paragraph: *she ate like a horse, so hungry-looking* and *I expected her to bulge out as she ate …* . A, though plausible, is not stated in the text. B is falsely suggested by the words *I don't know where she put it*. As with A, Triton does not pass judgement on Miss Nili, so D is ruled out.

3 The answer, A, is rooted in the whole paragraph that begins *Triton made it*, where Triton talks of his 'coming of age'. B is wrong, as it was *the one phrase Mister Salgado would say … again and again*. C is ruled out by Miss Nili's words in the next paragraph, where she says that Triton *makes a lovely cake*. D is not suggested by the text, apart from Triton's general comment on *the petrified morass of all our lives*, which is beyond the scope of the tea party.

4 The answer, D, lies in the words *I rode in it like a prince*. A is wrong, as although Triton implies that the taxi is slow, *a black tortoise*, there is no suggestion that he is annoyed by this. B is not suggested by the text and it would be inappropriate for Triton, a servant, to have such feelings. C is wrong, as it is Miss Nili who is helped into the taxi by Mister Salgado.

5 The penultimate paragraph (the one before the final paragraph) shows that Triton feels positive about life when his work goes well: *Suddenly everything becomes possible and the whole world … pulls together*, so the answer is A. B is the opposite of Triton's view, for he *felt stupid* to need the praise. C is not suggested by the text; in fact Triton appears to prefer being the sole owner of the kitchen. D is not suggested by the paragraph.

6 The answer, C, is rooted in the sentence *It was as if he couldn't believe his eyes, seeing Nili sitting there in front of him*. A is wrong, as, although Mister Salgado drank lots of tea, he ate nothing. There is no evidence in the paragraph for B, as it was Nili who *would murmur her approval*. D, though plausible in view of Mister Salgado's nervousness before her arrival, is not suggested in the paragraph and Triton is the one who orchestrates the delivery of each part of the meal, with the exception of Mister Salgado's words *No, bring the cake now*.

Point out to students that using similes sparingly in their own writing will demonstrate range, as already highlighted in the Unit 2 Extension activity on page 17. Elicit other similes that refer to animals, for example: *as quiet as a mouse, as slippery as an eel, as strong as an ox, as brave as a lion.*

Give students further examples of verbs associated with animals that could be used of humans, for example: *bark* (an order), *purr* (with contentment), *squawk* (in surprise), *squeal* (with delight).

Encourage students to experiment when writing about colour: replacing a standard colour adjective with a noun phrase – for example, instead of 'brown', you could say *coffee-coloured* or *the colour of mud*; supplementing the adjective with a noun, to give a more vivid description – for example *mint green, ice blue.*

Answers
The animals associated with Miss Nili are:
a horse   *she ate like a horse*
a snake   *like a snake swallowing a bird ... one leg coiled under her*
a cow   *She made a lowing sound between bites.*

The effect is to accentuate her appetite and unconventional behaviour.

By referring to the taxi as having a *butter-coloured* top, the author brings his own writing to life and also skilfully reminds us that Triton the narrator is also Triton the cook, who sees life through his cooking (see the answer 5A in the multiple-choice questions above).

Vocabulary

5   The *Cambridge English Corpus* is a huge collection of texts held on computer. The texts come from novels and non-fiction books, journalism, academic writing, everyday speech and other forms of written and spoken English, and access to this corpus has allowed us to analyse examples of current English usage. These examples of 'savour' have been chosen from the corpus to show typically modern uses of the word.

Answers
savour the aftertaste – enjoy the sensation of flavour left in her mouth
The noun collocates are: *success, freedom, memories, past, word, wine*

Visit the websites that hold text corpora, for example www.just-the-word.com and www.natcorp.ox.ac.uk. It is possible to do a trial search free of charge and you can print off the lines, or download them.

6   The sentences given in the answers below are drawn from the *Cambridge English Corpus*.

Possible answers
a   consume + equivalent, quantity, time
    A typical teenager consumes a staggering quantity of commercial media online.
b   devour + books, news
    People in Redwood City, California eagerly devoured news of the jury's decision.
c   relish + challenge, thought
    Montoya relishes the high expectations and says he loves pressure.
d   swallow + pill, pride, news
    There has been less retail activity over the last two weeks, perhaps as people swallow news of job cuts and a worsening economic outlook.

4.2 SB pages 34–35
Review of past tenses

Lesson plan	
Grammar	45–60 minutes
Vocabulary	15–30 minutes
SV	Set 4 for homework.
LV	See Extension activity for 5.

1   The picture shows a selection of old and new forks. The top fork is African in origin, from Sierra Leone, and is around 500 years old. Carved from a single piece of ivory, it has two tapering tines.

Possible answers
People would certainly have been using some form of knife to cut up meat and other foodstuffs 2,000 years ago – not metal knives of course, but some kind of sharp cutting implement. People could have been using basic forks, too, though metal ones must be a more recent phenomenon, probably only dating back a thousand years or so. The ancient Egyptians used spoons made of ivory, wood and other materials.

The design of the spork is very clever, as it gives you a spoon, a fork and a serrated 'knife' all in the one implement. Produced in bright colours, it looks very attractive too – just the thing for a picnic or a camping trip.

2 Summarise ideas on the board about how the appearance and use of the fork has changed over the last 400 years.

Suggested answer
Appearance: three longer prongs became four shorter ones in the 19th century
Use: 'shared' forks became less common in the 19th century; one-handed eating in the 19th century gave way to holding the fork in the left hand and the knife in the right, introduced by the English towards the end of the 19th century.

3 Elicit answers before referring students to the Grammar folder on page 180.

Answers
a past perfect (*the knife was put down once the food had been cut up*)
b used to; would (*used to use special spoons; people would more often share forks with others*)
c modal verbs (*as well they might have done; scooping with them must have been impossible*)
d present perfect (*have been used for over 2,000 years*)
e *is thought to have been used* (past passive infinitive)
f *was being carved* at table (past continuous passive)
were satirised / these *were* now *shortened* ... / the fork *was* then *used* / the knife *was kept* (simple past passives)
g *had been making* forks (past perfect continuous)
were successfully *introducing* (past continuous)
as we have been doing ever since (present perfect continuous)
h spread (spread); strove (strive); done (do); bore (bear); seen (see); sought (seek).

4 Refer students to the Exam spot and stress the importance of working from context clues. A *tine* is the technical term for the prong of a fork.

Answers
a tools b list
c female-like behaviour: used to show disapproval
d picking up e fussy or ultra-careful f sin
g still / without moving h spread (widely)
i changing j fashionable

5

Answers
a was thought; had mastered
b have carved; was carried out
c have always insisted; should be torn; arose; is/was dressed; may/might/can/could react
d had murdered; was given; ate; drank
e continued; had started / had been starting
f have been supported; have been chosen

6 Suggest that students use more compound adjectives in their writing and speaking, to show language range.

Suggested answers
1 a an orphan baby lamb b an undergraduate c junior staff
2 a about to be impeached b hyper-inflation c risking disqualification
3 a a company plaque b a bathroom tap c a pen
4 a to hold it together b to prevent it smelling c to keep them hot
5 a ice cream b oranges c some types of yogurt
6 a a tiger b a football hooligan c a vampire
7 a a dish b a recipe c a jar of baby food (to prevent criminal activity)
8 a silly, not serious b with perfect features and immaculate clothes c wise, bright-eyed

 Extension activity

Give students the adjective suffixes below and ask them to come up with further compound adjectives. They could also develop questions similar to 1–8 in groups and try them out on the rest of the class.

-made (home, hand, purpose, tailor, European)
-dried (sun, freeze, wind)
-free (tax, additive, lead, nuclear, risk)
-bound (leather, house, desk, duty)
-deep (knee, chest, six)

4.3 SB pages 36–37
Listening and Speaking

Lesson plan	
Listening	30–40 minutes
Vocabulary	10–30 minutes
Speaking	20–20 minutes
SV	Keep discussion brief in 1 and 4.
LV	See Extension activity for the Idiom spot.

1 Students discuss the picture in pairs, using the adjectives listed. The fruit shown, from top left, includes grapes, a lime, a grapefruit, an apple, a mango, a pineapple, a lemon, a nectarine, redcurrants, bananas, pomegranates, passion fruit, a kiwi fruit, a melon, a watermelon, a coconut, a peach and oranges.

Suggested answers
A mango is fleshy, juicy when ripe, and rather sensuous. Redcurrants are quite sharp but they are very appetising, and look exquisite as a garnish – like bright red beads. Lemons can be quite fibrous and their juice is sour.

2 **1** **07** Explain to students that when they take notes while listening, it is helpful to include brief headings like the ones given. Play the recording twice.

Answers
Ideal temperature for ripening: over 40°C
Chief mango-growing area: to the north of Calcutta (Eastern India)
Facts about the mango tree: up to 60 feet (about 18 metres) tall, has a massive trunk, shiny green leaves
History of mango-growing in India: established by the Moghuls in the 17th century and taken up by the Nawabs, who diversified the varieties grown

Recording script
For the last two months, across much of India, temperatures have soared daily to over 40 degrees Celsius – perfect ripening weather for the mango, perfect wilting weather for humans. The thing about India, and Calcutta in particular, is that everyone here eats seasonally and mangoes are everywhere – in every home, on every hotel menu, and sold on every street corner. In the markets, they're beautifully arranged, stacked up according to variety on big wide wicker baskets.

The main mango-growing areas are situated to the north of the city. I headed out to an old family estate where they still have a number of the original orchards. This estate, laid out around an old indigo-planter's house, is wonderfully peaceful and the air so clean – a million miles from Calcutta. Against the exotic foliage of the coconut palm and the banana plant, the mango tree looks like a shiny-leaved evergreen oak. It has a massive, gnarled trunk and can easily grow to a height of sixty feet. Many trees were planted over a hundred years ago.

Indians today have the Moghul dynasties of the seventeenth and eighteenth centuries to thank for the amazing diversity of mangoes available now. They established large plantations across the northern states of Uttar Pradesh and Bihar. It was the Muslim leaders – the Nawabs – who cultivated the fruit in Bengal. They were great fruit-loving people and they missed their apricots and their melons. They cross-pollinated the mango, they got 101 varieties, and these are the sophisticated mangoes that grow mainly in eastern India. When the Moghul empire was in its decline, the Nawabs moved southward and here they cultivated their mangoes, planting them according to their different varieties in orchards – they gave them the most romantic and poetic names, names like 'passari', the loved one, 'begum pasan', the Nawab's wife's favourite …

3 **1** **07** Play the recording again, pausing after each phrase, and elicit answers.

Answers
a The speaker uses the word 'perfect' ironically: although the high temperature is perfect for ripening the mango, it causes people to 'wilt', that is, become tired and without energy.
b The mangoes are arranged in piles according to their varieties.
c leaves that grow in the tropics or another faraway place from the speaker's point of view
d the Moghul Empire or royal families
e incredible variety (101 different types)

4 Remind students that *seasonally* comes from the noun *season* (the -*al* adjective suffix came up in Unit 1). The discussion could be run in four groups, with each group taking one of the statements. Each group then reports their views to the others at the end.

Suggested answer
Buying produce out of season appears to offer maximum choice and flexibility, but can be very disappointing in terms of flavour because the fruit in question has been flown halfway around the world in chilled conditions. Fresh soft fruit like strawberries and raspberries, or vegetables such as asparagus, taste so delicious when they have been freshly picked. Also, because they are only available at a set time of year, you look forward to eating them and savour them during their short season.

 Idiom spot

Answers
a icing; cake b lot; plate c eggs; basket d fish
e pill f pinch; salt g beans h hot cakes
i egg; face j pie

Suggested answers
a This government is sweetening the pill of higher taxation by introducing new benefits for employees at the same time.
b I've put all my eggs in one basket work-wise.
c Harry got egg on his face when Professor Samuels confronted him in the canteen queue.
d Valentina isn't staying on here as a student as she has bigger fish to fry in the US, with a Harvard scholarship.
e After the rugby team's outstanding performance, journalists will have to eat humble pie.
f I finally got Simon to spill the beans about his wedding.
g Sharon has a lot on her plate at the moment.
h Maria's earrings are selling like hot cakes on the market stall.

Extension activity

There are plenty of other idioms to do with food! Ask students to look up the following words in a dictionary, to find their related idioms:

bread, butter, cookie, fat, grapes, gravy, mustard, turkey.

Related idioms are: *the best thing since sliced bread* (referring to something new and exciting, though often used ironically)

know which side your bread is buttered (understand how you can benefit from something or someone)

bread and butter (the main part of your income)

that's the way the cookie crumbles (that's life)

a tough cookie (a brave or independent person)

chew the fat (chat with someone)

have sour grapes (be jealous of someone else's success)

a/the gravy train (a secure and easy way of making money)

keen as mustard (very eager)

doesn't cut the mustard (is not up to the job)

talk turkey (have a frank discussion: used mainly in American English)

You could also run a competition for homework, where the winner is the student who comes back with the longest list of food idioms.

5 Refer students to the Exam spot and explain that Paper 4 Part 2 is in two stages. Candidates have one minute to talk about some of the pictures and then a further three minutes to discuss all of the pictures.

Ask students to discuss the issues that are shown in Pictures A and B in pairs, using some of the phrases given. Stop them after one minute.

Suggested answer
The two photos illustrate different aspects of food consumption that are somewhat problematic. The green beans in Picture A have been grown in Egypt but are being sold in the UK, so the supermarket concerned has incurred air miles. The buying power of large supermarkets is such that they can afford to pay these transport costs and they know that people will buy them when they are not in season in the UK. It would be much better for the environment if shoppers restricted their buying of fruit and vegetables to local seasonal produce.

All the bananas for sale in Picture B have been shrink-wrapped, which is just so unnecessary! Excessive packaging like this causes so many issues, including rubbish disposal – the landfill sites cannot cope with the quantity of rubbish that is generated. Some shrink-wrapping has health implications too – take the way meat is packaged for example, with chemical treatment to extend the sell-by dates.

6 Now ask students to discuss all four pictures in pairs or groups of three, addressing the question: How could lifestyle choices be modified to promote a greener future?

Picture C shows appalling waste – a rubbish skip being filled with loaves of bread that cannot be sold by a supermarket because they are a day beyond their 'best before' date. Picture D shows someone working on their own vegetable plot, pulling a big fat fresh leek out of the ground. It has been grown in season and hasn't created any air miles – or even road miles, as it has been grown at home.

Possible modifications to life-style choices could be: supermarkets restricting the choice on offer, offering more seasonal, locally grown, produce, people growing their own food and baking their own bread.

Writing folder 2

SB pages 38–39

Part 2 Review

Explain to students that if they decide to write a review in Part 2, they will need to address the task set rather than merely describe what happens in the book or film being reviewed. They should make early reference to the title for clarity, as in a real review.

1 The picture is a 'still' from the film *The Perfect Storm*, showing the fishing boat amidst massive waves.

   Ask students to write three sentences on their own and then put a selection on the board. Leave them up, as they will be needed later (see 3 below).

Possible answers
The steel grey sea looks bitterly cold and very sinister. The huge waves tower menacingly over the fishing boat. Such a vast amount of heaving water threatens the lives of everyone on board the vessel.

2 Point out that the paragraph plan covers all parts of the exam task, including the general aspect at the end. Students may get lower marks in the exam if they fail to address the whole question.

3 Elicit comments on the answer.

Suggested answers
The review is not very successful. There is only a minimal lead-in. The film is not named. The third paragraph is all plot, most of which should have been omitted. There is insufficient description of the special effects in the fourth paragraph. The evaluation is barely attempted.

To improve the review, the balance of the content needs to be addressed: there should be less plot, more reference to the special effects used, and some expansion of the general evaluation at the end.

4 Encourage students to extend their range of vocabulary and expression.

Answers
See also the corrected and improved answer in 5 below.
a Hollywood blockbuster (film)
b the budget (money spent)
c an interesting sub-plot (part)
d portrayed (acted) by George Clooney
e he heads out (goes) to sea
f the safety of his crew (men)
g the eye of the storm (worst weather)
h the special effects kick in (start)
i really outstanding (very good)
j clever use of digital imaging (computers)
k those gigantic (big) waves
l the film also stars (has) Mark Wahlberg
m the film cuts to (shows)
n the girlfriend, scanning the horizon (looking out to sea)
o a prerequisite (essential part) of all films
p its best feature (thing)

5 Ask students to draft about 50 words to follow the rhetorical question, preferably in class if there is time. Suggest that students show each other their drafts and discuss how they might be improved.

Corrected and improved answer
As part of the feature on special effects, the film *The Perfect Storm* is a very good example to consider. In one way, it is not a typical Hollywood *blockbuster*, as there is no happy ending, but in other ways – the actors used, *the budget*, the special effects – it is.

Why is it 'perfect'? It is actually a weatherman who uses this word. As he tracks the worsening weather out at sea, we see him getting genuinely excited about the unique set of weather conditions. This was *an interesting sub-plot* for me.

The captain of the fishing boat, *portrayed* by George Clooney, does not care about *the safety of his crew* and only wants to find more fish and make money. His irresponsible risk-taking eventually leads the tiny boat into the very *eye of the storm*, which is brought vividly to the screen by *really outstanding* use of special effects, including some *clever use of digital imaging*. When *the special effects kick in*, you feel as though you are in the boat with the crew, facing *those gigantic waves*. At the end, the ship goes down and we see one of the sailors – *the film also stars* Mark Wahlberg – drifting on an empty sea. The huge waves tower menacingly over the poor fisherman. Somewhat unbelievably, he is shown thinking beautiful thoughts about his girlfriend. Then *the film cuts to the girlfriend, scanning the horizon* with an anxious look on her face.

Are special effects *a prerequisite* of all films today? In my own opinion, it depends on the type of film – a psychological drama has no need of special effects to heighten the tension between characters. However, most of today's younger cinema-goers choose action films and they do expect special effects to be an integral part of the entertainment. In *The Perfect Storm*, they were probably *its best feature*.
(309 words)

6 If necessary, write the following sample paragraph plan on the board. Elicit students' favourite advertisements and give them any relevant vocabulary. Set the review for homework.

Sample plan
Para 1   Introduction to review/advert chosen
Para 2   Brief description of the advert
Para 3   Visual effects
Para 4   Other features – music, actors, voice-over, etc.
Para 5   Assessment of influence adverts have on us

Sample answer
It is true that advertising has become an art form in its own right. Nowadays, some of the very best film directors are employed to produce a visually impressive fifty or sixty seconds of footage that we will remember and associate ever afterwards with the product being sold. My own favourite is a recent Guinness advert, which lives up to the high standards set by earlier adverts for this dark beer from Ireland.

The product becomes part of a visual extravaganza, set somewhere in South America or the Caribbean. At the outset, you are unsure what you are witnessing. Tension is in the air and you realise that a race is about to start – incredibly, a snails' race! Each snail lines up in its own lane, with a number on its shell, and bets are taken on which one will be the winner. Snails being what they are, the race gets off to a slow start, but then, one snail finds its way into an almost-empty glass of Guinness, takes in the necessary sustenance and streaks home, to the wild cheers of the crowd.

One striking image follows another and special effects are judiciously used to accentuate the snail's speed. The film is also shot from unusual angles – a snail's eye view, you might say, where human faces become slightly distorted and more unusual. At the end, we are almost participants in the vibrant celebration, which is fuelled by Guinness and exudes only good humour and love of life. Characteristically of a Guinness advert, loud music alternates with silence, busy scenes with stillness. There is no need for a voice-over, which would only labour the point. The overwhelming impression created is that you are watching something utterly unique, a message that you will then associate with the product itself.

In general, I believe adverts have a huge effect on our lifestyle and aspirations. If they didn't, far less money would be spent on them.
(324 words)

Units 1–4 Revision

SB pages 40–41

Lesson plan

Use of English	35–35 minutes
Writing	0–25 minutes

SV   Set 4 for homework.
LV   Elicit students' reactions to the texts in 1 and 4.

The aim of this revision unit is to focus on the language covered in Units 1–4, as well as extending the work done on reviews in Writing folder 2. Specific exam practice is provided for Paper 1 Parts 1, 3 and 4. This section could be done as a timed test of 30 minutes. Alternatively, the whole unit could be set for homework.

Use of English

1   The picture shows a side canal in Venice. Students should read through the text carefully before attempting to do the task.

Answers
1 undertook 2 glorious 3 encircled 4 uninviting
5 antiquity 6 inhabitants 7 perpetually 8 gratitude

2   Remind the class that contractions count as two words.

Answers
1 have no alternative | but to ask
2 known there | was going to / would be a delay OR known | about the delay
3 was made to / had to | shoulder the financial burden of
4 he was on the verge | of tears/crying
5 you find it necessary / it be necessary | to contact me urgently
6 hotel is bound to be good | as/because/since Pablo

3

Answers
1 C 2 B 3 B 4 D 5 A 6 C 7 D 8 A

Writing

4   The review originally appeared in *The Guardian* newspaper, in a slightly longer version. The writer is fairly negative about the book, dismissing it as 'publishing froth'.

Punctuated and paragraphed review
No one has yet written 'Froth: the Trend that Changed History' but Universal Foam comes pretty close to being the definitive example of publishing froth. The book blends two recent publishing trends, the newer of which is the wacky science subject. If there is a market for books on cryptography, chronometry or cod – **/** , and books on all these subjects have sold well in the last decade – **/** , then there is no reason why any subject should seem boring.

Once you have discovered a subject so obscure that no other publisher has come across it before, all that remains is to prove that it holds the key to universal understanding. 'Cod: **/** – a Biography of the Fish that Changed the World' **/** "Cod: **/** – a Biography of the Fish that Changed the World" **/** *Cod: /– a Biography of the Fish that Changed the World* is a pretty good example, but 'Universal Foam: **/** – the Story of Bubbles from Cappuccino to the Cosmos' **/** "Universal Foam: **/** – the Story of Bubbles from Cappuccino to the Cosmos" **/** *Universal Foam: / – the Story of Bubbles from Cappuccino to the Cosmos* outdoes it, since it permeates the universe from the smallest to the largest scale. After all, there aren't any galaxies stretched on the skin of unimaginably vast cod ; **/** , nor do physicists speak of the world arising from fluctuations in the quantum codfish. So 'The Boys' Bumper Book of Froth' **/** "The Boys' Bumper Book of Froth" **/** *The Boys' Bumper Book of Froth* might contain – **/** , **/** (as every bestseller should – **/** , **/**) everything you need to know about the universe. Then again, **/** [no punctuation] it might contain everything else. That's pretty frothy too.

In fact, 'Universal Foam' **/** "Universal Foam" **/** *Universal Foam* runs into another current publishing style: **/** – the book of lists. Among the subjects covered here are: **/** [no punctuation] volcanoes, shaving-foam, champagne, fire-fighting **/** firefighting equipment and meringues. Then you list everything you know about everything in the first list: **/** – 101 important facts about galaxies ; **/** – then 20 things you never knew about the cappuccino, **/** [no punctuation] and so on.

Finally, all this is wrapped up in the academic style, **/** – **/** (as old as exams, **/** – **/**) where you simply cram in all the knowledge that you can possibly get hold of and regurgitate it, **/** [no punctuation] with the echoing solemnity of a TV anchorman on 'The Simpsons' **/** "The Simpsons" **/** *The Simpsons*, suggesting a rhetorical question: **/** – 'Can everyday foams like milk foam ever be fully understood and controlled?' **/** "Can everyday foams like milk foam ever be fully understood and controlled?" At which point, **/** [no punctuation] there is foam flecking this reviewer's lips.

You can't really blame the author, **/** [no punctuation] **/** (Sidney Perkowitz, **/**) who has worked hard and writes clearly. It is not his fault that he has nothing particular to say after he has got through the bits that particularly interest him: **/** – the fairly technical discussions of how to measure foams and describe them mathematically. However, the fact is there is no sound reason for this book to have been written in the first place.

Crossword

This includes some of the idioms, phrasal verbs and other vocabulary from Units 1–4.

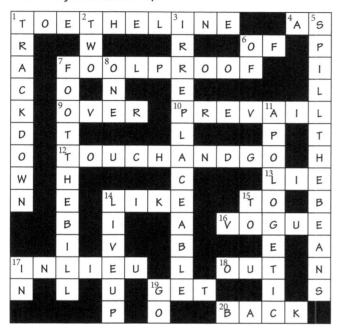

The crossword grid contains the following answers:

¹T	O	E	²T	H	E	L	³I	N	E		⁴A	⁵S
R			W			R		⁶O	F		P
A		⁷F	O	⁸O	L	P	R	O	O	F	I
C		O		N		E					L
K		⁹O	V	E	R		¹⁰P	R	E	V	¹¹A	I	L
D		T			L			P		T
O		¹²T	O	U	C	H	A	N	D	G	O	H
W		H			C			¹³L	I	E
N		E		¹⁴L	I	K	E		¹⁵T	O	B
		B		I		A		¹⁶V	O	G	U	E
		I		V		B			E		A
¹⁷I	N	L	I	E	U		L		¹⁸O	U	T	N
N		L		U		¹⁹G	E	T		I	S
		P		O			²⁰B	A	C	K

5 The consumer society

5.1

Exam skills	Listening Paper 3 Part 2
	Reading and Use of English Paper 1 Part 1
Vocabulary	Phrasal verbs, phrases with *right*

5.2

Grammar	Countable/uncountable nouns
	Possession
	Prepositions

5.3

Exam skills	Reading into Writing: Working with two texts – Paper 2 Part 1
Vocabulary	Abstract nouns

Workbook contents

1	Reading Paper 1 Part 5
2, 3, 4	Grammar – countable/uncountable nouns
5, 6, 7	Vocabulary
8	Use of English Paper 1 Part 3

5.1 SB pages 42–43

Lesson plan

Introduction	10–15 minutes
Listening	20–20 minutes
Vocabulary	20–25 minutes
Use of English	0–20 minutes
Speaking	10–10 minutes

SV   Keep the discussion brief in 1; set 4 for homework.

LV   See Photocopiable recording script activity for 3 and Extension activity for 4.

Speaking

1   Ask students to work in pairs to discuss the questions. They might not know the word *shopaholic* and discussion could result from the origins of this word.

Listening

2   **1 08** Refer students to the Exam spot. Make sure they read through the questions carefully before they hear the recording. Check they understand the vocabulary. Play the recording twice.

Answers

1 consumer slot   2 database   3 lawyers   4 title
5 kitchen (door)   6 online   7 hairspray/hair-spray
8 squeaked   9 publicity

Recording script

Paula: Good morning. On the programme today we have Mike James, a familiar face on television as the champion of consumers' rights. Mike, you've been doing *Pricewise* a long time now, is it something you set out to do?

Mike: Far from it Paula. It all began in 2002, when I was a reporter on a nightly news programme. They wanted a consumer slot, so I took it on. It wasn't until nearly ten years later that it became a programme in its own right. Now, we regularly get more than ten million viewers.

Paula: Where do the stories you look into come from?

Mike: Well, from you, the public. We get thousands of letters, phone calls and emails that tell us about poor service, ridiculous small print, malpractice and the need for information. We actually read all the correspondence and we follow up some stories immediately but most are filed for future use on our database.

Paula: What happens when you get a particularly juicy story?

Mike: We check it out thoroughly of course, and then we contact everyone involved, write the script and arrange filming. Sometimes we use actors and sometimes real people. Of course, it's essential that our lawyers check the script over. It's all done to very tight deadlines.

Paula: Do any particular stories stand out in your memory?

Mike: Oh, yes, many. There was one about an advert which promised to give you a title for anything up to £1,000. So, Bob and Trace became Lord Robert and Lady Tracy de Vere. You also get a piece of land but that only measures 20cm by 20cm. One of our researchers handed over the cash and tried to find out if being a lord would help him out in London.

Paula: And did it?

Mike: He went to Harrods, the department store, and they were very nice to him, but then they're nice to everyone. He then tried to book a table in a trendy restaurant and he got one – but not in a prime position next to the window – but by the kitchen door! So, really, it won't do you a lot of good being a lord nowadays.

Paula: Any other interesting stories?

Mike: Well, we did a programme not long ago about shopping on the Internet. The big supermarkets will deliver to your door if you order <u>online</u>, as you know.

Paula: Yes, it's a great idea, but I've not actually tried it out.

Mike: Well, it does usually work well. However, we did find that some customers hadn't received quite what they'd ordered. One poor man had asked for apples and got <u>hairspray</u>! The supermarket was very apologetic when we pointed out these problems and sent the customer some shopping vouchers.

Paula: Do you think consumers are more ready to complain these days?

Mike: Oh, yes. Research has been done that shows that attitudes have changed remarkably in the last forty years. Take a well-known brand of trainer. You could understand if they leaked, but actually these particular ones <u>squeaked</u>. Now, as they cost upwards of a hundred pounds, people weren't prepared to put up with this, but when they returned them to the shop, the shop didn't want to know.

Paula: So they wrote to you for help.

Mike: Yes. We bought a pair of the trainers and sent them to be inspected by an expert who said that some of the glue inside the shoe had come unstuck. We contacted the manufacturer with evidence of the problem and they were more than happy to back down and refund the money paid by the purchasers.

Paula: Another success then.

Mike: Yes, it's funny how quickly manufacturers and retailers react when they think they might attract bad <u>publicity</u>.

Paula: Indeed! It just shows what a good job you're doing. Now next week …

Vocabulary

3   **1** The aim of this exercise is to get students to learn phrasal verbs in context, rather than in a list. Make sure they write down the whole sentence in their notebooks. The phrasal verbs are highlighted in the script above.

Answers
a to set out   b to take on   c to look into / to check out
d to follow up   e to stand out   f to find out   g to try out   h to point out   i to put up with   j to back down

Photocopiable recording script activity page 143

If students find exercise 3 too difficult to do just by listening, give them a copy of the recording script and ask them to find the words and expressions in the text. This will build their confidence.

Phrase spot

Ask students to work through a–j in pairs. Encourage them to use an English–English dictionary.

Answers
a By rights   b as right as rain   c in the right
d right under their noses   e the film rights
f right on time   g within your rights
h makes all the right noises   i the right way round
j serve (Michelle) right

4   This exercise gives practice in Paper 1 Part 1.

Answer
1 D   2 A   3 C   4 B   5 A   6 D   7 B   8 C

Extension activity

Ask students to write a sentence to show how the following words from exercise 4 can be used. Encourage them to use an English–English dictionary.

1 body   5 cluster
2 brought out   6 sequel
3 devised   7 correlate
4 rally   8 heighten

Possible answers
1 FIFA is football's ruling body.
2 The company has brought out a new range of leisure wear.
3 A scheme has been devised to allow students on the course to study part-time.
4 Supporters have been quick to rally to our cause.
5 The team was encouraged to cluster around the coach at the end of each match.
6 You know there's now a sequel to that book you're reading about the two sisters.
7 The response to the questions correlated closely with the participants' age and status.
8 The director introduced the music specifically to heighten the suspense of the scene.

5 Students should work in pairs to answer the questions.

Possible answers

I prefer to shop in a town centre because there are more independent stores. I hate out-of-town shopping centres or malls because they are just full of the big chain stores, all selling similar things.

I think it's terrible that there are so few small independent shops in my town. I can quite understand why people go out of town to do their shopping – after all, it's probably more convenient and possibly the prices are lower – but I prefer the variety that small independent shops provide.

Parking provision is probably the main reason why shopping centres or malls are so popular. Added to that is the fact that, in some cold, rainy climates, it is more comfortable to shop in a warm, indoor mall rather than having to battle against the elements on the High Street.

5.2 SB pages 44–45

Nouns review

Lesson plan	
Grammar	40–70 minutes
Vocabulary	20–20 minutes
SV	Set 3 for homework.
LV	See Extension activity for 4.

 Corpus spot

The sentences in this exercise contain the type of errors that students make when they write. The importance of knowing whether a noun is countable or uncountable cannot be stressed too highly as it affects the whole grammar of a sentence.

Answers
a Correct
b How <u>much luggage</u> did you bring with you?
c Doctors and scientists, with their <u>research</u>, have managed to give us a better life.
d The news this morning <u>was</u> terrible – more price rises and a teachers' strike.
e Thanks to the revolution in <u>transport</u>, travelling has become easier.
f correct
g correct
h <u>Equipment</u> such as the tape recorder and stereo are very outdated.
i correct
j The future <u>behaviour</u> of our children will depend on a good upbringing.
k I live on the <u>outskirts</u> of the city.
l The fishmonger weighed out three kilos of <u>fish</u>.
m correct
n The <u>scenery</u> in New Zealand <u>is</u> spectacular.
o correct
p The police <u>are</u> aware of the break-in.
q My father is a Professor of <u>Economics</u>.

1 Ask students to work in pairs to discuss the different meanings and then to write a sentence showing the difference in meaning.

Answers
a **work** – job; **works** – factory/of art/literature/road
b **iron** – material; **an iron** – machine for smoothing garments
c **a disorder** – an illness; **disorder** – untidiness
d **a speech** – a talk; **speech** – language/noise
e **a room** – a place; **room** – space
f **a language** – German, Greek, etc.; **language** – the method of communication
g **home comforts** – a comfortable bed, central heating, etc.; **a comfort** – someone or something that gives you sympathy
h **an experience** – something that happened to you; **experience** – what you have learned doing something
i **a capital** – chief city; **capital** – money
j **a coffee** – a cup of coffee; **coffee** – the plant or beans

Suggested answers
a The work I do is confidential.
   There are road works on the motorway.
   I've never read the *Complete Works of Shakespeare*.
   The Tate Modern has some wonderful works of art.
b The box was made of iron.
   I used an iron to make the dress look more presentable.
c He is supposed to be suffering from a heart disorder.
   Her room is in a terrible state of disorder.
d The Minister made a brilliant election speech.
   Her speech was affected by the accident.
e Go to your room at once!
   There is no room in our house now we have four children.
f What languages do you speak?
   Language is one of the features that sets human beings apart from other animals.
g I love my home comforts like the microwave and Jacuzzi.
   It is a comfort to know that someone cares about me.
h I had a terrible experience on a train once.
   Does she have enough experience for the job?
i The capital of Italy is Rome.
   The company had depleted its reserves of capital.
j Would you like a coffee?
   Coffee grows in certain places in Brazil.

2 Explain that, in some cases, for example for *glass*, it is not wrong to use *a bit of* or *a piece of*. However, for other cases it is essential that the right word is used and a higher mark would be gained if the best word was used with *glass*.

Answers
a a burst of applause   b a pane of glass
c a stroke of luck   d a grain of sand   e a gust of wind
f a speck of dust   g a stream of abuse
h a ray of sunshine   i a source of amusement
j an item of clothing/news   k a rumble of thunder
l a puff of smoke   m a state of emergency

3 Spelling is important in all the papers in the examination. The underlined nouns are the ones which were spelt wrongly.

Answers
Look around. You're in the midst of a global maelstrom. A swirling mass of converging technologies and new business <u>opportunities</u> unleashed by the internet. All waiting to be harnessed by large IT service <u>providers</u>. As one has said: 'We've focused our energy and <u>resources</u> on creating technology to solve the unique problems of <u>thousands</u> of individual businesses. Last year alone we invested $2.5 <u>billion</u> of our global IT and <u>telecommunications</u> <u>revenues</u> on R & D. <u>Innovations</u> that keep your company one step ahead of the Internet. And light years ahead of the <u>competition</u>.'

It is worth spending some time each lesson on spelling. The *Cambridge Learner Corpus* shows that certain words continue to be misspelt even at C2 level. These include: *access, beautiful, because, beginning, believe, business, definitely, environment, existence, future, mystery, opinion, psychological, responsibility, should, strength, successful, typical, until, whether.* American spelling is acceptable in the examination, if it is consistent.

4 Students are often confused as to how to use the apostrophe *s* in English. As a result they tend to use *of*, which is often not correct. Ask them to read through the notes in the Student's Book and then to do the exercise.

Answers
a back seat **b** boss's wife / wife's boss – depending on whether the boss is male or female **c** corner of a/the room **d** pay day **e** week's holiday **f** wine glass **g** moment's delay **h** Anne's best friend **i** door handle **j** sports field

 Extension activity

Ask students to explain what the following are: *a seat back*; *a wine glass*; *a field sport*; *a horse race*; *a racehorse*; *a house boat*; *a boat house*; *pay day*; *a working party*; *the building of the museum*; *the museum building*

Answers
A seat back is the part of the seat itself, not where it is.
A wine glass is the object.
A field sport is discus, javelin, etc.
A horse race is a race for horses.
A racehorse is a type of horse.
A house boat is a boat you can live on.
A boat house is where you keep your boat.
Pay day is the day you are paid.
A working party is a committee to discuss the organisation of something.

The building of the museum is the construction of the museum.
The museum building is the building itself.

Vocabulary

5 Prepositions are often a problem in English for students of all levels. It's a good idea to make posters divided into adjectives, verbs and nouns, all with their particular prepositions on, to be displayed in the classroom. Conversely, a game can be played as a warmer to a lesson. Ask students to match cards with different prepositions on to cards which have verbs, nouns or adjectives on. You can easily adapt this game to suit your circumstances.

Answers
1 in **2** with **3** of **4** by/into **5** in **6** of **7** with/in **8** to **9** in/at **10** of **11** into/on **12** with **13** towards/to **14** on **15** without **16** at

5.3 SB pages 46–47
Reading into Writing: Working with two texts

Lesson plan	
Speaking	10–20 minutes
Reading two texts	30–30 minutes
Writing	20–20 minutes
Vocabulary	0–20 minutes
SV	Keep discussion in 1 brief; set 6 for homework.
LV	See Extension activity for 1.

1 Ask students to work in pairs to discuss the questions.

 Extension activity

Bring in ads from magazines and pass them round the class. Students have to talk about which ad they think works best and why. It's a good idea to bring in ads which aren't explicit and students can then guess what they think they are for.

2 Give students about five minutes to read the two texts and answer the questions.

Answers
Text 1 is possibly from a newspaper. The style is fairly informal, e.g. *shell out, dawn on, nagging, even down to*
Text 2 is possibly from a research paper. The style is academic, e.g. *cognitive ability, embedded within, inherently*

3 Check students understand the meaning of the words before they start to look for synonyms.

> **Answers**
> **Text 1:** occur to – dawn on; pester – nagging; including – down to; whim – impulse, evaluate – weigh up
> **Text 2:** assess – evaluate; extent – scope; claim – contention; essentially – inherently; exaggerated – overstated

4 Students will need to find the two main points in each text in the examination.

> **Answers**
> **Text 1:** b, d
> **Text 2:** a, c

5

> **Suggested answer**
> The two texts discuss the pros and cons of advertising to young people. Text 1 claims that young people have an enormous impact on what the people around them, friends and family, decide to spend their money on, even affecting decisions normally made by adults. Not only this, but young people, unlike older ones, do not spend time carefully considering their purchases or asking around to get advice.
>
> Text 2 argues that, even though there is some unease about targeting young people with advertising, in fact, this group have some immunity to it as they have been subjected to it over a long period of time. There is also the point that advertising can enable young people to make sensible decisions about their purchases by giving them the facts they need about the goods advertised.
> (135 words)

Vocabulary

6 As mentioned in Unit 3, it is important to be able to manipulate words, both for the word formation task and in answering Paper 2 Writing tasks.

> **Answers**
> **a** boredom **b** obsolescence **c** awareness **d** pride
> **e** confidence **f** austerity **g** generosity
> **h** independence **i** inefficiency **j** insecurity
> **k** meanness **l** Individualism, responsibility
> **m** aspirations **n** scepticism

Exam folder 3

SB pages 48–49

Paper 1 Part 1 Multiple-choice cloze

Refer students to the different examples of tested vocabulary. They should read them through carefully before attempting the exam task.

Refer the class to the Exam advice and then ask them to do the task.

The photograph is of a fresco by Giovanni Stradano (1523–1603) of the Piazza del Mercato Vecchio in Florence.

> **Answers**
> 1 B 2 B 3 A 4 A 5 D 6 B 7 A 8 C

6 The sound of music

Topic Music

6.1

| Exam skills | Reading and Use of English Paper 1 Part 6 |
| Vocabulary | Phrases with *take* |

6.2

Grammar	Modals: Degrees of likelihood
Exam skills	Reading and Use of English Paper 1 Part 4
	Reading and Use of English Paper 1 Part 2

6.3

Exam skills	Listening Paper 3 Part 2
	Speaking Paper 4 Part 2
Style extra	Collocations with adverbs and adjectives
Vocabulary	Idioms with music words
Pronunciation	Contrastive stress

Workbook contents

1	Listening Paper 3 Part 2
2, 3	Grammar – modal verbs
4, 5	Vocabulary
6	Use of English Paper 1 Part 1
7	Use of English Paper 1 Part 2
8	Use of English Paper 1 Part 3

6.1 SB pages 50–51

Lesson plan

Introduction	20–20 minutes
Reading	40–55 minutes
Phrase spot	0–15 minutes

SV Set Phrase spot for homework.
LV See Extension activity for 3.

Speaking

The photos are of a young woman listening to an MP3 player and studying and a teenage boy playing an electric guitar.

1 Ask students to discuss the statements together.

Possible answers
I'm afraid I find it very hard to concentrate if music is playing – it doesn't matter what type it is, I still find it very distracting.

It's quite true that every child should learn to play an instrument, although getting them to practise may be a problem. Learning how to read music is very good.

I think the piano is much easier to learn than the violin. Your playing can sound fairly reasonable much faster on the piano than on the violin.

Pop music can improve my mood, but it depends – sometimes it just makes it worse!

I don't believe that classical music is superior to pop music. They both have their positive aspects.

Reading

2 Refer students to the Exam spot. This part of Paper 1 Reading and Use of English is the one students often have the most trouble with. They must read all of the base text and then all the extra paragraphs before doing the exercise. Some of the important references have been highlighted in bold as this is the first example of this type of task. They are not in bold in the examination. Students should read both sides of the gap to make sure they have the right answer. Just reading the paragraph before the gap will not always help. They should try to underline the linking words or phrases that helped them find the answers.

Answers
1 F 2 D 3 B 4 G 5 A 6 E 7 H
Links to underline:
3 'statistical connection' (para 2); 'truly convincing study' (para B); 'musical ability enhances mathematical ability' (para B); 'the two are interestingly related' (para 3)
4 'piano' (para 3); 'are mathematicians more drawn to this rather than to other instruments' (para G); 'can we at least argue' (para G); 'Indeed, yes, we can' (para 4)
5 'not the kind of obscure connection' (para 4); 'the straightforward link' (para A);
6 'we don't ... mysterious connection between mathematical ability and linguistic ability' (para 5); 'because the link exists but not the uncertainty: grammar feels mathematical' (para E); 'paradoxical' (para E); 'contradiction' (para 6)
7 'solve problems of the "A is to B as C is to D" kind' (para 6); 'Music is full of little puzzles like this' (para H)

3   Ask the class to discuss the statements together.

 Extension activity

Ask students to paraphrase the following words or phrases from the text.
Main text:
1   compelling evidence
2   a control group
3   implausible
4   innumerate
5   uncharted territory
Gapped paragraphs:
1   spill over
2   tied up with
3   grossly exaggerated
4   anecdotal evidence
5   one's expectations are confounded

Suggested answers
Main text:
1   convincing/strong evidence
2   a group who are not part of an experiment
3   unlikely/suspect
4   unable to add up or do mathematics
5   unknown territory

Gapped paragraphs:
1   overflow
2   linked with
3   greatly exaggerated
4   evidence drawn from stories people have told
5   expectations are contradicted/disproved

 Phrase spot

Phrases with *take* are often tested in the examination.

Answers
a exception to   b notice   c place   d part
e the view   f account of   g issue   h advantage
i by surprise   j second place   k into account/
consideration   l for granted   m a stand

6.2 pages 52–53

Modals: Degrees of likelihood

Lesson plan	
Grammar	40–60 minutes
Use of English	20–30 minutes

SV   Set 4 for homework.
LV   See Extension activity for 3. Extend 5 with discussion on the questions.

1   Ask students to read through the information in the box on likelihood. Refer them to the Grammar folder on page 181 if they are not clear about the uses of these modal verbs.

Answers
A c, f, h, l
B a, b, d, e, g, i, j
C m
D k

2   Ask students to work in groups to discuss these statements. Encourage them to use the expressions they have just learnt.

Possible answers
a   There is every likelihood that another Mozart will be born. I can't believe that only one musical genius will ever exist.
b   I guess an asteroid could hit the Earth, but the government is bound to do all in its power to prevent it.
c   People may well have brain transplants in the future – after all, we have transplants for most parts of the body, don't we?
d   I think there's only a faint chance that English will be the language of the Internet in the future. I think Chinese will take over.
e   There's no chance of New Zealand winning the football World Cup – not when there are teams from France, Spain, Italy and Brazil.
f   It's a foregone conclusion that electric cars are the cars of the future. It stands to reason that oil reserves won't last forever.

3   Students should then go on to try to work out who or what is being talked about in this exercise. Make sure they read the example and try to use language in the same way. There may be different answers to the ones suggested below.

Possible answers

a landing on the Moon
b a royal wedding
c possibly Madonna
d possibly Federer – anyone who is a sports champion who is about to retire
e possibly polio, AIDS or smallpox

 Extension activity

Get students to make up radio news extracts for the other students to guess. They should then circulate round the classroom alternately reading out their news extracts and trying to guess each others' extracts. These could relate to a person or an event.

4 Refer students to the Exam spot for advice. After they have completed each sentence, ask them to check how many words they have used. They should also check that they have used the word given and that they haven't changed it in any way.

Answers
1 chances are (good/excellent) (that) Alan will | be/get
2 's/is doubtful that Professor Potts will | take
3 bound to get the Head's job | if / providing (that) / provided (that)
4 all likelihood | the cause
5 a foregone conclusion (that) | a/the gold medal
6 likely (that) the audience will take | no notice

5 The article is about how bands are often 'manufactured' by people in the music industry for profit. There are more spaces than would be the case in the exam, to give extra practice.

Answers
a The writer is rather cynical.
b The comparison between groups in the past who got together themselves and what is happening now.
c That music bands are like any other product.

1 Not 2 as 3 out 4 in/to 5 may 6 With
7 who/what 8 far/much 9 Although/Though/Whereas/While/Whilst 10 before 11 having/likely
12 together 13 charge/control 14 fact/reality 15 any

6.3 pages 54–55

Listening and Speaking

Lesson plan	
Introduction	5–10 minutes
Listening	20–20 minutes
Style extra	10–10 minutes
Idiom spot	0–15 minutes
Speaking	15–15 minutes
Pronunciation	10–20 minutes

SV Keep the discussion in 1 brief. Set the Idiom spot for homework.
LV See Extension activity for 6.

1 Ask students to use an English–English dictionary to help them with this exercise if they are unsure of the answers.

Answers
brass: trumpet
electronic: synthesizer
keyboard: piano
percussion: triangle; drum; xylophone
string: violin; guitar; cello
woodwind: clarinet; flute; saxophone

2 **1 09** Students should read through the questions before listening to the recording and try to predict the answers. Get them to write down what they think the answer is going to be and check whether they were right after they have heard the recording. Play the recording twice, as in the exam.

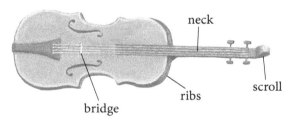

Answers
1 carved 2 cold 3 flexibility 4 wastage/waste
5 ribs 6 glue 7 neck 8 varnish 9 tone

Recording script

Interviewer: Any string player will tell you that no instrument is identical to another. Thirty violins may look the same, but each has a characteristic, however subtle, all of its own. Middleton College runs a violin-making course for students of all ages. And I must say that to see a violin in its stages of development, and especially the intricately <u>carved</u> wood, really fascinated me. The head of the violin school is one of its ex-students, Sue Pearson. I met her in the violin workshop. Sue, before you start to make a violin into the instrument we all know and love, where do you go to find your wood?

Sue: Various places. The pine really needs to come from places where the weather is <u>cold</u> enough for the tree to have grown fairly slowly, so that it grows straight and has close, uniform grain lines.

Interviewer: Why is that – that you need such finely grained wood?

Sue: It's all relating to <u>flexibility</u>, and it needs to be incredibly strong too, of course. We make the front of the violin from pine and the back from maple. These two woods have the qualities we're looking for.

Interviewer: What we've got here are basically just blocks of wood, aren't they? As with any great piece of woodwork, you can never believe for a moment that you could just produce something out of a boring block of wood.

Sue: This piece here is basically for just one part of the violin. In any operation in violin-making, I think you're looking at 80–85% <u>wastage</u>.

Interviewer: And you've got some other bits as well. Very thin pieces.

Sue: These are what we call the <u>ribs</u>. These are about one and a half to one and three-quarter millimetres wide, and before they can go onto the instrument, they'll be reduced in thickness.

Interviewer: We've got the *shape* of the body here. What happens next?

Sue: Basically we shape the top and bottom and then we use <u>glue</u> to stick them together. We don't use a nail or machine for this. We've still got the <u>neck</u> to do and this is easily the most elaborate part of the instrument. It's always quite difficult for a novice student to undertake. We're really dealing in three dimensions.

Interviewer: There's an instrument that looks finished over there, but it's an unusual colour. Why is that?

Sue: Well, it's not finished yet. It needs a good clean – it can get a bit grubby when it's being made. It needs to have <u>varnish</u> applied and this can affect the sound – makes it more mellow in my opinion.

Interviewer: Some of the greatest violins are fairly old. Are you expecting when you make these instruments that they might still be around a couple of hundred years hence?

Sue: That's one of the things that always interests us. We're all mortal and it would be nice to think one of your instruments was still being played in two to three hundred years and that it would even improve in <u>tone</u>. Obviously it will increase in value too, but that's not something that worries me too much.

 Style extra

Collocations are often tested in the examination and more marks can be gained if candidates use them in their written work for Paper 2.

Suggested answers
a A monster is widely believed to live in Loch Ness.
b She gave her boyfriend a carefully chosen birthday present.
c Designer clothes are more keenly priced in out-of-town retail outlets.
d The seats for the rock concert were staggeringly expensive.
e The new album has been singularly successful and has reached number one.

Idiom spot

The idioms here all derive from words to do with music. One word is used more than once.

Answers
a note b tune c song d string
e score f note g chord

3   Refer students to the Exam spot. They should work in pairs and try to use a wide range of vocabulary and not repeat the same words over and over. Make sure students contribute equally. The photos are of

   A   a classical concert
   B   a man and his grandchild listening to an MP3 player
   C   an outdoor music festival
   D   a rock concert

   Possible answer
   (These are ideas for one side of a conversation.)
   I think that the person listening to music on an MP3 player is probably the most representative of the way people listen to music today. Since its introduction the iPod® and similar devices have really become popular as they mean that you can listen to whatever music you want, wherever you are, without annoying anyone else. At one time, it was possible to overhear a tinny noise when someone was using an MP3 player, but with the new types of earphone, this is no longer the case. I'm sure that even better devices will be invented very soon as well.

Pronunciation

4   **1** This exercise looks at contrastive stress. This is particularly important for the modal auxiliaries you have seen in this unit as the meaning can change depending on how they are said. Play the recording and ask students to give you a word which sums up what feeling the speaker is expressing.

   Suggested answers
   a irritated   **b** reproachful   **c** irritated
   d suggesting   **e** worried   **f** angry

   Recording script
   a   You could have rung me from the station.
   b   You could have rung me from the station.
   c   You might ask before you borrow the car.
   d   You might ask Pete if you can borrow his car.
   e   Liz should have got here an hour ago.
   f   Liz should have got here an hour ago.

5   **1 11** Ask students to listen carefully to which words in the sentence are stressed and answer the question which follows.

   Recording script and answers
   a   I <u>thought</u> you'd gone home.
         Yes, she/he has gone home.
   b   I thought you'd gone <u>home</u>.
         No, he's/she's gone somewhere else.
   c   She's an <u>English</u> teacher.
         Yes, she teaches English (not Spanish).
   d   She's an English <u>teacher</u>.
         Yes, she teaches English; she's not a student.
   e   I'm not buying a <u>car</u>.
         No, he's getting a bike, etc.
   f   I'm not <u>buying</u> a car.
         No, he's hiring one.
   g   She's not <u>pretty</u>.
         No, but she's intelligent/friendly, etc. or possibly she's ugly.
   h   <u>She's</u> not pretty.
         No, but her friend is.
   i   I <u>had</u> wanted to see the paintings.
         No, he didn't see them.
   j   I had <u>wanted</u> to see the paintings.
         Yes, he saw them.

Extension activity

Ask students to write out similar sentences and then practise saying them using different stress patterns each time.

Writing folder 3

SB pages 56–57

Part 1 Essay

The compulsory task in Paper 2 Part 1 involves reading two short texts in order to summarise and evaluate the ideas they contain. *Objective Proficiency* develops the language and skills needed for this task in the Reading into Writing lessons, which occur in alternate Student's Book units. This Writing folder focuses on expressing ideas from the texts, using a variety of organisational patterns such as sentence openers and paragraphing.

In Paper 2 Writing, students must write in a register that is suitable for the task set. Most questions will demand an unmarked register and it is vital to produce this *consistently*, as inappropriately informal language would have a negative effect on the reader (examiner).

If timetabling permits, work through all the Writing folder exercises in class, as they raise awareness of the requirements of the exam tasks and allow students to share ideas and best practice. Many *Cambridge English: Proficiency* candidates tend to under-perform on Paper 2, often because they have paid insufficient attention to writing skills. Encourage students to keep all their written homework. It can be very effective for them to work on a second draft following your marking and feedback on their first attempts, as they will learn from earlier mistakes and better understand how to improve their writing.

Start by eliciting facts about the Part 1 task. If necessary, remind students of the above facts about the exam.

1 Ask students to work in pairs or small groups. Give them enough time to read both texts and write four summary sentences.

Suggested answers

Text 1
- Although music is all around us, it does not enjoy a high status in contemporary society.
- It is challenging for talented musicians to survive in their chosen profession.

Text 2
- Music is often cut from the school curriculum so that more resources can be given to mathematics and science.
- There are unforeseen benefits to children from the study of music in school.

2 Suggest that students compare their own sentences with a–f and underline useful vocabulary that paraphrases words in the texts.

Answers
Sentences b and e do not reflect the content of the texts.

3 Stress to students that in the exam they must use their own words wherever possible.

4 Encourage students to vary their writing by using a range of sentence openers like these.

5 If time permits, ask students to draft their opening paragraph in class.

Suggested answer
Nobody can deny that music features in our lives and yet, as the texts point out, it is undervalued in society. The first text considers the plight of professional musicians, while the second focuses on the low prestige of music in schools. This essay argues that music is important and requires investment to secure its presence in education and culture. (60 words)

6 Set the complete essay for homework, asking students
   to follow the advice given.

Sample answer

Nobody can deny that music features in our lives and yet, as the texts point out, it is undervalued in society. The first text considers the plight of professional musicians, while the second focuses on the low prestige of music in schools. This essay argues that music is important and requires investment to secure its presence in education and culture.

What then is the role of music today? Professional musicians are sometimes highly regarded yet earn a pittance. From the classical performer's point of view, the reality is that it is very hard to find orchestral positions nowadays. This must be disheartening after so many years of study. Perhaps more should be done by the state to support young musicians who are embarking on their working life?

Similarly, on the question of teaching music in school, not enough is done. People tend to regard music as a less essential part of the school curriculum than mathematics or science. At the same time, there are unforeseen advantages for children who learn music from a young age, as it encourages creativity and allows them to develop social skills through participation in a group event. This is not to say that everyone should be able to read music, but they should have access to it.

Music plays a fundamental role in both the educational and cultural spheres, and its beneficial contribution to shaping our lives needs to be better understood by all members of society. If more resources were made available to schools and young musicians were given adequate financial support through government subsidy or other means, society would profit significantly.

(268 words)

7.1

Exam skills	Listening Paper 3 Part 1
	Reading and Use of English Paper 1 Part 3
Vocabulary	Idioms with *eye*
Style extra	Extended noun phrases

7.2

Grammar	Participle clauses

7.3

Exam skills	Reading into Writing: Exemplifying your ideas – Paper 2 Part 1
Style extra	Adjectives showing disapproval

Workbook contents

1	Reading Paper 1 Part 6
2	Grammar – participles
3, 4	Vocabulary
5	Use of English Paper 1 Part 4
6	Use of English Paper 1 Part 1

7.1 SB pages 58–59

Lesson plan

Introduction	10–10 minutes
Listening	20–30 minutes
Idiom spot	5–10 minutes
Use of English	20–30 minutes
Style extra	5–20 minutes

SV	Set the sentences in Style extra for homework.
LV	See Extension activity for 4.

Listening

1   Put these relevant words on the board: *close-up, dot, enlarged, hues, magnified*. Encourage students to use them in their discussion of the pictures. If they don't know what they mean, explain them later with reference to the pictures.

Give students a few minutes to discuss the pictures before eliciting the answer: the pictures all have an 'eye' in common.

The pictures show:

*   a 'macrophoto' of the human eye, showing the dark central pupil surrounded by a blue iris

*   the eye of a needle with thread
*   a cat's eye, the device used on main roads to guide drivers at night

2   **1 🔢 12** Refer students to the Exam spot and explain that in the exam, they will have 15 seconds before each extract to read through the questions. In this time, they should try to predict what they might hear.

Play each extract twice. Elicit answers after each repeat.

Answers
1 B   2 A   3 C   4 B   5 B   6 A

Recording script
Extract One
Interviewer: Dr Joanna Walters, your new book *The Complex Eye* has been featured in many newspapers this week. In it, you remind us that the eye is not only a passive receiver of information, but a great communicator too.
Joanna: Um, I should point out that I collaborated on the book with a leading zoologist – it's the human communication side that's my field.
Interviewer: Sorry. That's journalism for you. I've been misinformed. Anyway, we all remember being told by our mothers that it's rude to stare.
Joanna: Right. Staring is the most aggressive facial expression with which to threaten a rival and in the animal kingdom, those species that can't frighten off their would-be attackers in this way, from moths to fish to birds, have evolved false eye spots, which fulfil the same function.
Interviewer: And you draw parallels with human beings here.
Joanna: Absolutely. Because it's taboo for us to physically stare someone out, other, subtler, strategies are often in play. Look in your rear-view mirror late at night and you may see a pair of dazzling headlights eyeballing you. What do you do?
Interviewer: Let them overtake?
Joanna: That's right, avoid confrontation, especially in these days of road rage. Once we're behind the wheel, those headlights become an extension of our persona, whether aggressively so, or in self-defence.

Extract Two

Woman: When Sam was two and a bit, he began to use one of the living room walls, which was unfortunately white at the time, as a drawing surface. It was always the same wall and he appeared to be attempting pictures, as well as showing a definite sense of colour. <u>I had no wish to stifle any artistic genius he might have, so I tended to turn a blind eye to what he was doing</u>, making sure that he was armed with washable felt-tips and cleaning up after him without delay. But one weekend I was out and my husband caught him at it … a boat with two funnels, as I recall, and he hit the roof, both with Sam and with me. In the end we compromised: I bought some huge rolls of white paper and taped it to the wall, all the way along. As soon as Sam completed one <u>magnum opus</u> I would take it down and replace it with a fresh canvas, so to speak. <u>It cost me a fortune, but I've never regretted it. In fact I feel proud of myself, as I believe it helped to make him the way he is.</u> But Sam loves to wind me up about it. You see, he has absolutely no leanings towards art, being heavily into information technology!

Extract Three

Man: Percy Shaw always had an eye for practical solutions. Driving home through the unlit outskirts of Halifax at night, he found the perfect substitute for night vision, following the glint of his headlights in the metal tramlines. <u>But he ran into a problem: no longer in use, these rails were soon taken up for good.</u> With this serious setback, Shaw decided it was time to come up with something that would help him – and others – to steer in the dark. His now ubiquitous invention, modelled on the eye of a cat, consists of a mirror and a spherical lens mounted on a rubber pad. Each time a vehicle runs over it, the assembly is forced into its iron base and the lens is wiped clean <u>by the rubber, which acts like an eyelid.</u> Shaw patented his invention in 1934 when he was only 23 and, thanks to the cat's eye, became a very rich man.

3   Ask students to read the two extracts from the recording script and explain the meaning of the phrases in their own words.

Suggested answers
Extract Two
sense of colour – a feeling for how colours work together
magnum opus – major work (of art, here)
no leanings towards – without any interest in
Extract Three
the perfect substitute – the ideal replacement
serious setback – a problem that affects your ability to do something
ubiquitous invention – an invention that is in use everywhere

Idiom spot

The idiom used in the recording was: *turn a blind eye to*.

Catch someone's eye means to be attractive or different enough to be noticed by people; there is a related compound adjective: *eye-catching*. (*Catch someone's eye* also means 'get someone's attention by looking at them'.)

Look someone in the eye/eyes means to look at someone in a direct way, without showing fear or shame.

Have an eye for means to be good at noticing a particular type of thing.

See eye to eye (with) means that two people agree with each other.

Be in the public eye means to be famous and often featured in the media.

All of these idioms are included in the English Vocabulary Profile, mostly at C2 level.

Possible answers
a   … that pair of orange silk pyjamas hanging out of the school window.
b   … the child's petty stealing of sweets from the shop counter: he needed to be taught what was right and wrong.
c   … 'I'm afraid we're going to have to let you go.'
d   … my younger sister, but her decision to quit college is her stupidest yet.
e   … interesting accessories – I love those earrings.
f   … behave responsibly and always tell the truth.

4   Suggest students look back briefly at Exam folder 1 on pages 14–15 of the Student's Book before doing the task.

Background information
Georges Seurat was a highly innovative artist, responsible for the whole Pointillist movement. He was not really appreciated by the Parisian art establishment during his lifetime. His most famous painting is *Un dimanche après-midi á l'île de la Grande Jatte* (Sunday afternoon on the island of Grande Jatte), shown on page 59. This painting took three years to complete (1884–1886) and is now on permanent exhibition in the Art Institute of Chicago, USA. The painting was the subject of a successful musical by Stephen Sondheim, *Sunday in the Park with George*.

Answers
1   essence   2   Hitherto   3   unpredictable
4   intuitively   5   stability   6   incomparable
7   influential   8   interaction

Extension activity

Ask students to imagine the characters of some of the people shown in the Seurat painting – this is what happened in the Sondheim musical. For example, the man with the pipe in the foreground is a boatman taking the day off with his dog; the two soldiers in the background invite the two seated young women for a walk.

Style extra

Using extended noun phrases is an effective way of varying the beginning of sentences. It would be particularly appropriate to use them in an article or review.

Possible answers
a A highly-regarded and ground-breaking film-maker, Werner Herzog has now produced a film in 3D about some ancient cave paintings in France.
b Best-known for their awe-inspiring poetry, Byron, Keats and Shelley formed part of the English Romantic movement in the early 19th century.
c The most significant political thinker of his generation, James Harrington recognised the fundamental link between economic distribution and political power.
d A leading innovator in her field of expertise, Amanda Wixted has developed some of the best-selling computer games of all time.

7.2 SB pages 60–61

Participles

Lesson plan	
Grammar	60–90 minutes
SV	Set 5 for homework.
LV	See Extension activity for 6.

1 a In the example, *dazzling* is an adjective; *eyeballing* is a participle. Refer students to the Exam spot.

b

Answers
i The participle *Driving* is active and refers to Percy Shaw.
ii The participle *modelled* is passive and refers to his invention (the cat's eye); the clause could be rewritten as a defining relative clause: *His invention, which is modelled on the eye of a cat, …*

c

Answers
i The cat is sitting on the roof.
ii The person is sitting on the roof.

2 Elicit reactions to the two pictures, which show:
• Fort Vimieux (oil on canvas) painted by Joseph Mallord William Turner (1775–1851)
• an image taken by the Hubble Space Telescope of gas pillars in the Eagle Nebula, which is about 7,000 light years from Earth.

Possible answer
The painting by Turner is a spectacular interpretation of sunset and is indeed beautiful. The space image also has beauty and the gas clouds are almost flamboyant in their towering grandeur. There is something very awe-inspiring about this image.

3 Ask students to read the article fairly quickly and then discuss the question in pairs.

Suggested answer
In the nineteenth century and earlier, the artistic tradition was to paint the beauty of nature, but modern artists rarely represent nature on canvas, so their works are not usually described as 'beautiful'. The writer refers to Ruskin's views on art and beauty in connection with images from the Hubble Space Telescope, seeing them as contemporary examples of beauty derived from nature.

4 Refer students to the section in the Grammar folder on page 182 after doing this exercise.

Answers
having viewed: active; previous action
taken: passive; previous action
having been launched: passive; previous action
sending: active; simultaneous action
being (successfully) repaired: passive; simultaneous action
seeing: active; simultaneous action
imitated: passive; previous action

5

Possible answers
1c Receiving mixed reactions from members of the public, the exhibition includes some rather shocking images.
2f Often occurring in open landscape, Andy Goldsworthy's sculptures are particularly effective during dramatic weather conditions.
3b Wanting to create order from chaos, physicists are constantly trying to reduce the universe to a set of basic principles.
4e Having taken quite a few warm-up shots, the photographer then caught the model unawares in a more relaxed pose.
5a Coming in from the street for an hour's rest, people don't realise that the beds – and they themselves – are part of an installation.
6d Having bought two previous works by this artist, I am now looking out for a third.

6   Explain to students that passive participles can also be continuous (see answers to a and e below).

Answers
a (being) chosen **b** shown **c** sold **d** made
e being searched **f** announced **g** damaged

 Extension activity

Run a class debate on one of these statements (the first is from the text in exercise 3):

•   Art is no longer concerned with the representation of nature.
•   Contemporary art is without substance and has nothing new to offer us.
•   Artists nowadays have no technical skills and rely on gimmicks.

7.3 SB pages 62–63
Reading into Writing:
Exemplifying your ideas

Lesson plan	
Introduction	5–15 minutes
Reading	15–25 minutes
Style extra	10–10 minutes
Use of English	20–30 minutes
Writing	10–10 minutes
SV	Keep the discussion in 1 and 2 brief.
LV	See Extension activity for 4.

1   Refer students to the dictionary definition – unless your class is French-speaking! Then ask students to decide which image they find the most clichéd.

The pictures show:

•   a twee picture of a kitten
•   a clichéd image of two people dressed as punks
•   a hackneyed picture of the global business handshake.

Possible answer
I find the kitten all in pink to be the most clichéd image. You see the same thing all the time in magazines and on cards. It's so posed too – when would a kitten sit like that of its own accord?

2   Explain that the two texts are the same length as the texts in Paper 2 Part 1. This lesson focuses on how to include relevant examples of your own ideas in response to the points made in the two input texts. Stress the importance of doing this in the exam.

Suggested answer
The two texts are complementary in their ideas, both focusing on when and how original images become clichéd.

3   If students cannot decide which text includes examples, refer them to the Style extra first – examples of clichéd images are introduced by adjectives showing disapproval, for example 'squat greetings card'.

Suggested answer
The second text includes specific examples – squat greetings card, popular poster, radiant sunset over a tranquil sea – in order to support the argument and make the contrast between originality and cliché more understandable.

4   Suggest students skim the text to find the specific examples that are mentioned (portrait shots by Irving Penn and Diane Arbus; the business handshake; the world as a globe). Elicit the phrases used to introduce these and encourage students to make similar references in their own writing.

Answers
Reference to specific examples underlined:
'... <u>such as those</u> by Irving Penn and Diane Arbus among others'
'<u>Take for instance</u> the cliché-ridden use of visuals <u>like</u> the business handshake or the world as a globe'

5   Ask students to do the Part 3 task and compare their answers. If necessary, refer them back to Exam folder 1 (pages 14–15) on the testing of compounds in Part 3.

Answers
1 experimentation **2** landmark **3** inspirational
4 dismissively **5** countless **6** persuasive
7 devalues **8** commonplace

 Extension activity

Photocopy the Paper 1 Answer sheet (Use of English tasks) on page 154 and distribute to students, so that they can record their answers to exercise 5 in capital letters, as practice for Paper 1 Part 3 Word formation task.

6   Allow students a few minutes to read the paragraph and then elicit their suggestions for where phrases a–d should go.

Answers
1 b **2** d **3** a **4** c

Exam folder 4

SB pages 64–65

Paper 1 Part 7
Multiple matching

Refer students to the exam advice and then ask them to
do the exercise.

Answers
1 D 2 B 3 E 4 A 5 C 6 B 7 C 8 D 9 A 10 C

8 Urban jungle

8.1

Exam skills	Reading and Use of English Paper 1 Part 7
Vocabulary	Compound adjectives and their collocations

8.2

Grammar	Inversion
Exam skills	Reading and Use of English Paper 1 Part 4

8.3

Exam skills	Speaking Paper 4 Part 3
Vocabulary	Idioms by key word
	Phrases with *place*

Workbook contents

1	Listening Paper 3 Part 1
2	Use of English Paper 1 Part 2
3	Use of English Paper 1 Part 1
4, 5	Grammar – inversion
6, 7, 8, 9	Vocabulary

8.1 SB pages 66–67

Lesson plan

Introduction	15–25 minutes
Reading	35–45 minutes
Vocabulary	10–20 minutes

SV   Keep the introduction discussion brief.
LV   See Extension activities for 1 and 4.

1 Start by eliciting students' views about living in one of the cities shown:

- Sydney: the Opera House and harbour
- Rome: a square with open-air restaurants
- Delhi: a hectic street scene

Then ask students to rank the factors in the box and take a class vote on the most important benefit.

Possible answer
1 effortless access to amenities
2 sufficient open spaces
3 diverse employment opportunities
4 low levels of pollution
5 spacious living accommodation

For me, the best thing about city living is the easy access to entertainment and culture – having a choice of concerts and galleries on your doorstep is a real plus, which makes up for possibly having to live in a small high-rise apartment.

Extension activity

Ask students to contrast city living with living in a small town or village, referring to each of the five phrases in turn.

Possible answer
Obviously a big city has diverse employment opportunities, not to mention good access to many cultural amenities, such as an opera house, and plenty of nightlife. Cities often have historical buildings too. There is usually a lively atmosphere, with so many people. On the other hand, big cities are noisy and polluted, usually without many green areas for recreational use, and it often takes a long time to travel from one district to another. Smaller towns and villages have lower levels of pollution and can offer more spacious living accommodation, together with sufficient open spaces.

Reading

2 Emphasise to students that the multiple-matching task in Paper 1 Part 7 of the exam requires them to process a text or set of texts at speed to find specific information. Refer them back to the advice given in Exam folder 4 on pages 64–65 of the Student's Book and remind them that for this task, there will either be a set of separate texts, as on page 65, or one longer text divided into sections, as here.

Explain that this text is taken from an article in an academic journal, and evaluates a particular approach to city architecture in the USA called the New Urbanism. Check understanding of the highlighted words and phrases in the questions and explain that students should use these key elements of each question when scanning the text for their answers.

3 Ask students to answer the questions individually. They should underline the places in the text that confirmed their answers. Elicit answers and where they can be found in the text (see sentences and underlining below).

Answers

1 B *They give some priority to <u>accessible public spaces, community institutions and a variety of parks and other green spaces,</u> in order to <u>foster exemplary civic behaviour.</u>*

2 A *However, during <u>the grim California recession</u> of the 1990s, the original developer for this scheme <u>went bankrupt</u> and the entire project was taken over by a <u>less sympathetic developer, who contravened virtually all of CNU's principles. Had Laguna West been completed</u> as Calthorpe planned it, <u>it would have been</u> one of the great visionary new towns of the late 20th century.*

3 D *The US government-sponsored company Fannie Mae's research into housing preferences shows that <u>up to 80% of US households would prefer to</u> live in a single-family dwelling with a garden, regardless of income, race or current tenure status.*

4 A *As things have turned out, it is just another conventional, <u>car-dependent suburb.</u>*

5 B *They have a <u>strong preference for 'infill' development</u> – that is, the use of land within a built-up area, especially as part of a community redevelopment project – <u>rather than the endless expansion of cities sometimes referred to as 'urban sprawl'.</u>*

6 E *Most NU communities <u>are being built on green field sites some distance away from the central city</u> ...*

7 C *<u>The same idea of 'self-containment'</u> was one of the principles behind <u>the creation of the British new towns of the 1960s,</u> such as Milton Keynes and Telford.*

8 E *... <u>and infill development has been limited</u> – probably <u>of necessity because of land scarcity</u> – <u>to tiny pockets.</u>*

9 D *Urban capital stock is already largely in place and remains a constant, while <u>much of the residential housing in the US has been built in the last 40 years,</u> so <u>innovation through renewal is off the agenda for the time being.</u>*

10 C *The overwhelming tendency was for residents to work elsewhere, with the jobs available in the new towns filled by commuters from outside, with <u>the net result being more use of fossil fuels rather than less.</u>*

Vocabulary

4 Remind students that the compound adjectives *mixed-use* and *car-dependent* are hyphenated forms that are only used before a noun, as in *mixed-use neighbourhoods*. Elicit other examples with *mixed-* (*mixed-ability classes, mixed-race marriages*). Then summarise the other types of compound adjective on the board: participle + preposition as in *boarded-up*, adjective + participle as in *slow-paced*, and adverb + participle as in *forward-thinking*. Note that students will be able to make combinations from the table that include both an adverb and a preposition, as in *well thought-out*.

Ask students to form more compound adjectives from the words given and to add noun collocates for each one. Summarise their suggestions on the board.

Suggested answers
quick-thinking (politician)
long-running (TV series)
short-sighted (policy)
well thought-through / well thought-out (argument)
far-sighted, far-thinking (planner)
poorly constructed (building), poorly-fitting (cupboards),
poorly thought-through / poorly thought-out (plan)
smashed-up (car)
blown-down (trees), blown-out (windows), blown-up (buildings)

 Extension activity

Using real corpus examples if possible, blank out the compound adjective and ask students to fill the gaps. You can find your own examples from the *British National Corpus* (www.natcorp.ox.ac.uk) or *Just the Word* websites (www.just-the-word.com).

8.2 SB pages 68–69

Inversion

Lesson plan	
Grammar	60–70 minutes
Use of English	0–20 minutes

SV Set 4 for homework.
LV See Extension activity for 3.

1 Ask students to read the explanation in the first box and the section in the Grammar folder on page 182 of the Student's Book.

2 Elicit examples orally from students and write a few on the board. Underline the inversion in each one to stress the point.

Possible answers
a Never before have I felt as contented as I do now.
b Only once in my life have I regretted taking a trip.
c Scarcely had the clock struck midnight when the lights went out.
d No sooner had I put my raincoat on than the sun came out again.
e Hardly had I sat down before someone else hammered on the door.
f Not until last month did I feel in control of my workload.
g Seldom do any birds visit the garden, due to the number of cats around.
h Rarely will there be an opportunity for proper discussion.
i Had it not been for the fact that my cousin was coming to the party, I would have stayed at home.

3 Ask students to look at the second box. See the Grammar folder for further examples of prepositional phrases. Then ask students to complete the text using the verbs given.

Answers
1 stood 2 sat 3 hung 4 had
5 stretched 6 were 7 did

⊙ Extension activity

Inversion is a common feature of literary narrative. Develop a story round the class, with each student having to add a sentence. Not all the sentences need to include inversion – it would be a very unnatural text if they did! However, you could reward students who do produce one of the different types of inversion covered in this lesson. (There are further examples below exercise 3.) Record the story if possible, or key it onto a computer. The story could start with: *Never before had they been in such a wild and windswept landscape.*

4 Refer students to the further examples of inversion in the box beside exercise 3.

Answers
1 once did the train run | on time / on/to schedule
2 had Brian and Sue met | when/before/than
3 no circumstances | are you to
4 sooner had they left | their car than/before/when
5 one postcard did Kerry | send us while
6 had the bus company put | their prices up
7 high has the demand | for tickets been that
8 only are the buildings beautiful / only are there beautiful buildings | but the climate

8.3 SB pages 70–71

Listening and Speaking

Lesson plan	
Introduction	5–5 minutes
Listening	20–25 minutes
Idiom spot	10–10 minutes
Vocabulary	10–20 minutes
Speaking	15–30 minutes

SV Keep discussion in 1 and planning in 6 brief; set 9 for homework.
LV See Photocopiable recording script activity in 3; allow more time for 5.

1 The meaning of *The grass is always greener* ... is that there always appears to be a better situation than your own.

2 **1** 13

Possible answer
Sally is Meg's daughter and they currently live in Wales. Kevin works in London but is disenchanted with the rat race and plans to swap living accommodation with Meg and Sally temporarily.
It does sound very unusual. I suppose the success of the lifeplan will depend on how well the three of them get on – and on how well they look after each other's properties. It does give Kevin an escape from city living and gives Sally and Meg more flexibility. The downside is that they will all lack a permanent base and it might be difficult to make long-term plans.

Recording script

Interviewer: OK, well there are three people sitting in the studio with me now – Sally, Meg and Kevin – who are about to embark on a rather unusual 'lifeplan' as they call it, something that will bring about a change of gear for all three of them. By way of introduction, we need to go through some recent history, and I'm going to start with you, Sally, because it's your discontent about where you're living now that has played a large part in all this. Sally, tell us where you and Meg call home at the moment.

Sally: It's a tiny village in the Welsh hills, which no one will have heard of. Last November we quit London and headed for the border. Mum and Dad decided to go their separate ways, you see – I think Mum took this literally, she wanted to get as far away as possible from Dad at the time.

Meg: It wasn't quite like that, but yes, the divorce had a lot to do with needing to get out of the city and start again.

Interviewer: So out of the blue you chose a remote Welsh village?

Meg: Not quite, I had good friends there …

Sally: Who have since left.

Meg: Yes, but, well, anyway, as Sally will tell you, it hasn't quite worked out for her, though for me at the beginning, winding down was a godsend, it gave me the chance to rethink my life and decide on priorities.

Interviewer: Mm, so, Sally, why has it been less than perfect for you?

Sally: I'm 15 now and I left really good friends behind me, some I'd known my whole life. Plus, I've had to learn Welsh to even function at school and that's been hard. And as you can imagine, there isn't exactly a lot to do where we are – most people of my age just hang around the village green or go to each others' houses. It's not that great. Fortunately, I've been staying some weekends at my Dad's place – so I can meet up with some of my old friends, go to clubs, you know.

Interviewer: Mmm … so the country idyll, not such good news for you, but for you, Meg, you're content with your life there?

Meg: Yes and no-o. I have to confess that once the honeymoon period was over (a rather unfortunate term in my case) well, you know after a while I woke up and realised that this wasn't right for me either. It's hard to pin down exactly why – I don't suffer from boredom, and I still get a rush out of the sheer beauty and calm that surrounds us, but I … I feel that I'm missing out too, that I should be working, socialising more, going to exhibitions, all those things I used to take for granted, but which are totally out of the frame at the moment.

Interviewer: And that's where Kevin comes in …

Kevin: One lucky break all round …

Sally: Well, it's pretty flukey. Basically Mum and I sat down one night and agreed we had to get back somehow … but we realised that there was no way we could expect to move back to London as easily as we'd left.

Meg: Selling the cottage wouldn't be easy, and nor would finding somewhere in our price range in London.

Sally: Mum had this real brainwave. She decided to look for anyone who might be interested in changing places, house swaps, that sort of thing.

Kevin: And thanks to the power of the Internet, they tracked me down.

Interviewer: And everything's fallen into place. But what's in it for you, Kevin? You've already told me you have a large flat in a very desirable part of London, a good job, …

Kevin: What I've got is a nice flat I hardly ever see, a high-profile, high-stress job in share-dealing, no girlfriend, 'cos she dumped me a month ago, so life's not exactly a bed of roses. But I've been very successful and can afford to negotiate my future. Well, I want to get out for a while but not burn my boats completely, so Meg's proposal is perfect.

Interviewer: And how is this lifeplan going to unfold now?

Meg: In a nutshell, we've agreed to change places for three months initially, swapping everything – we leave the car, the furniture, the tins of soup in the kitchen …

Kevin: Not the clothes though!

Meg: If we're all happy, then we'll extend to a year, which will give Sally and I a wonderful base in London and Kevin some peace and quiet to realise his dream.

Interviewer: Which is?

Kevin: I've got an idea for the next bestseller, a racy paperback on city slickers.

Interviewer: Ah, plenty of first-hand experience to draw on – sounds promising! And Sally, you'll get back your social life, but isn't it potentially disruptive, to your schooling and so on?

Sally: We're going to be moving at the start of a new school year, so there's a natural break anyway. And if things don't pan out, I can always move in with Dad.

Meg: But I think we're all quietly confident that it *will* work out.

Kevin: Yeah, 'cos it's what we all want deep down. And if I make it as a writer, well it might end up a permanent arrangement, you know, six months on, six off, <u>the best of both worlds</u>.

Interviewer: Well, they say *the grass is always greener*, but you seem to have things pretty much sorted out. Meg, Sally, Kevin, the very best of luck.

All: Thank you.

Photocopiable recording script activity → page 144

Apart from the idioms, which are covered in the next exercise, the recording script is rich in vocabulary and expressions. Hand out copies and ask students to explain the meaning of the following words and phrases, which are in order of occurrence:

embark set out
a change of gear a different pace of life
quit left
go their separate ways split up
remote isolated
a godsend a lucky break
idyll perfect life
the honeymoon period the first few weeks, when everything was a novelty
pin down put a finger on, say precisely
a rush a thrill
flukey lucky
brainwave a very good idea
realise his dream make his plan happen
racy fast-moving, lively and perhaps slightly shocking
pan out work out as planned

3 **1** 🔟 The idioms are underlined in the recording script (see 2 above).

Answers
a 5 b 4 c 6 d 3 e 2 f 1

Idiom spot

Elicit views on the best way of learning idioms (refer students to the four bullet points).
The key word is *burn*. Elicit example situations.

Answers
a burn a hole in your pocket – have money that you want to spend
b burn the midnight oil – work late into the night
c get your fingers burned/burnt – have something go wrong
d fiddling while Rome burns – focusing on something trivial during a crisis
e have money to burn – have lots of money
f burn your bridges – take action which you cannot reverse

Vocabulary

4 Explain to students that *place* has a number of meanings in English and is a very common word, so it is worth their reviewing their knowledge of this word. The spaces require one or two words to complete the phrases.

Answers
a taking b in c all over d first e out of

Extension activity

Give students copies of the English Vocabulary Profile entry for the word *place* to extend their understanding of this word – go to www.englishprofile.org to sign up for access to the resource.

5 Ask students to skim the text and complete the spaces (there are two extra words). Explain that the words in the box will be useful for the speaking task that follows.

Answers
1 acronym 2 network 3 spaces
4 sector 5 regeneration 6 neighbourhood
7 demolition 8 consultation

6 Refer students to the Exam spot and remind them that the three ideas on the Part 3 prompt card are there to help candidates, but it is not mandatory to cover them. Suggest that students look back over Unit 8 for ideas and relevant vocabulary. Allow them enough time to brainstorm their ideas in their groups of four.

7 Now ask them to form two pairs, with each pair planning a talk together, following the advice given.

Answer
a B b B c D d E e B f D
g E h D i E j D k B l E

8 This is intended as a rehearsal stage, where timing can be established and organisation improved if necessary.

9 Refer students to the Exam spot before they start. If there is no time to do the activity in class, ask students to record their long turn for homework.

Writing folder 4

SB pages 72–73

Part 2 Set text question: Film tie-in

Explain that in the set text option students can refer to a film tie-in of the book. This Writing folder concentrates on approaches to studying a film version. Writing folder 8 focuses on writing a book review.

1   Ask students to look at the suggestions in pairs and add their own ideas.

2   *The Secret Life of Bees* has been a set text on the *Cambridge English: Proficiency* exam, with a film tie-in available on DVD. If students don't already know the film, ask them to read the description and elicit whether they would be interested in seeing it. Further background information to the historical period is given below.

Background information

Key dates: African-American Civil Rights Movement

1955 Rosa Parks refused to give up her seat on a public bus for a white passenger and was arrested. The ensuing protest made Martin Luther King a national figure.

1957 Nine African-American students won the legal right to attend Little Rock Central High School, but were harassed by white students all year. The local school system then closed public schools rather than continue to integrate.

1961 Freedom rides organised by activists on interstate buses travelling to the American South tested an earlier Supreme Court decision that had supposedly ended segregation on buses. By the end of summer, more than 300 freedom riders had been arrested in Jackson, Mississippi, held in tiny cells and beaten. Public sympathy and support for the freedom riders led President John F. Kennedy's administration to issue a new desegregation order.

1964 Almost 1,000 activists, most of them white college students, travelled to Mississippi to help register voters and teach in 'Freedom Schools'. Through this action, some 17,000 black people attempted to register to vote, though less than 10% succeeded. More than 80,000 African-Americans joined the Mississippi Freedom Democratic Party at this time, to show their desire to vote. On 2 July, President Johnson signed the Civil Rights Act into US law.

3   If you are using the film in class, use the questions as the basis for detailed analysis and discussion.

Possible answers

1   Having been brought up in Georgia, Dakota Fanning would have already been very familiar with the accents and dialect of the Deep South, as well as with the agricultural setting in which the events of the film take place. In the film, Lily 'comes of age' – that is, she begins her journey from childhood to adulthood – leaving home and experiencing her first love. As a 'real' fourteen-year-old, Dakota Fanning embodies that transitory period between childhood and adulthood.

2   In the film, Rosaleen does not appear to be much older than Lily. We see how differently the young black woman and the young white woman are treated by society, even though they are both victims of abuse. When Rosaleen and Lily escape, it is Lily who is in charge and this is credible, given their proximity in age in the film. As a younger woman, it also seems natural for Rosaleen to take May's place in the Pink House after May's death. It would have seemed less plausible for an older woman to have been accepted so easily by May's older sisters.

3   The bee theme provides a narrative framework for the story. It is auspicious that Lily is visited by bees at the beginning of the film and that her father does not see them. When she conquers her fear of them and keeps one as a pet in her father's house, we know that bees will be important symbolically for her in her story. It is the honey label which she finds in her mother's possessions which leads Lily to Tiburon and ultimately to the Pink House. While she is there, August teaches Lily how to care for the bees and this is a metaphor for the nurturing which Lily has lacked since her mother's death. The community of industrious bees is a reflection of the ordered and successful community in which the sisters live.

4   August is the most maternal of the three sisters, and in addition to being the bee-keeper, she makes all the big decisions in the household, such as deciding that Rosaleen and Lily can stay for a while, even though June is suspicious. June is more 'cold' than August – she is wary of the unexpected visitors and nervous of committing to marriage with her long-term boyfriend – although she can express herself more freely through her music. May is the most emotional and sensitive of the three. She is very prone to tears and extreme feelings, due in large part to the death of her twin sister, April, during childhood. Eventually, she feels unable to continue bearing the weight of the world on her shoulders.

5   Objects in the Pink House look as though they have come directly from 1964, even down to the smallest piece of kitchen equipment. The same is true of the clothing – whether it is the immaculately-turned-out attire that the three sisters and their friends wear, or the shabby clothes in which Rosaleen and Lily arrive. In Tiburon, the cars, the shops and the movie theater all look convincingly like they belong in the early 1960s.

4   Ask students to read the task and sample answer. Discuss how they could conclude the answer and then ask them to draft a conclusion of about 50 words.

Suggested answer
The Secret Life of Bees gives a vivid picture of the rise of the American Civil Rights movement in the late 1950s and 1960s and is well researched in terms of period detail. The various examples cited above indicate how successfully the film represents the book and brings the characters and action to life.

5   Ask students to complete the text; the words and phrases are useful language for an essay relating to a film version.

Answers
1 scene setting   2 crew   3 cinematography
4 action   5 props department   6 wardrobe manager
7 script writer   8 screenplay

6   Set the essay task for homework, based on this book and film or a different one of the students' choice.

Units 5–8 Revision

SB pages 74–75

Lesson plan	
Use of English	20–30 minutes
Vocabulary	10–15 minutes
Writing	20–30 minutes

SV Set 3 for homework.
LV Elicit students' reactions to the text in 1.

The aim of this revision unit is to focus on the language covered in Units 5–8 and to support Writing folder 3 on essays. Specific exam practice is provided on Paper 1 Parts 1 and 4. These tasks could be done as a timed test of 30 minutes. Alternatively, the whole unit could be set for homework.

Use of English

1   The picture shows someone wearing a Lacoste jacket.

Answers
1 B 2 C 3 A 4 C 5 D 6 B 7 D 8 C

2

Answers
1   a widespread belief | that having your/a photo
2   can't have set | off yet
3   takes great | pride in
4   did we know | at the time what a
5   had I | returned from the supermarket than
6   the time | you've come to mind

Vocabulary

3

Answers
a nose b burst c singularly d stroke
e for granted f eye g exception
h chord i widely j thunder k tune l view
m seen n childish o note

Writing

4   The picture shows a sculpture by Andy Goldsworthy.

Answers
1 C 2 A 3 E 4 B 5 D

Crossword

This includes some of the idioms, phrasal verbs and other vocabulary from Units 5–8.

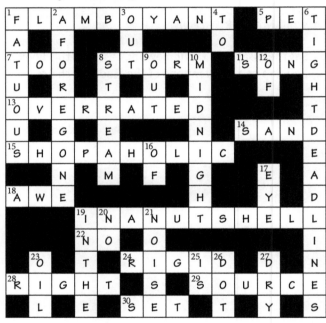

9 Fitting in

Topic Attitudes

9.1
Exam skills	Listening Paper 3 Part 4
Vocabulary	Phrases with *come*

9.2
Grammar	Gerunds and infinitives
Vocabulary	Prefixes
Exam skills	Reading and Use of English Paper 1 Part 2

9.3
Exam skills	Reading into Writing: Linking – Paper 2 Part 1
Vocabulary	Personal appearance, personality types Linking words and phrases

Workbook contents
1	Reading Paper 1 Part 7
2	Use of English Paper 1 Part 4
3, 4, 5, 6, 7	Vocabulary
8	Grammar – linking words and phrases
9	Grammar – gerund or infinitive?

9.1 SB pages 76–77

Lesson plan
Introduction	10–10 minutes
Vocabulary	10–10 minutes
Listening	40–55 minutes
Phrase spot	0–15 minutes

SV	Set Phrase spot for homework.
LV	See Photocopiable recording script activity in 5.

Speaking

1 This exercise is aimed at discussing the reasons why we choose to wear certain clothes.

The photos show:
- a female Goth
- a man in overalls and a hard hat
- a woman in a sari
- a man in a business suit
- three UN peacekeepers

Possible answer
These people are in clothes which identify them as part of a certain group. The girl in black wants to be accepted by Goths. The man wears his overalls to protect his clothing from damage and also possibly to protect himself from being injured by machinery. The woman in a sari wishes to conform to Indian traditions. The man in a business suit is presumably expected to conform to office policy. The UN peacekeepers wear their uniforms so that they are easily identified by members of the public.

2 Ask students to form groups and decide what they would wear for the occasions specified. Put their answers on the board to see if there is general agreement on the subject.

Possible answer
I would wear whatever I fancied to a classical concert. I don't think people bother too much about formality these days.

For a rock festival I would wear comfortable clothes – jeans and a T-shirt.

On a long-distance plane trip I would wear a tracksuit as you really need to be as comfortable as possible on a plane.

On a first date it's really difficult. Perhaps something that reflects what your date was wearing when you first met?

At a club, definitely not jeans. Possibly chinos and trainers. Ties are out generally – you get so hot in clubs.

At a job interview, a very smart suit, absolutely. Polished shoes, new haircut and briefcase.

I'd wear a hat and something stylish to a wedding. A summer dress or a good suit.

To the gym, I'd wear my trainers, shorts and a T-shirt.

Vocabulary

3 This exercise will help with some of the vocabulary in the listening task. Encourage the use of an English–English dictionary.

Answers
a down **b** stuck **c** outlay **d** clear
e hooked **f** eyebrows **g** nose **h** opt

Listening

4 **1** **14** Refer the class to the Exam spot. This is the first time they will have seen this task. They should read through both tasks and check that they understand the vocabulary.

> **Answers**
> 1 C 2 D 3 A 4 H 5 F
> 6 H 7 C 8 A 9 B 10 G

Recording script

Speaker 1

When I left school, I was taken on by an environmental charity. I turned up in a suit, but instead of being stuck behind a desk, I was out on the streets, fundraising. My boss at that time was a bit of a rebel. She had quite a funky hairdo and tended to wear ethnic stuff she'd picked up on her travels. I <u>guess she came across as something of a hippie. We got on really well and I thought I'd opt for the same kind of outfits</u> – I can't remember anyone saying anything to make me do that but, to be honest, <u>I think the others at work saw me more as one of them.</u> But I do remember my mother not recognising me when she saw me in the street!

Speaker 2

I play in a metal band called Zandroid. I have a dragon tattoo on my face and wear a leather jacket with a dragon on it. <u>It does mean that people can spot me immediately</u> and I'm constantly getting asked for autographs when I'm out which is great! It makes me feel loved by the fans I guess! I had the tattoo done properly by this guy who I really respect and it wasn't cheap, I can tell you. It was funny how my look came about – I was on the train to a music festival and I picked up one of <u>those free papers. There was a whole thing about dragons in it. I was hooked on the idea in a flash.</u>

Speaker 3

The dress code at my school is fairly formal so I have to wear smart clothes, but I go for tops and trousers rather than suits and high heels. I wouldn't want to raise too many eyebrows among the other staff members so no jeans. Not that the school is super posh or anything, <u>but very casual clothes wouldn't go down too well.</u> What I wear is great really because I have to spend quite a bit of time <u>delving into cupboards. I tend to go for high-end clothes which aren't skin tight</u> – ones that move with me. And they should last – if they were cheap, they'd soon come apart.

Speaker 4

When I left university, I had long hair and wore old jeans. Job interviews were coming up and <u>I didn't want to get up any interviewer's nose and lose out on a good job.</u> There was this job advertised which seemed perfect as a designer at this factory making cars, so I got myself a suit and tie and landed the job. I realised later that I'd got hold of the wrong end of the stick as no one was the least bit bothered, but there you go, better safe than sorry. Anyway, one thing I've found is <u>that suits are good as there's only a minimum outlay</u> and now we have dress-down Friday I can still wear my jeans then.

Speaker 5

I'm Indian, but I live in the US, doing research in a university. For years, I've worn western clothes, mainly skirts and blouses. I'd always steered clear of the sari as it seemed to me to be not quite right for the workplace, although some other colleagues wear them. <u>Something changed for me last year when I went back to India to see my relatives.</u> The women in saris looked so elegant and I realised that the only person who was stopping me wear one was myself. <u>Now, when I put on my sari, I feel pride in my heritage</u> and realise that what I wear is not going to come between me and promotion or being accepted by others.

5 Ask students to discuss their answers and to explain how they made their decisions.

Photocopiable recording script activity **P → page 145**

If students have found this piece particularly difficult, then give out the recording script so they can read the text to find the answers.

Students should underline adjectives in the recording script which are used to describe people and their clothes.

> **Answers**
> funky, ethnic, formal, smart, casual, high-end, skin tight, cheap, old, elegant

6 Ask students to discuss the questions in pairs or groups.

⊙ Phrase spot

Students should work in pairs for this activity.

a come round/over **b** came over **c** came out in sympathy with **d** come easily **e** come between **f** first come, first served **g** comes up with the goods **h** coming along **i** come to terms with **j** came in for

9.2 pages 78–79

Gerunds and infinitives

Lesson plan

Grammar	50–60 minutes
Vocabulary	10–20 minutes
Use of English	0–20 minutes

SV Set 7 for homework and omit 8.
LV See Extension activity for 4.

1 This first exercise aims to review some key points about verb patterns. Refer students to the Grammar folder on page 183 if there are problems with this.

Answers
a wearing b to wear c you to wear
d wearing / to wear e him to shave f her wear

 Corpus spot

This exercise looks at common mistakes which are made with gerunds and infinitives.

Answers
a I would have helped her <u>find / to find</u> the right wedding dress.
b We shouldn't spend so much time <u>trying</u> to find bargains in the sales.
c I suggest <u>you use</u> a plaster if you have a blister on your foot.
d The old uniforms in the museum are worth <u>seeing</u>.
e We enjoy ourselves <u>laughing</u> at the stars at the Oscars.
f My new glasses enable me <u>to read</u> more easily.
g We should let them <u>enjoy</u> themselves while they are young.
h I missed <u>talking</u> to my sister when I was away from home.
i I convinced him <u>to apply</u> to the Editor of the magazine.
j You aren't allowed to <u>come</u> into the hotel without wearing a tie.

2 These verbs often cause problems. Allow ten minutes for students to discuss the differences.

Answers
a I mean to = I intend to
b It will mean = It will involve
c We regret to inform you = We are sorry to have to tell you
d I regret wearing = I wish I hadn't worn
e The first thing that happened is the walk, now I remember it.
f First remember, then buy the milk.
g First not forget, then post the letter.
h First meeting boyfriend, then not forgetting.
i Try to = Make an attempt
j Try doing = Experiment with
k First he talks about one subject, then another
l goes on talking = continues talking
m After a period of time he accepted this
n A way of moving, describing the action
o I heard them once
p I heard them regularly

3 This exercise gives practice in the type of transformation found in Part 4 of the Reading and Use of English paper.

Answers
a I don't object to your leaving early.
b Do they allow you to smoke outside your office entrance?
c It's not worth asking her out, she's always busy.
d My father forbade my sister to go / from going to the club in town.
e Book early and you will avoid having to queue / to avoid having to queue.
f His doctor recommended that he do / doing more exercise.
g Don't worry, I promise to post that letter for you.
h I suggest we take our bikes with us / I suggest taking our bikes with us.
i You had better move your car immediately or else I'll call the police.
j Peter denied causing / having caused the accident.
k His mother made him apologise.

4 **1** 15 The woman is talking about the uniform she had to wear when she was at school and how she felt about it.

Suggested answer
The uniform was bottle green for the girls with a shirt and tie. The rules were very strict. The English teacher was inspirational and wore interesting clothes.

Recording script

Woman: What do I remember about being at school? Well, it was some time ago now – in the 1990s in fact. I was at a posh private school. I do remember the uniform – it was <u>bottle green, rather dingy</u>, and all the girls had to wear <u>a shirt and tie</u>, which was a pain, I can tell you. The uniform was really uncomfortable and I often felt self-conscious, especially when I was walking down the street.

<u>The girls' skirts had to be the right length. If one of the teachers thought you were wearing a skirt which was too short, then they'd make you kneel down and measure the length from the hem of the skirt to your knees.</u> You had to go home and change if it was too short. <u>Some teachers were worse than others</u> of course.

I remember <u>my English teacher</u>, in particular. She <u>used to wear the most amazing clothes – red swirly skirts and purple and silver shoes. She had blonde hair tied back in a pony tail and large glasses with a range of different coloured frames, over which she could peer.</u> I guess she brought a bit of colour into our lives. I thought she was undervalued though by the rest of the staff. I guess they thought she was a bit flashy.

<u>She really inspired me though.</u> She gave us a book list once and said: 'Read these.' The books were brilliant, not fuddy-duddy at all. I used to go to the library every Saturday and hunt them out.

Now ask students to talk about their own school days.

Possible answer
I didn't have to wear a uniform at school, but I suppose wearing jeans and a T-shirt was some sort of uniform. Many of the girls wore dresses but I never did. We only had school in the morning – we started at 7.00 and finished at 1.00 because in the afternoon it got too hot for class. I remember going home and spending about an hour doing homework and then going to the swimming pool to meet my friends. Once a week I had dance class and also my piano lessons.

 Extension activity

Ask students to write two paragraphs entitled 'My happiest memory', in which they must describe something wonderful that has happened to them, e.g. a great family holiday, winning a prize, getting something they really wanted, falling in love. Ask students to check each other's work for errors, paying particular attention to the use of gerunds and infinitives.

Vocabulary

5   This exercise looks at prefixes. Ask students to decide what the prefix means for each word.

Answers
a   refers to person talking – conscious of themselves
b   wrongly heard
c   going against something, not productive
d   for something, in favour
e   too much of something
f   under/below
g   more than – here it is more than human
h   against something
i   before – arranged before
j   to do more in the sense of competition here
k   less – the idea that something isn't given its true worth

6   It is important to know how prefixes are used, although in Paper 1 Reading and Use of English candidates will never be asked to form a word which has a hyphen. Take care, as dictionaries often do not agree on the use of hyphens. Ask students to use the prefixes in exercise 5 to complete this exercise.

Answers
a self-contained   b sub-tropical   c has outlived
d underestimate   e misunderstanding   f pre-packed
g super-concentrated   h anti-lock   i overhear
j counter-argument   k pro-American

7   This exercise is longer than the open cloze found in the examination but it gives practice in deciding on what word is needed to fill each space.

Answers
We have become more informal and less rigid in both what we wear and when we wear it.

1 would/does   2 intents   3 time   4 tell/see
5 between   6 say   7 our   8 into   9 come   10 such
11 ourselves   12 out   13 being   14 when   15 do

8   Ask students to discuss these questions in pairs or groups.

Possible answer
I think clothes aren't as important as personality. Clothing is important but not to the extent that you wouldn't be friends with someone who was, in your eyes, badly dressed. I think that people in the public eye should take more care with what they wear than ordinary people and that also applies to people who work in certain environments such as an office.

9.3 pages 80–81
Reading into Writing: Linking

Lesson plan	
Introduction	15–15 minutes
Reading two texts	25–35 minutes
Writing	20–25 minutes
Vocabulary	0–15 minutes
SV	Keep review of Phrase spot brief and set 5 for homework.
LV	See Extension activity for 2.

Speaking

1 The photos are of:
- a boy with a pierced lip
- a makeover – when someone is either digitally enhanced or when make-up, cosmetic surgery or Botox is used to make someone look younger

Ask students to work with a partner to discuss the questions.

Possible answers
I don't think it is important to look attractive, although society nowadays seems to think it is. An attractive face means having symmetrical features and good skin. I think cosmetic surgery is slightly weird unless it is done for really good reasons, like someone who has a cleft palate. Any facial piercing is dangerous in my opinion. Make-up is fine as long as it isn't too heavy and wigs are also acceptable.

A politician should get a vote because of his or her policies not his or her looks.

I would describe myself as fairly tidy and tending towards the casual when it comes to dress. I would never look scruffy or unkempt.

2

Answers
In Text 1 the points made are:
- people are unconsciously attracted by the way a candidate looks
- people believe that looks equate with trustworthiness, intelligence, likeability and ability.

In Text 2 the points made are:
- it may be necessary to stop people using modern technology to make people look better in photos than they are
- the tendency to make people look better is something that has always happened.

 Extension activity

Ask students to paraphrase the following words or phrases from Texts 1 and 2.

Text 1
mocked (= laughed at)
enhanced (= improved)
receding (= moving away, becoming less)

Text 2
transform (= change)
on the quest (= searching)

3 This exercise gives practice in linking words. Students should decide which is the right word in each gap.

Answers
1 B   2 A   3 C   4 B   5 A

4 Refer students to the Phrase spot. They should use suitable phrases from here to link their sentences effectively. This exercise will also give students practice in giving their own opinions.

Possible answer
First of all, I believe that the use of modern technology to make politicians more attractive is just another way that politicians can bribe the public into voting for them. It does not seem sufficient for people in politics to have suitable policies to attract the voters; they additionally need to use psychological methods. However, I do think that the majority of people are able to see through these tricks and are able to come to their decisions independently. Moreover, it is highly unlikely that someone will vote for a 'pretty boy' or 'proto-Barbie doll' if they don't have a strategy for improving the economy or creating more jobs. To my mind, it would be incredible if the general public were that credulous.

Personally, I believe that today people are much more aware of the use of digital enhancement than in the past. Consequently, people nowadays are more likely to take any picture of their favourite star of stage or screen looking amazingly thin or curvy, with a pinch of salt. Then again, we have actually been enhancing people's looks for longer than the advent of digital airbrushing. After all, didn't Henry VIII of England receive a painting of Anne of Cleves, only to find that, disappointingly, it bore little resemblance to the real woman? Portrait painters in the past knew that it was part of their job to make people look a bit better than they actually were and I believe that everyone was aware of this.

(248 words)

5 This exercise can be done for homework if time is short.

Answers
a correct
b wrong – they have a lot to say on every subject, whether they know what they are talking about or not
c correct
d wrong – they are lively and excitable
e wrong – they hoard things
f correct
g wrong – they have good taste
h wrong – they see no need for change even if needed
i wrong – they like to remain in the background
j wrong – they try to control people
k correct

Exam folder 5

SB pages 82–83

Paper 1 Part 6 Gapped text

This type of reading comprehension requires the reader to understand what is happening both in terms of content and also in terms of reference. Sometimes the links between the paragraphs are not obvious and it will require some skill to sort them out. Students should read the base text first and then the gapped paragraphs. They should think about the scenario, i.e. what the passage is about. Are there any references, e.g. *it/she/they* or *moreover/secondly/however* which might give a clue?

This text on lying has some clues to help students with the first few questions.

Answers
1 E 2 B 3 F
4 A this sort of background (i.e. university qualifications) – a smooth-talking lawyer and consummate liar – lying in corporate culture
5 C body language – visual clues – shifty eyes
6 H more reliable than body movements
7 D doesn't take too much mental planning ... make up a story about something they know well

10 Globalisation

Topic Language and culture

10.1
Grammar	Reference devices
Exam skills	Reading and Use of English Paper 1 Part 1

10.2
Grammar	Expressing wishes and preferences
Exam skills	Reading and Use of English Paper 1 Part 4
Vocabulary	Expressions with *turn*

10.3
Exam skills	Speaking Paper 4 Part 2
	Listening Paper 3 Part 1
	Reading and Use of English Paper 1 Part 3
Pronunciation	Word stress

Workbook contents

1	Listening Paper 3 Part 3
2	Listening follow-up
3	Use of English Paper 1 Part 1
4	Use of English Paper 1 Part 2
5	Use of English Paper 1 Part 3
6	Grammar – wishes and preferences
7, 8, 9	Vocabulary

10.1 SB pages 84–85

Lesson plan

Introduction	5–10 minutes
Reading	45–55 minutes
Speaking	10–10 minutes
Use of English	0–15 minutes

SV Set 7 for homework.
LV See Extension activity for 5.

Speaking

1   This exercise can be done either in pairs or as a class activity. It acts as a lead-in to the reading on the death of languages around the world.

Answers
The languages (from left to right) are: Chinese, Hungarian, Bulgarian, Greek, Polish, Turkish.
There are about 6,000 languages in the world.
A language dies about every two weeks.
The language spoken more than any other is Chinese.

Reading

2   Students should scan the text to find the answers to the questions.

Answers
a   It is a pun (play on words). A 'death sentence' is the words used by a judge to condemn someone to death. The use of the word 'sentence', which is connected with language, also relates to the topic of the article, the death of languages.
b   He seems ambivalent/undecided. (*Or so they think.*)

3   This article was written by David Crystal. Students should ignore the words in italics when they read through the article at this stage.

4   Reference devices are often tested in the Reading and Use of English paper.

Answers
a   the death of a language
b   Kasabe
c   the 6,000 languages
d   the fact that half are going to die out
e   languages
f   language death
g   language death
h   what we learn from a language
i   some people

5   These questions test understanding of points in the text.

Answers
a   made an impact / been considered a matter of some importance
b   People start out by being forced to speak the majority language. Then there is a period when both languages are spoken and finally the old language is totally forgotten and the majority language takes over.
c   You need to have a wide range of species of animals for a healthy environment. The same is true of different cultures.
d   If you lose a language you lose more than just a method of communication.
e   medical treatments, early civilisations, new ideas about language itself
f   One language is not enough to hold all human/world knowledge.

Extension activity

The article can be used as a summary exercise. Write **notes** for a summary of 50–100 words on why a language dies out and why we should worry about this. Try to use your own words as far as possible.

Answer
A language dies when there is no one left to speak it. It usually dies as a result of the speakers being assimilated into another culture.

We should worry about the death of a language because we need strong cultural diversity in order to survive as a species. Both information about medicine and literature from other cultural groups help our own culture to grow strong.

6 Students should spend 5–10 minutes discussing the questions. The cartoon is someone asking in Esperanto if the shop accepts credit cards.

Background information
Esperanto is the best known of the world's auxiliary languages and was invented by Ludwig Zamenhof in 1887. It was designed to overcome problems of international communication. Newspapers and journals are published in Esperanto, together with the Bible and the Koran. It is also taught as a school subject in many countries.

7 This text is taken from an encyclopaedia. It is written in an impersonal and informative style. Ask students to decide on their answers and explain why the other words are wrong.

Answers
1 D is correct. A is used for a piece of guesswork; B is for a person who you only know slightly; C is also used with *between* but in the sense of two things having something in common.
2 D is correct. A, B and C all have the idea of *come from*. An idea can *stem from* or *spring from*. A declaration is *issued*.
3 A is correct. B takes the preposition *from* and C and D don't collocate with the idea of language.
4 A is correct. Only A takes the word *on* in this context.
5 D is correct as it collocates with *rely on*.
6 C is correct. *Once* here has the meaning of *when*.
7 B is correct. A language may *expand*; feet *swell* when they are hot; you can *enlarge* a photograph and *increase* is a general word which can't be used here.
8 A is correct as it takes the preposition *from*.

10.2 SB pages 86–87

Expressing wishes and preferences

Lesson plan	
Grammar	45–50 minutes
Use of English	15–25 minutes
Phrase spot	0–15 minutes

SV   Set Phrase spot for homework.
LV   See Extension activity for 4.

1 This extract is from an English newspaper and is a true story. Encourage students to come up with sentences with *wish*.

Suggested answers
I wish they wouldn't look so embarrassed.
I wish I could speak to them.
I wish the interpreter was/were here.
I wish this meal would end.
I wish someone would say something.

2 and 3 These exercises should act as a review of the structures. Refer students to the Grammar folder on page 183 if they have problems with them.

Answers
a the past simple
b the past perfect
c *would* – be careful with this, as it can't be used when the subject is repeated, i.e. you can't say *I wish I would …*

If only and *I wish* have more or less the same meaning. Some people believe *If only* is slightly stronger / more formal in tone.

 Corpus spot

The examples in this exercise are all from the *Cambridge Learner Corpus*.

Answers
a I do hope …
b I wish I could suppress …
c She wishes she were / could be
d I hope you like
e I hope you have
f they had allowed us
g He wishes he were able to / could remember
h hope
i her children were
j they would stop smoking
k I wish there could always be / I hope there will always be
l hoping

4 Ask students to work in pairs and spend about five minutes talking about the subjects.

 Extension activity

Ask students to write a letter to either the college principal or a government minister expressing their hopes and wishes for the future. It should not resemble a letter of complaint, more a polite suggestion.

5 *It's about time* and *It's high time* are slightly stronger than *It's time*. Note that *I'd rather* is **never** used with *prefer* as in *I'd rather prefer*.

Answers
a to go b you went c spend d left / had left
e had given f he did g she took

6 There are eight sentences here for practice. In the exam there would only be six. Remind students to count the number of words that they write and to use the key word.

Answers
1 you stood | up for your rights / for yourself
2 you stopped behaving | as though you were
3 they | carried out
4 would/'d rather | all students wrote
5 I hadn't splashed | out
6 he had/he'd let me | know
7 she had been aware | of the strength / she had known | the strength
8 would/'d rather | you took off / you didn't wear

 Phrase spot

Some of these phrases are easy to guess, e.g. *turn as red as a beetroot*. Others are more difficult, e.g. *a turn-up for the books*. Go through the phrases as a class activity and then ask students to do the exercise in pairs or for homework if time is short.

Answers
a Well, there's a turn-up for the books – I never thought he'd get a girlfriend.
b He has a nice turn of phrase.
c He turned as red as a beetroot when ...
d From the turn of the (last) century, we see ...
e I didn't know which way to turn when the airline ...
f I tossed and turned all last night.
g but he's suddenly taken a turn for the better and ...
h Muriel didn't turn a hair when ...
i Now, everyone must take it in turns to have a go ...

10.3 SB pages 88–89

Listening and Speaking

Lesson plan	
Speaking	10–10 minutes
Listening	35–50 minutes
Pronunciation	15–15 minutes
Use of English	0–20 minutes

SV Set 5 for homework.
LV See Extension activity for 3.

1 The photos are of:
   • a McDonald's in Marrakech
   • a Mongolian yurt with satellite dish
   • someone skyping

   Students should talk about whether the photos show positive aspects of globalisation or not.

2 Ask students to spend about three minutes discussing the questions.

Possible answer
I think the term 'global village' is very depressing in many ways. It would be better to highlight differences between people rather than to make everyone the same, with the same interests, culture and so on.

I think that globalisation permeates all aspects of life in my country, from food to clothes to films. This is accelerating at an alarming rate, due, I believe, to the influence of the Internet.

Global culture is making inroads into the generation gap. Old people are often the very people who are checking for the best deals on their car insurance on the Internet or booking their holidays with budget airlines online. They don't, perhaps, feel so much in need of a smartphone as younger people though.

3 **1 16** Allow about five minutes for the class to read through the questions. Check for any vocabulary they may not understand.

Answers
1 B 2 C 3 B 4 C 5 A 6 A

Recording script
Extract One
F: There is much heated debate about the true effects of globalisation and if it is really such a good thing. Good or bad though, there isn't much debate about whether it's happening or not. Today we have Steven Bright MP, in the studio. Mr Bright, what exactly are your objections to globalisation?

M: Well, on the one hand, there's greater access to foreign culture now which can't be bad, but then again some people think that we've ended up as one big superculture. And then there's that awful word, 'outsourcing', which *can* be detrimental to the economy, but not always. Fundamentally, however, I believe that countries are becoming too dependent on each other to thrive. <u>Governments are becoming less influential</u> in the face of an increasingly market-driven world.

F: But, surely, helping developing countries to succeed by giving them loans is a good thing, isn't it?

M: You'd think so, wouldn't you? It may look that way on the face of it, but actually if you get a large organisation handing out money, <u>it is usually with strings attached and those strings often want a particular path to be followed</u>. A solution to, for example, an African problem is often thought up in New York or London. It can be disastrous.

Extract Two

F: I've spent the last twenty years researching into how being bilingual sharpens the mind, but I didn't set out to find out whether bilingualism was good or bad. I did my doctorate in psychology, on how children acquire language. When I finished, there was a job shortage in the US. The only position I could find was with a research project studying second language acquisition in schoolchildren. It wasn't my area but it was close enough. As a psychologist, I brought neuroscience to the study, like 'How does the acquisition of a second language change thought?' <u>It was these types of questions that led me to the bilingualism research. The way research works is, it takes you down a road. You then follow that road.</u> One interesting thing is that bilingualism helps with multitasking. <u>It was something I'd always had a sneaking suspicion about, but as a result of one experiment, there's now no question.</u> Now, I don't advise anyone to try this at home but we put monolinguals and bilinguals into a driving simulator. Through headphones, we gave them extra tasks to do – as if they were driving and talking on their cellphones. We then measured how much worse their driving got. Everyone's driving got worse, but with the bilinguals, their driving wasn't quite so bad. This is because the bilingual brain has had more practice at multitasking.

Extract Three

M: One summer my sister Elena talked me into spending ten weeks learning Chinese with her. I have to say I hadn't covered myself with glory during my previous forays into language learning at school, so

I wasn't exactly chomping at the bit to go through it all again, especially with a language which is widely seen as difficult. But Elena convinced me to give it a go <u>and, as she'd previously studied Spanish very successfully, she had quite a few language learning techniques</u> I'd never thought of up her sleeve. Of course we did the assigned homework, but we didn't spend any extra time quizzing each other on grammar points or vocabulary, which you may think was a bit rash. Instead, we used post-it notes to put a Chinese label on everything in our house we could think of. The fridge, the bookshelves, the walls, the cooker, the doors, nothing escaped a post-it note naming the object in question in Chinese. Then, whenever we could, we'd make lame observations in Chinese. 'The chair's brown; I don't want to be old; Where's my favourite pencil?' <u>You might laugh, but that really worked.</u> We also rented as many Chinese movies with English subtitles as we could. Ten weeks later we finished the course and we got 'A's. I enjoyed it so much I decided to do Chinese at university.

 Extension activity

Using both information from Extract One and also from their own reading, students should work in pairs to discuss this statement:

Globalisation is a force for good.

One person should speak in favour and one against and the pair with the best arguments should give their talk to the class, who then vote on who is the most persuasive.

Pronunciation

4　Noun + noun usually has the stress on the first word.

Adjective + noun usually has the stress on the second word.

Some extra words can be made with *red* and *old* but not all are included here.

Answers
red <u>carpet</u>　<u>horse</u> race　<u>race</u>horse　<u>sheep</u> dog　<u>tea</u> bag
<u>boat</u> house　<u>house</u> boat　<u>road</u> sign　back <u>seat</u>
<u>glass</u>house　old <u>woman</u>　red <u>wine</u>

5　Ask students to read the text and check their understanding. Remind them that prefixes might be tested here as well as suffixes.

Answers
1 meaningful　2 scholarly　3 literary
4 obsession　5 response　6 conception
7 unsatisfactory　8 spectacle

Writing folder 5

SB pages 90–91

Part 2 Article

1 Ask students to match the statements to the logos shown.

Answers
a Google b Coca-Cola c Apple iPod® d BMW

2 Ask students to read the article. Then elicit their views on the best title, reminding them that they should always include one when they write an article.

Answers
The best title is **c**.
Title **a** doesn't reflect the argument expressed; **b** is uninformative; **c** is catchy and in the spirit of the article.

3 Elicit students' reactions to the views expressed (to recycle vocabulary that came up in Unit 10).

4 Suggest students try to use some of these expressions in their writing, as they offer further ways of linking and reinforcing ideas. Explain, however, that they would be inappropriate in an essay, due to their journalistic style. They are best used in articles, reviews and letters (to newspapers).

Answers
a end b all c come d cold/clear e all

5 Explain that rhetorical questions are appropriate to both articles and essays (remind students of the essay on art in Units 5–8 Revision on page 75 of the Student's Book).

Possible answers
a Don't American products impose a way of life on us that many regard as alien at the end of the day?
b All things considered, mightn't globalisation bring more equality to the world?
c When you come to think of it, isn't it rather depressing to find a McDonald's in every town?

All in all, is it so disastrous that everyone can link up to the Internet?
In the cold light of day, won't these transnational companies bring much-needed investment to poorer countries?

Do we all want to wear the same branded clothes, in the final analysis?

6 Get students to write the 'balancing' paragraph in class and elicit their ideas.

Sample 'balancing' paragraph
Although, when you come to think of it, isn't it rather depressing to find a McDonald's in every town? The 'invasion' of global fast food chains sometimes creates problems at the local level too, driving down the takings in established cafés and even forcing closures. That can't be good news for the community at large.

7 Students can write the article for homework. Remind them to follow the advice given.

Sample answer
Are we living in one big, happy global village? Or are we currently witnessing, as one journalist so neatly put it, 'global pillage'? Globalisation is a complex issue, but one thing is certain: it is irreversible. Many transnational corporations are now more powerful than national governments; they will not give up their dominance, as too much is at stake economically.

Yet at the same time, the decline of the centralised nation-state is allowing more independence at local level. Regions (which were often countries in their own right formerly) are re-asserting themselves, from Scotland and Wales to Catalunya. Far from mourning the loss of tradition, these parts of the world are strengthening their cultural identities. Take the speaking of Catalan in north-east Spain, for example. Banned for decades, it has resurfaced stronger than ever in the last 25 years, and is now the medium of instruction in schools, the language of local government and often of business too.

However, in the cold light of day, it cannot be denied that global pillage is going on. Doesn't every town boast a McDonald's? Isn't everyone dressed in Nike trainers and Tommy Hilfiger sweatshirts? Companies such as these have made huge profits from our desire to conform. Nevertheless, if people want to make those choices, that is their decision.

My own reaction to globalisation is to take it with a pinch of salt. I do not see any evidence of regional differences dying out and, as I have argued above, the opposite is actually true. There are many positive aspects to the new world order. Not least of these is the Internet, which has revolutionised communication and encourages a political openness that may serve to prevent world war rather than instigate it. All in all, we have much to look forward to in the 21st century, if we concentrate on dealing with the real threat to our individual survival: environmental change.
(319 words)

11 For better, for worse

11.1
Exam skills	Listening Paper 3 Part 3
Vocabulary	Collocations with phrasal verbs
	Idioms to do with relationships

11.2
Grammar	Gradability
Exam skills	Reading and Use of English Paper 1
	Parts 2 and 3

11.3
Exam skills	Reading into Writing:
	Reformulation 2 – Paper 2 Part 1

Workbook contents
1	Reading Paper 1 Part 5
2	Grammar – gradability
3, 4, 5, 6	Vocabulary
7, 8	Use of English Paper 1 Part 2

11.1 SB pages 92–93

Lesson plan
Introduction	15–20 minutes
Listening	20–30 minutes
Vocabulary	25–40 minutes

SV	Elicit the summary orally in 2 and set 6 for homework.
LV	See Photocopiable recording script activity in 3 and Extension activity for 4.

Speaking

1 Elicit where the unit title comes from: it is part of the marriage vows. Refer students to the pictures and ask them to discuss the three questions given.

Possible answer
The couple on the left look as though they've been together for decades! They seem to have a good relationship and are very close, whereas the couple on the right are clearly going through some sort of communication breakdown. I think you need to respect your partner and be willing to support them whenever necessary. There will be good times and bad, after all. The external factors that can impinge on a relationship are many: stress at work, lack of money, poor living conditions, or other family members' influence.

2 Give students a couple of minutes to discuss the ranking of the seven attributes in pairs and elicit ideas. Then ask students to summarise these attributes in their own words, justifying why they are the most important in a relationship. The summary can either be done orally or in writing, depending on the time available.

Possible answer
What counts above all in a relationship is the ability to compromise – both partners need to show some give and take, because otherwise there will inevitably be friction in the relationship and unpleasant arguments.

Listening

3 🔊 **17** As this is the first full-length Paper 3 Part 3 task, spend extra time on it. Give students time to read the questions before starting the recording. Play it twice, as in the exam.

Answers
1 D 2 A 3 B 4 B 5 C

Recording script
Interviewer: Last week, Steve came into the studio to prove to us that life still has some happy endings. Here's his story … So, Steve, your relationship with Abby has been through some ups and downs but is definitely on a high now?

Steve: That's right, and we're finally tying the knot next month. Just over five years ago, I met this bubbly little lady – Abby. We went out, shared some laughs, and pretty soon, I knew she was the one for me.

Interviewer: And was it love at first sight for her too?

Steve: She was happy enough to spend lots of time with me, but treated me more like a big brother, if anything – she even told me about another guy she was hoping to get together with. At which point, realising I would get nowhere romantically, I decided I'd better cast my net elsewhere. I met a nice girl called Samantha, very down-to-earth – the opposite of Abby – and we started seeing each other once in a while. We had well-paid jobs and money to burn. After a good holiday in Spain, we decided to move in together. I think we both understood that it wasn't true love, but we rubbed along fairly well. Unfortunately, quite soon after that, Abby made up her mind that I was Mr Right after all, and made this very plain to me, though not to Samantha.

Interviewer: How did you take this bolt from the blue?

Steve: It was baffling. I actually wondered whether she was joking, she used to do that, but I knew deep down she wouldn't pull that trick any more. <u>I rationalised it as her whipping up a fleeting fantasy – she had time on her hands, as she'd been fired from her job and was on her own a lot</u> – her then current boyfriend worked long hours.

Interviewer: And there were displays of obvious jealousy, weren't there?

Steve: Yeah, we'd be at the same pubs and there would be anguished looks from Abby across the room, deep sighs if she was ever standing next to me at the bar, that sort of thing – I misread the situation for ages – she's always had a streak of theatricality.

Interviewer: What was your reaction once you realised it was genuine?

Steve: Well, it dawned on me that I was calling the tune now; if I wanted it, Abby and I would have a life together – otherwise, things would stay the same. It wasn't straightforward, there was Samantha to consider. She'd always been very supportive and loyal. For a while, I couldn't decide what to do. To fend off the problem, I threw myself into my job.

Interviewer: And did colleagues at work pick up on anything different about you?

Steve: Very much so – <u>I'd never been that keen and efficient before!</u> Although my daily routine was much the same, I was glad to get to work, because it distracted me – but I made sure I kept my private life out of our usual conversations. As time went on, there was growing pressure on me to do something – for all I knew, Abby might give up in disgust.

Interviewer: Then, one summer's day …

Steve: Yes, one beautiful morning last June, I couldn't keep up the pretence any longer. I sat Samantha down at the kitchen table and blurted everything out. She was terrific, far from holding back tears, she didn't even seem mildly phased by the revelation that I'd been carrying a torch for someone else and it was over. Just rolled up her sleeves and started sorting out my life for me: <u>phoned my office to say that I was at death's door</u> and wouldn't be coming in, then told me to get round to Abby's place pronto, preferably with a big bunch of flowers – she let me buy those myself.

Interviewer: And so Samantha walked out of your life and Abby walked in.

Steve: Yeah. Abby and I rented a cottage out in the country. Last summer was idyllic, and, well, it matched our mood. We got to know each other properly, spent every evening gazing into each other's eyes at sunset and … well, I'm sure you can picture the rest.

Interviewer: Absolute rapture, straight out of *True Romance* … how wonderfully slushy! So when did you finally pop the question, Steve?

Steve: I was at a big family wedding, one of my cousins, and Abby hadn't come, I think she had flu. Anyway everything seemed to fall into place at that event. I managed to sit down with my mother and talk about Abby – Mum'd been giving me the cold shoulder, as she'd really liked Samantha and, social norms being what they are, had seen her as a prospective daughter-in-law. Anyway, she came round after our heart-to-heart and I went off to offer a lift to my cousin's old schoolfriend, who lives in the States – <u>I hadn't seen him for five years. Well, he looked me between the eyes and said, 'You've always loved Abby, so how come you're not married yet – get a grip, Steve.'</u> So I did, leapt in the car without him, drove back and proposed. It's funny though, it had taken someone at one stage removed from my life to state the obvious.

Interviewer: Well, Steve, I wish you and Abby every happiness – you certainly deserve it.

Steve: Thank you.

Photocopiable recording script activity **→ page 146**

Hand out copies of the recording script and examine the text in detail, eliciting where the answers come and pointing out distraction. The recording script can then be used again to find the idioms a–j in the Idiom spot.

4   Elicit students' views.

> **Possible answer**
> It's got as good a chance as any marriage. At least Abby knows what she really wants now, and Steve seems pretty keen.

 Extension activity

Have a structured discussion on the subject of marriage.

Give students up to five key words and then ask them to discuss their views on marriage in groups, incorporating all the words, for example: love, society, religion, divorce, children.

Elicit comments and comparisons with other countries.

5   Elicit students' understanding of the phrase *a streak of theatricality* and their ideas about the adjective collocates. If time is short, set the text for homework.

> **Answers**
> Steve means that Abby sometimes likes to behave in a dramatic way.
> Some collocations with *streak* can be positive, e.g. *romantic*.
>
> 1 first sight   2 streak   3 slushy
> 4 displays   5 one   6 popped

Vocabulary

6 Elicit the expressions and additional noun collocates.

> **Suggested answers**
> blurt out a problem, a secret
> bottle up a problem, emotions
> choke back tears, emotions
> fend off criticism, blows, accusations
> keep up appearances
> shoot down an argument, accusations
> sweep aside an argument, accusations, criticism
> tease out a problem, a secret
> tone down criticism, accusations
> whip up rage, emotions

Sentences a–f can either be set for homework or done quickly at the end of the lesson. They should include:

a bottle up / blurt out a secret
b tone down criticism
c whip up emotions
d fend off blows
e choke back tears / bottle up emotions
f shoot down an argument

⟳ Idiom spot

If necessary, play the recording again and stop after each idiom. Alternatively, use the Photocopiable recording script.

Then allow students to work through sentences k–r on their own or in pairs.

> **Answers**
> a tying the knot – getting married
> b cast my net – look around for someone else
> c bolt from the blue – a total surprise
> d time on her hands – plenty of free time
> e calling the tune – in charge
> f carrying a torch for – in love with
> g rolled up her sleeves – behaved very practically
> h at death's door – very ill
> i giving me the cold shoulder – ignoring me
> j get a grip – take charge, get in control
>
> k hands l grip m sleeve n clutching
> o grasp p grips q hands r grabs

11.2 SB pages 94–95

Gradability

> **Lesson plan**
> Introduction   5–10 minutes
> Use of English   15–20 minutes
> Grammar   40–40 minutes
> Use of English   0–20 minutes
>
> SV Keep discussion in 1 brief; set 8 for homework.
> LV See Extension activity for 2.

1 Refer students to the picture and elicit their ideas about the advantages and disadvantages of social networking sites.

> **Possible answer**
> Facebook is great. I couldn't plan my social life without it and it means I can keep in touch with people I don't get to see very often. I guess there are disadvantages to do with privacy and security, but it doesn't actually worry me that much.

2 Allow students a couple of minutes to skim the text. Richard and Cindy met through an Internet chat room.

> **Answers**
> 1 since/from 2 anything 3 hardly/barely/scarcely
> 4 Having 5 as 6 Within 7 most 8 sooner

⟳ Extension activity

Elicit students' ideas on other possible outcomes of Internet chat rooms (positive and negative).

3 Elicit students' ideas. Refer them to the Grammar folder on page 184 if necessary.

> **Answers**
> You cannot say 'completely affectionate', as 'affectionate' is a gradable adjective; conversely, 'devastating' is an ungradable adjective, so you cannot say 'extremely devastating'.
>
> The adverbs *deeply, fairly, immensely, rather* and *very* go with A (gradable adjectives) and the adverbs *absolutely, entirely* and *utterly* go with B (ungradable adjectives). The three adverbs that can go with both are *pretty, quite* and *really*, but there are register restrictions.

4

Answers
a utterly miserable   b doubly disappointing
c slightly embarrassed   d highly suspicious
e absolutely staggering   f somewhat envious

Possible answers
(Two remaining phrases)
Helena seems **fairly laid-back** about tomorrow's interview, but I know she has spent ages preparing for it.
Your forecast about the weather was **remarkably accurate** – how on earth did you know it was going to be sunny today?

5   Refer students to the first pair of examples and explain the difference between the literal and figurative uses. Then elicit their ideas about the second pair of examples.

Answers
The first use is ungradable – nationality is an absolute. In the second use, the degree adverb *very* can be used – here, the adjective is gradable, as 'Britishness' exists on a scale from mild to very strong, or stereotypical.

6   Give students three minutes to discuss a–f in pairs then elicit their answers.

Answers
a **First example:** used to describe food that keeps for a long time in a freezer (in a frozen state)
Second example: INFORMAL and non-literal, used when a person feels very cold
b **First example:** If something is empty, it does not contain anything.
Second example: having no meaning or value
c **First example:** used to mean very difficult to deal with – note that although this sentence is fairly informal, the meaning is not restricted in register – e.g. UNMARKED *Trapped in a war zone, the journalists are facing an impossible situation.*
Second example: If an action or event is impossible, it cannot happen or be done.
d **First example:** INFORMAL, non-literal, meaning very stupid or crazy
Second example: (old-fashioned use) seriously mentally ill
e **First example:** non-literal, used of a situation where there is little or no hope for the future
Second example: literal use – if a place is bleak, it is cold, empty and not attractive.
f **First example:** lacking in taste or flavour – note that although this sentence is quite informal, the meaning is not restricted in register – e.g. UNMARKED *The meat was dry and tasteless.*
Second example: offensive, likely to upset or anger people

7   Remind students of earlier work done on suffixes in Unit 1.

Answers
a alternative   b cautionary   c collapsible   d detestable
e honorary, honourable   f laborious   g loathsome
h hypocritical   i philosophical   j repulsive   k tenacious
l theatrical   m virtuous   n voluntary

8   This word formation task can be set for homework if time is short.

Answers
1 indeterminate   2 setting(s)   3 decidedly   4 disclose
5 alliances   6 crucial   7 outcomes   8 inroads

11.3 SB pages 96–97
Reading into Writing: Reformulation 2

Lesson plan

Introduction	10–20 minutes
Reading two texts	30–30 minutes
Writing	20–40 minutes

SV   Set part of 5 for homework.
LV   Allow more time for the discussion in 1.

1   The pictures show members of a street gang on a housing estate and team bonding at a business meeting. Ask students to discuss the questions in pairs or groups. Elicit answers.

Possible answers
People conform in society by wearing similar clothes, having similar tastes in entertainment and by behaving in the same way. Being part of a group offers security and the feeling of belonging, rather than being an outsider. People may join a sports club to play sport, but they often want to make new friendships too. Being accepted into a gang is also a form of conformism.

2   Elicit how the two texts overlap in content – there is overlap in the discussion of belonging to a group, but the contexts are very different.

3   Refer students to the three statements and elicit which two reflect ideas in the first text (1 and 3). Suggest they underline where the ideas come in the text.

4 Explain that reformulation is essential to avoid losing marks in the exam. Allow them to work through the exercise in pairs first and then elicit answers.

Suggested answers
a people's biased attitudes and failings
b there is a trend of extreme behaviour
c members are inclined to inflate the group's worth / regard the group as better than it is
d the belief that the group is invincible
e a rigidity in outlook
f a desire for homogeneity
g the suppression of individual views
h any opposition is firmly dealt with

5 Do the analysis of the sample answer in class but set the rewriting for homework if time is short.

The answer has a strong introduction that puts the topic into context and includes the writer's own language. The remaining paragraphs concentrate on the second text – the first text is only summarised briefly and there is no evaluation of it.

In the rewriting, most phrases can be used from exercise 4; 'disregarding' can be replaced by 'ignoring'.

Exam folder 6

SB pages 98–99

Paper 3 Part 4
Multiple matching

1 Refer the class to the information and the Exam advice. They will always hear the recording twice.

2 **1.18** Play the extract for Speaker 1 twice. Ask students to underline the information containing the answers and to look for where the distraction is occurring.

Answers and Recording script
You are going to hear Speaker 1. Look at Task One and Task Two and decide which answers are true for the first speaker. You will hear the recording twice.

Speaker 1
I was at a twenty-first birthday 'do'. I'd just broken up with a beautiful girl who I'd been head over heels in love with and my loyal friends thought it was time to find me someone else. I'm quite shy but I was instantly taken with this girl they introduced me to, called Sarah. She struck me as really fun and sparkling, ready to chat to anyone, even me! Anyway, we were married a year later. She's a wonderful person – she must be to have stayed married to me all these years! She's been there through thick and thin, and I can tell you there have been times when money's been extremely tight.

3 **1.19** Play the extract for Speaker 2 twice and follow the same procedure as for 1, above.

Answers and Recording script
2 C 7 C

Now listen to Speaker 2 and, with a partner, decide on the answer for Questions 2 and 7.

Speaker 2
I'm a bit of a workaholic and so actually finding someone to have a relationship with was always tricky. I'm at the top of my game, head of a large fashion house, and I've found that men find me a bit intimidating because I'm so determined to succeed. I guess that's why I've always liked older men – they're usually less insecure. My partner is great, so shrewd about people, much better than me, although when I first met him, even though he was as stylish as everyone around me, it was his intellect that drew me to him. I like to think we're really well matched.

4 **1.20** Students should now listen to the other three speakers and complete the task.

Answers
3 G   4 B   5 A
8 F   9 D   10 G

Recording script

Now listen to the other three speakers and, for Questions 3 to 5 and 8 to 10, choose from the lists A to H. Use each letter only once. There are three extra letters which you do not need to use. You will hear the recordings twice.

Speaker 3

I'm a writer and I'd lived alone for years. Anyway, I went to a friend's party and there was this woman there surrounded by admiring men – someone told me they thought she was 'gorgeous' but I didn't think she was my type. Anyway, when I did get to talk to her we got on like a house on fire. She just seemed to be so full of stamina, so dynamic. We married six weeks later – a whirlwind romance! Anyway, we've had our ups and downs obviously over the years but it's her warm personality that keeps me close. We do have rows, mainly about money, and I get very impatient with her, but we always soon make up.

Speaker 4

I started online dating when I moved to London. I didn't know anyone so I was determined to give it a go, and it was cheap! That's how I met my husband. We're kindred spirits really and I really like the fact that he's such a perfectionist – everything has to be just right – I guess I am too really. Some people say it would drive them mad but not me. Of course, I didn't notice that about him when we first met. Most people see the handsome face first but it was his attitude to people that attracted me. He was so broadminded and really opened my eyes to the problems some people have in society.

Speaker 5

I went on quite a few dates when I first moved to New York. My workmates fixed me up with people. One was this model with not a hair out of place who looked terrific, but was extremely dull. Not long after her, I met this wonderful girl on a plane to Tokyo. She wasn't conventionally pretty, I guess, but she just managed to see the funny side of everything. We got married soon after and we're still in love. What I love about her is that she's happy to spend ages reading to our kids and, not only that, she can find time to sit and chat to my elderly parents and that's not easy as my mother's beginning to forget things.

Topic Scientific advances

12.1

Exam skills	Reading and Use of English Paper 1 Part 6
Vocabulary	Idioms with technical words

12.2

Grammar	Passive structures
Exam skills	Reading and Use of English Paper 1 Part 4

12.3

Exam skills	Speaking Paper 4 Part 3
Pronunciation	Stress and emphasis
Vocabulary	Phrases with *set*
Exam skills	Reading and Use of English Paper 1 Part 1

Workbook contents

1	Listening Paper 3 Part 4
2, 3	Grammar – passive forms
4, 5, 6, 7, 8	Vocabulary
9	Use of English Paper 1 Part 3
10	Use of English Paper 1 Part 4

12.1 SB pages 100–101

Lesson plan	
Introduction	10–20 minutes
Reading	40–50 minutes
Vocabulary	10–20 minutes

SV	Keep introductory discussion brief.
LV	See Extension activity for 4.

1 Explain that the three questions are typical ways in which an examiner might ask candidates to extend topic discussion after the individual long turns in Paper 4 Part 3.

Possible answers
Ordinary people have greater life expectancy due to improvements in medicine. DNA analysis has led to better crime detection and conviction of criminals.

This area of genetics and biotechnology is bound to give rise to new discoveries, as further work is done on the human genome.

Multinational companies are very powerful and the attempt to introduce GM (genetically modified) food illustrates that government ministers need to keep a close eye on what they are doing. Current legislation and governmental controls may be inadequate.

Reading

2 The photo shows the minuscule guitar from Cornell University that is referred to in the opening sentence of the text.

Ask whether any students have read 'popular science' books in their own language – this is a growth area of publishing in Britain. Explain that although the text covers a complex scientific subject, the writer has tried to use non-specialist style and language as far as possible.

Suggested answer
The writer has tried to simplify the difficult subject matter by referring to things from the real world – parts of cells are likened to scissors, motors, pipes and so on, and the DNA helix is compared to a ladder. Atoms and molecules become busy commuters, rushing around the body. The A, T, C, G base pairings in DNA are 'just a string of four-letter words' (almost certainly included to raise a laugh from the reader, as 'four-letter words' is a common euphemism for swear words, and is rather appropriate to a discussion of life as these tend to refer to the sexual organs and the act of reproduction!).

3 Stress that students must spend enough time reading the text and missing paragraphs, in order to work out the links involved. In the exam, they should underline key phrases in both as they read for the first time.

The parts of the text which link to the underlined phrases in paragraphs A–H are given alongside the answers below. Point out that there isn't always a link both before and after a gap.

Answers
1 D before gap: *tweezers, scissors*, etc.;
   after gap: *collectively*
2 H after gap: *urban environment, commuting*
3 A before gap: *no overseer supervises their activities*;
   after gap: *nowadays, convincing explanation*
4 F before gap: *they say*
5 C before gap: *more than the sum of its parts, the job of explaining life*;
   after gap: *with the discovery of DNA, early 1950s*
6 G before gap: *handrails, rungs*
   after gap: *A, T, C, G*
7 B before gap: *slot together snugly, complementary projecting arms*;
   after gap: *this is guaranteed to be identical to the original*

4 Ask students to name the illustrations.

Answers
a a pump b valves c (a pair of) scissors
d (some) tweezers e (a padlock and) chain

 Extension activity

Before looking at the Idiom spot, put these words (which are nouns and verbs) on the board: *lever, plug, spike, tool, wrench*. Elicit uses in other contexts for both parts of speech. NB the verb *lever* is only used in a technical sense.

Answers
lever (noun) – *bargaining/political lever*; NB also the uncountable noun *leverage*, the ability to influence people
lever (verb) – only technical, e.g. *lever a frame/door*
plug (noun) – *pull the plug on a project* (terminate); *give a book/film/CD/etc. a plug* – promote on air or in the press
plug (verb) – *plug a/the gap* (fill); *plug a book/film, etc.* (promote)
spike (noun) – only technical, of metal and other long, pointed things, e.g. *wooden spike, flower spike, hair in spikes*
spike (verb) – *spike a drink* (with alcohol or drugs); *spike a project* (terminate)
tool (noun) – as *lever* i.e. *bargaining tool*, etc.; *a/the tool of someone or something*, e.g. *a tool of a regime/government/country*, etc., used to show disapproval; a gun (slang)
tool (verb) – drive, usually with *along/around* (informal)
wrench (noun) – a painful separation; *throw a wrench in* (American English) – damage a deal or arrangement (the British English equivalent is *throw a spanner in the works*)
wrench (verb) – pull or twist something; *wrench your mind/eyes/thoughts away from something or someone*

 Idiom spot

If there is time, ask students to write example sentences using these idioms.

Answers
a nail – something that has finally caused failure
b spade (a) spade – to speak directly
c tubes – to fail
d chain – unreliable part of something, usually used of people
e fuse – to lose your temper
f strings – unconditional
g wires – to misunderstand
h bolt – to fail
i gear – to start to deal with something effectively
j knife – to deliberately make someone feel worse

12.2 SB pages 102–103

Passive structures

Lesson plan	
Grammar	60–70 minutes
Use of English	0–20 minutes
SV	Set 6 for homework.
LV	See Extension activity for 3.

1 Students can match the examples to the explanations in pairs. Elicit answers.

Answers
a 1 b 3 c 5 d 4 e 2

2 Remind students that use of the passive gives rise to an impersonal tone. Scientific articles are perhaps the most widespread example of this style.

Ask students to work through the exercise in pairs, deciding whether the agent needs to be mentioned.

Answers
a Marie Curie was given the Nobel Prize for Chemistry for her discovery of radium.
b Homes in and around the city have been affected by lengthy power cuts all this week.
c The 'miracle' drug was found to have unpleasant side-effects.
d Meteorites have been found in Antarctica which are believed to have come from the Moon.
e Dark matter is said to exist in the universe, but (it) has not been detected as yet.
f The car will no longer be manufactured in Europe, due to recent global restructuring.
g The Truman Capote Award for Literary Criticism was won in 2011 by Mark McGurl / was won by Mark McGurl in 2011.
h The latest version of Adobe Flash should be installed to get the best from this application.

3 Explain that further uses of the passive include official or public language and news reporting. Ask students to rewrite the sentences to shift the register and tone.

Suggested answers
a Food and drink must not be brought into the lab.
b No photographs may be taken inside this museum.
c Infra-red equipment is being used to search for further survivors.
d The award for best innovation will be shared by/between three postgraduate students.
e Thorough safety checks are to be / will be carried out immediately.

Extension activity

Find scientific reports on the Internet and/or bring in newspaper and magazine articles featuring passives. Students could work on a chosen text in pairs or small groups, summarising the content.

Relevant websites include www.guardian.co.uk, www.newscientist.com and www.britishmuseum.org.

Corpus spot

Answers
a be reminded   b being delayed   c being damaged
d to have been invited   e having been asked / being asked   f be discovered

4   Refer students to the Grammar folder on page 184 first if they are unsure of modal passive forms.

Answers
1 was discovered   2 could not have been caused
3 was detected / had been detected (specific to one research project) OR has been detected (traces of iridium continue to be found there)   4 must have been formed   5 would have been thrown   6 to be blotted out   7 were eaten   8 would have been killed

5   Refer students to the example *confirm – confirmation* and explain that several nouns ending in *-ation* are used in academic writing. You can search for these in the English Vocabulary Profile by doing a wild card search (*ation) and specifying the part of speech as 'noun' in Advanced Search.

Possible answers
a   Publication/The publication of these scientific papers will be delayed until next year.
b   An announcement of big job losses has just been made on the local news.
c   Consideration is being given to the planning application for a new sports centre.
d   A recommendation will be made for the immediate closure of the hospital.
e   An in-depth / A more in-depth investigation of the case is to be carried out.
f   No explanation was given as to how much the project would cost.

Answers
1   for a probe | to be landed
2   will need/have to be worn | for the duration
3   be seen | by/with the naked eye OR be discernible/ visible | to the naked eye
4   increasing number of planets | have been found
5   to be | on the brink of
6   being / having been advised | against physics / not to continue with physics

12.3 SB pages 104–105

Listening and Speaking

Lesson plan	
Introduction	10–10 minutes
Listening and Speaking	20–30 minutes
Pronunciation	20–20 minutes
Phrase spot	10–20 minutes
Use of English	0–10 minutes

SV   Set 5 and 6 for homework.
LV   See Photocopiable recording script activity in 3.

1   Remind students that the prompt card for the individual long turn in Paper 4 Part 3 is there to generate ideas in the exam, and should not be seen as a 'straightjacket'.

Possible answers
career opportunities – more now than ever before
commercial interests – very strong, may go against government policy
moral issues – tampering with nature

2   🔊 **21** Before starting, point out that the recording lasts the required two minutes. Students should listen out for their own ideas and say afterwards whether they were included or not. Play the recording a second time if necessary, before eliciting whether students agree or disagree with Jana and Erik's views. Refer to the Photocopiable recording script if necessary.

Recording script
Interlocutor: Now, in this part of the test you're each going to talk on your own for about two minutes. You need to listen while your partner is speaking because you'll be asked to comment afterwards. So Jana, I'm going to give you a card with a question written on it and I'd like you to tell us what you think. There are also some ideas on the card for you to use if you like.
All right? Here is your card.

Jana: Well, I don't have a scientific background, but I think science is something that affects us all nowadays. You can't afford to ignore what's going on in advanced science. There's a lot of media interest right now in the latest developments in, say, genetics and DNA profiling. Er, I do think it's worrying how genetic testing can be used, actually. For example, if you have a genetic disorder of some kind, you may not be able to take out life insurance … or get a job even. But then, on the other hand, DNA analysis is helping to solve crimes, and that's good for society, so it's good and bad, I suppose.

The main problem centres around information. Most people don't know the facts and so naturally they're worried. So what is needed is more information in simple language for ordinary people to understand – and perhaps this needs to come from the government. Because I think the biggest worry of all is that the whole area of genetics is being driven by the business world. Much of the research going on today is backed by big companies – drugs co…, pharma… pharmaceutical companies and so on – and they're going to want something back from their investment. Which means that the research is not being done just as research, it's not pure, not independent. … I think too, that they're not controlling this research.

The public needs to be properly informed. There are potential benefits, yes, but we must be told what's happening and why. You know, things are being pushed ahead at such an alarming rate and … mm, I don't know, it seems to me, it's maybe not always going to be helpful for society.

Interlocutor: Thank you. Erik, what is your view on current career opportunities in science?

Erik: I'm actually in the final year of a biology degree so I can comment on that personally. We're always being told by our lecturers that more progress will be made in biology in the next five to ten years than has occurred in the last fifty. It's a fast-moving field. As Jana said, there are many new companies … biotech companies springing up, so yes, job prospects are good for someone like me, I think, plenty of different directions to go in. So it's not all doom and gloom, far from it.

Interlocutor: What do you think, Jana?

Jana: Well, Erik is speaking from experience! It's good to hear his positive take on things.

Interlocutor: Thank you.

Pronunciation

3 **1.22** Give students a couple of minutes to match the expressions to their meanings.

Photocopiable recording script activity (P) → page 147

Having clarified the meaning of the expressions, ask students to look through the recording script and decide where it would be appropriate for Jana to use them. Then play the recording, where Jana uses these expressions.

Ask students to listen carefully to the six sentences, which include the expressions a–f. Stop after each one and ask for comments on how Jana stresses important points (underlined in the recording script below) and pauses for emphasis (shown by … in the recording script).

> **Recording script**
> a You can't <u>afford</u> to … <u>ignore</u> what's going on in the <u>vanguard</u> of science.
> b So it's … a <u>double-edged sword</u>, I suppose.
> c So what is needed … is more <u>information</u> in <u>simple</u> language … for the <u>lay</u> person to understand.
> d Which means that the research is not being done for its <u>own sake</u> … it's not <u>pure</u> … not <u>independent</u>.
> e I think too, that the research is … not subject to <u>enough regulations</u>.
> f It's maybe <u>not</u> always going to be for … the <u>greater good</u>.

4 **1.23** Ask students to repeat what they hear after the recording, placing appropriate stress on key words.

> **Recording script**
> a concern
>   cause for concern
>   considerable cause for concern
>   There's considerable cause for concern in the whole area.
> b duty
>   duty bound to
>   Governments are duty bound to regulate the industry.
> c repercussions
>   possible repercussions
>   There are a number of possible repercussions.
> d significance
>   the social significance
>   The social significance of biotechnology should not be underestimated.
> e cusp
>   on the cusp of
>   We're on the cusp of completely new forms of treatment.
> f reservations
>   extreme reservations
>   I have extreme reservations about the confidentiality of all this information.

Phrase spot

Ask students to work through the phrases, ticking the ones that use *set*.

Answers (clockwise)
set the wheels in motion, set the world on fire, set the scene, set out your stall, set your heart on, set the record straight, set a dangerous precedent, set in stone, set your sights on, set your teeth on edge

The other verbs are *pull* and *run*:
pull your weight – work as hard as other people in a group
pull your socks up – improve your behaviour or work
Pull the other one! – if you use this expression, it means you don't believe what someone has just said to you. Also: *Pull the other one, it's got bells on it.*
pull the strings – control people or an organisation
pull a fast one – trick someone
run rings round – beat or do better than someone
run the risk of – do something although something bad might happen because of it
run counter to – have the opposite effect to something else
run a tight ship – manage something efficiently

5

Suggested answers
a Jenny **set her heart on** having the new gadget.
b The consultant **set out her stall** to the whole department.
c Allowing her teenage son to stay out late has **set a dangerous precedent**.
d Nothing is **set in stone** as yet.
e The vivid description of the Martian landscape **sets the scene** at the beginning of the book.
f The sound of a young child attempting to play the violin really **sets my teeth on edge**.
g A leading biotech company immediately **set the wheels in motion** to recruit the young scientist.
h Carla's a good singer, but she's never going to **set the world on fire**.

6 The text features two of the expressions with *run*.

Answers
1 B 2 C 3 A 4 C 5 D 6 B 7 A 8 D

Writing folder 6

SB pages 106–107

Part 2 Report

1 Explain to students how the work they have done on passive structures in Unit 12 can now be used in their writing. Suggest students work in pairs looking at the layout and organisation of the sample report.

Improved answer with sub-headings and bullets
This report summarises the current career opportunities for science graduates, drawing largely on the experiences of past and present students. Many final-year students have already been invited to interviews and some have even been offered jobs, conditional on graduation.

A broad scope of employment
The first point to stress is that interesting opportunities exist outside the specialist scientific fields. This is dealt with in the final section of the report.

Academic research
Returning to pure science, it has been estimated that there will be over a thousand post-graduate posts available for the next academic year, countrywide. Students should consult their tutor for advice in the first instance. High-achievers should contemplate applying for scholarships to the U.S.A., where so much research is at the cutting edge. Students wishing to follow up on specific research possibilities in the States are advised to consult Professor Grimbleton.

Exciting new opportunities
The fast-moving developments in biotechnology and genetics look set to provide good job opportunities, as many companies are being expanded in their bids to become market leader. Four local companies have specifically requested graduate trainees from this college. They are:
• Bio-futures
• Genotech
• PJF Seed Research
• Railton Systems.
Application forms can be obtained from the Administration Secretary.

Education as a career
Several past students have opted for jobs in teaching and it is recommended that anyone considering such a career should attend the information day planned by this department. At this event, it will not only be possible to meet Head Teachers and Science Coordinators from schools in the region, but also former college students who are now qualified and practising teachers.

A more unconventional path
As indicated above, any report on current opportunities would be incomplete without mentioning other non-scientific jobs that past students have taken up with relish. While none of these jobs can be said to demand the recall of actual science, the generic skills that students have been given through their undergraduate courses are directly relevant.

Here are some of the more unusual career moves:
- accountancy
- stockmarket brokering
- counselling
- air-traffic control
- casino management.

Next steps

More details can be found on the student website.
A booklet is also in preparation.
(360 words)

2 Ask students to underline other examples of signposting in the report.

Answers

Other signposting devices:
This report summarises
The first point
This is dealt with in the final section
Returning to pure science
Here are

Referring forward: c, e, g
Referring back: a, b, d, f, h, i, j

3

Answers

a high-achievers
b fast-moving, recently-formed
c un- (unconventional), post- (post-graduate), non- (non-scientific)
d -al (unconventional, conditional), -ally (specifically), -ist (specialist), -ship (scholarship)
e at the cutting edge, career move

4 Spend some time in class planning the report, getting students to compare their ideas in pairs or small groups.

5 Set the report for homework, reminding students of the advice given.

Sample answer
KELVINGTON FILM CLUB ANNUAL REPORT
Following another successful year, the club is able to make ambitious plans for the coming twelve months. This report will summarise its current financial situation, review recent events, and outline future plans.

Financial affairs
The club has seen a slight rise in expenses: film rental costs were increased last July and mailing costs have also risen, due to a notable increase in membership: 32 new members have joined and their fees have contributed to the club's healthy bank balance. Moreover, in March, the club was awarded a grant of £500 from the Princefield Film Institute, due to the impressive bid submitted by the Chair.

Main events
The highlights of last year's programme are given below:
- Welcome for new members, February
- Short season of Bertolucci's films, March
- Talk by screenwriter Todd Grafton, April
- Visit to the Cannes Film Festival, June
- Summer barbecue and party, August
- Lecture series on animation techniques, October
- Annual club dinner, December

Of these, the Cannes visit was particularly popular and thanks must be given to Joy Wellman for organising everything so well. In contrast, the lecture series in October was poorly attended, and enrolments barely covered the costs of the venue and speaker. It would be appreciated if members could give the committee feedback about this event, so that the same mistakes are not repeated.

Future plans
As always, the film programme is defined largely by members' requests. While the booking secretary already has a potential list of screenings, it is not too late for further films to be proposed.

One exciting development is the imminent setting up of a DVD library, which has been requested by many members. The scheme will allow members to rent up to two films at a time, for periods of three to five days.

Finally, the club is proud to confirm that the Canadian director Brad Eastwood has accepted the invitation to give a talk to members, date to be confirmed. This event promises to be both informative and exciting, as Brad is known to be a lively and controversial speaker.
(340 words)

Units 9–12 Revision

Lesson plan	
Use of English	30–35 minutes
Writing	30–30 minutes
SV	Set 4 for homework.
LV	Elicit students' reactions to the text in 1.

The aim of this revision unit is to focus on the language covered in Units 9–12, as well as extending the work done on reports in Writing folder 6. Specific exam practice is provided for Paper 1 Parts 2 and 4. This Use of English section could be done as a timed test of 30 minutes. Alternatively, the whole unit could be set for homework.

Use of English

1 Elicit where this text might have come from (a magazine).

Answers
1 with 2 us/readers 3 Not 4 but 5 come
6 nothing 7 all 8 gives 9 among/perhaps/possibly
10 but/while/whilst/although 11 go/date 12 everyone
13 When/Once 14 might/could

2

Answers
1 agreed to take it | in turns to tidy
2 went on | to discuss
3 Peter had put on | a suit for
4 is remembered | for always having
5 not/never lose | sight of the fact that luck
6 as friendship is concerned, | I'd rather have

Vocabulary

3

Answers
a came in for b turn c vivacious d set e chain
f shoulder g choke back h pompous i sets j blue
k a spade a spade l coming along m nettle
n blurting out

Writing

4 Stress to students once more that using compound adjectives in their writing will show their range of language.

Answer
Here is my report on our club's recent exchange visit to Australia. Without exception, members who participated in this trip were highly appreciative of the **meticulously-planned** itinerary, not to mention the warm welcome extended by our **easy-going** Australian hosts. This **long-standing** relationship continues to flourish and we will be hosting a **record-breaking** number of visitors this summer (see below).

Travel
The **inter-continental** flights went smoothly and we arrived in Melbourne on schedule. A coach had been organised to transport us to the civic reception, where our individual hosts awaited us. Travel within Australia was mostly by plane – unfortunately, our visit coincided with industrial action, so our transfers were not entirely **trouble-free**.

Trips
The highpoint was the Great Barrier Reef, where two exhilarating days were spent **deep-sea** diving. Those members who chose not to dive were given the alternative of a **half-day** cruise in a **glass-bottomed** boat, which was said to be very enjoyable for all concerned.

Some members have suggested that the visit to the Kakadu National Park could have been extended, as it was rather rushed. In subsequent years, it might also be more informative to visit during the dry season, which would allow **wider-ranging** access to the park.

Return visit
There will be 48 visitors to us in July, including six families with young children. In view of this, it will be necessary to find extra hosts. Strategies for achieving this should be agreed at the next club meeting. In anticipation, could the following suggestions be tabled:
• advertising in relevant journals
• feature in local newspaper
• posters in public places, e.g. library
• mailshot to schools and colleges
• interview on KJY radio
• club website?
Perhaps other members should be asked for further suggestions in advance of the meeting.
(288 words)

Crossword

This includes some of the idioms, phrasal verbs and other vocabulary from Units 9–12.

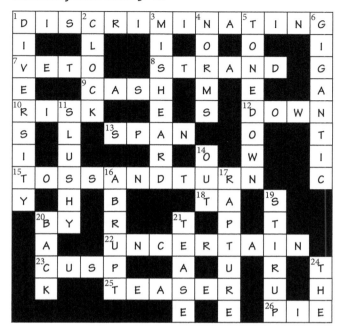

13.1

Exam skills	Listening Paper 3 Part 1
	Reading and Use of English Paper 1
	Part 1
Vocabulary	The environment
	Register
	Synonyms

13.2

Grammar focus	Reported speech
Exam skills	Reading and Use of English Paper 1
	Part 2

13.3

Vocabulary	Word formation; prepositions
Exam skills	Reading and Writing: Giving
	opinions – Paper 2 Part 1

Workbook contents

1	Reading Paper 1 Part 6
2	Grammar – reported speech
3, 4, 5	Vocabulary
6	Use of English Paper 1 Part 2

13.1 SB pages 110–111

Lesson plan

Vocabulary	10–10 minutes
Speaking	10–10 minutes
Listening	30–30 minutes
Vocabulary	10–20 minutes
Use of English	0–20 minutes

| SV | Set 8 for homework. |
| LV | See Extension activities for 6 and 8. |

Vocabulary

1   Ask students to work together to match the words.
There may be more than one answer.

Answers

fossil fuel	climate change
severe famine/shortages	solar energy
pristine environment /	population density/change
ice cap	melting ice cap
finite resources	rising sea levels
greenhouse gases	life expectancy
water shortages/resources	

Speaking

2   The photos are of:

- an overpopulated city
- smog from cars and scooters
- deforestation

Students should work in pairs to discuss the photos
and their solutions.

Possible solutions may be to halt global warming by
curbing the use of cars, reducing emissions of carbon
into the atmosphere, using energy from renewable
resources such as solar/wave/wind power, and not
cutting down the forests.

3

Possible answers
Recycle glass, paper and cans.
Don't carry shopping in plastic carrier bags.
Don't use disposable containers or cups.
Turn off lights, computers and TVs.
Turn down the thermostat in your room.
Plant a tree.
Ride a bike to work or college.
Use recycled stationery and toilet paper.
If you use a car, go electric and share car space.
Use energy-efficient light bulbs.
Volunteer to help in local environmental programmes.
Fix any dripping taps.
Always use biodegradable products.
Don't use herbicides or insecticides in your garden.
Use paper carefully.
Turn off the tap when you clean your teeth.
Use washing machines that use less water.

Listening

4   ◀ 1 24 Allow students a few minutes to read through
the questions before you play the recording. Play each
extract twice, as in the exam.

Answers
1 B   2 B   3 A   4 C   5 A   6 C

Recording script
Extract One
Kids love it when I say I talk rubbish for a living, but
it's the truth. As a recycling officer, I'm pretty obsessed
with cutting down on consumption and waste. People
come into this field from a mix of backgrounds. Mine is
teaching, which is ideal, and most days during term

time I'll have some contact with schools. <u>Kids are very receptive to the 'save the planet' message and they're actually natural collectors of everything from bottle tops to newspapers, which is useful.</u> If it's a keen school, I'll ask questions and they'll bombard me with questions of their own, which is great. But if I ask, 'What's recycling?' and someone answers 'Riding your bike' I know I've got a long morning ahead of me. Usually they're completely spellbound, they've a rough idea of what the local 'dump' is, but with a video and descriptions and the occasional trip, I can really spell out what landfill means. The cost of burying rubbish is enormous. <u>Even taking into account the roller coaster changes in price for recycled plastics, glass and paper, it's still worth recycling, and children are receptive to that. What really gets me is the lack of local initiatives – there is often no direct link between policy and action.</u>

Extract Two

Interviewer: Now, Professor Dean, the greenhouse effect has made finding alternative sources of energy all the more urgent, hasn't it?

Professor: Indeed. If not for the greenhouse effect, we may have been able to postpone finding a replacement for fossil fuels for some time. Places like India and China, for example, have huge quantities of cheap coal at their disposal, but with the greenhouse effect we need to make the transition earlier. <u>But renewables, such as solar and wind power, all tend to be very episodic</u> and the power density is low. Investment and take-up of renewables has been variable.

Interviewer: And what about biomass energy?

Professor: Well, that brings you to the inevitable land-use issue. Say that by 2050 you wanted to supply ten terawatts of power, which equals the current total energy consumption of all humankind, and you wanted to do it with biomass energy, you would need an area equal approximately to ten per cent of the Earth's land surface area. <u>Eventually you'd have people and you'd have wheat but nothing else.</u> I'm not sure how popular that policy would make a government.

Extract Three

Presenter: With me to talk about environmental issues today is Dr Jane Dove, of the University of Melchester. Welcome, Jane.

Woman: Good morning.

Presenter: Today we're discussing the Gaia hypothesis, a theory about the Earth put forward in 1965 by James Lovelock. Now Lovelock was a scientist outside the British establishment. <u>He took issue with the accepted view</u> that the Earth was just a passive host to millions of species of plants and animals, and

that these living organisms simply adapted to the environment they found themselves in. Jane, <u>nowadays Lovelock's theory that denuding forests will ravage delicate ecosystems is generally accepted, isn't it?</u>

Woman: Indeed, but you know, even in the 1960s he was thought of as a tree-hugger – someone who goes around hugging and worshipping trees. <u>A bit of a weirdo really.</u> Of course, it didn't help that he called his idea the Gaia hypothesis.

Presenter: <u>Yes, in fact this name, after the Greek goddess of the Earth, pushed Lovelock even further away from his peers.</u>

Woman: <u>I guess to them it seemed to represent the very opposite of rigid scientific enquiry.</u>

Presenter: True, more a 'holistic' view of the Earth – that's as a whole rather than its individual components. He wasn't an amateur though, and his ideas have since gained acceptance.

5 **1** 24 Play the recording again and ask the class to decide which register each extract has. A knowledge of register is important at Proficiency level.

Answers
Extract 1: informal – 'to talk rubbish' is a play on words; quite a few words are informal: *pretty, kids, cutting down, spell out, a rough idea*; use of *bombard* – exaggeration for effect
Extract 2: the man uses formal speech; *postpone, at their disposal, the transition, humankind.*
Extract 3: man uses fairly formal speech; woman more informal – *a bit of a weirdo, I guess*

6 These words are all taken from the *Cambridge Learner Corpus*.

Answers
a *people* is unmarked; *persons* is used in notices and government handouts
b *amelioration* is formal; *improvement* is unmarked
c *bloke* is informal; *man* is unmarked
d *stuff* is informal; *things* is unmarked
e *frequented* is formal; *went to* is unmarked
f *reckon* is informal; *think* is unmarked
g *boozing* is very informal/slang; *drinking* is unmarked
h *mates* is informal; *friends* is unmarked
i *fellow* is rather dated informal; *guy* is modern informal
j *snaps* is informal; *photographs* is unmarked
k *pluses* is informal; *advantages* is unmarked
l *lousy* is informal; *terrible* is unmarked
m *prudent* is formal; *careful* is unmarked
n *mad* is informal; *annoyed* is unmarked

Extension activity

Students should try and bring into class examples of English – possibly from the Internet or from English language newspapers or magazines or adverts – and make up posters giving examples of different registers. They can include technical, office, scientific, pop music and government information, etc. as well as simply formal, informal and neutral.

7   Although it's a good idea to encourage students to look for synonyms, they should also be made aware that there might be usage differences.

Answers

a   broke (*destitute* is a formal, literary word)
b   skinny (*skinny* is more negative in tone than *slender*)
c   enemies (*opponents* is mainly used in sport)
d   sneaking into (*entering* is just unmarked; *sneaking* has the idea of doing something underhand)
e   commence (*kick off* is used to talk about sport or informally to mean 'begin'; *commence* is more formal and suitable for the context)
f   lost his cool (*became displeased* is formal; *lost his cool* is the same register as 'socked him in the jaw', i.e. informal)
g   struck (this is much stronger than *touched*)
h   trickling (*trickling* is for water that is moving slowly; *flooding* is more for a river)

8   This exercise could be set for homework if time is short.

Answers

1 D   2 A   3 C   4 B   5 A   6 A   7 C   8 B

 Extension activity

In pairs or groups, get students to draft a plan, to present to the rest of the class, to make their region more environmentally friendly and attractive for residents and tourists. They should agree on the register to use – formal or unmarked – and what vocabulary they will need. They should think about:

• rubbish removal / improved recycling
• pedestrianisation / cycle paths
• better and cheaper public transport
• tree planting and more green areas
• the needs and problems of tourists

Although students are presenting to the rest of the class, they should choose who they want the class to represent as their target audience. This will affect the register they decide to use when they speak. They could be speaking to a formal audience, like the city council, or to an informal audience, such as neighbours.

13.2 SB pages 112–113
Reported speech

Lesson plan	
Listening	10–10 minutes
Grammar	40–50 minutes
Use of English	0–20 minutes
Speaking	10–10 minutes

SV   Set 7 for homework.
LV   See Extension activity for 5.

1   **1 25** This listening task is aimed at introducing reported speech. Play the recording once or twice and ask students to make notes.

Answers

1 southern Africa   2 desert landscape   3 collect plants and paint   4 (rhino) footprint   5 geologists
6 (the) media   7 thriving / doing well

Recording script

Presenter: Nowadays we're all aware of the need for biodiversity. Without a range of animals and plants our planet would be a poorer place. Well, I've recently been to southern Africa, which is the last truly wild home of endangered black rhinos. Here something is being done, albeit in a small way, to encourage biodiversity. In most other places black rhinos live either in fenced enclosures or under armed guard. But here in this out of the way desert landscape they are completely free to roam. And yet the fact that any rhinos survive in that part of the world at all is partly due to our guest today, Susan Newhall. Susan, how did you come to get involved?

Susan: I was in the desert collecting plants and painting and I came across a rhino footprint. That was how I first found out that there were rhinos in the area. I didn't realise that this was unusual until I met up with geologists who were working there, and they said there was a terrible slaughter going on and showed me places where dead rhinos were lying around. So I launched ahead and used the media to help me expose what was going on.

Presenter: It's amazing to think that if you hadn't found that footprint, things could've been different.

Susan: Yes, that's right. It's extraordinary you know. Thanks to one rhino which I didn't even see.

Presenter: That was back in 1980, and after her discovery Susan got together with a group of other people to help form an organisation to help the rhinos. At the time, poaching in the region was so rife it seemed unlikely the rhinos could be saved, but

> Susan and her dedicated supporters refused to admit defeat and today rhinos are not just surviving in their harsh desert home, <u>they're positively thriving</u>.

2 Students should take notes and then use the notes to report what was said to their partner. They should take turns speaking. Refer students to the Grammar folder on page 185 if they are unclear. The reporting doesn't have to be word for word as long as the gist of what is said is there.

Suggested answer
Southern Africa is the last truly wild home of endangered black rhinos. In most other places they live in either fenced enclosures or under armed guard. The man said that in the desert they are/were completely free to roam. He stated that rhinos were helped to survive in southern Africa because of Susan Newhall.

She said she had / 'd had no previous knowledge of rhinos being in the desert and that when she was looking / had been looking for plants and doing some painting she came / had come across a rhino footprint. She eventually met up with / had eventually met up with geologists who were working / had been working in the area and they told / had told her about the terrible slaughter and took / had taken her to see the dead bodies. As a result she used / had used the media to expose what was / had been going on.

The man congratulated her on finding the footprint, as things would have turned out differently if she hadn't found it. She agreed and said that it was an amazing story, especially as she hadn't actually seen a rhino.

The man went on to say that Susan had got together with some friends and started an organisation to protect the rhino. He said that poaching in the country had been rife and if it hadn't been for Susan there wouldn't be any rhinos today.

3 Refer students to the notes at the bottom left of page 112 before they do the exercise, which contains some examples of unusual patterns. More information on these forms can be found in the Grammar folder (page 185).

Suggested answers
a She said that her grandmother had been able to walk / could walk to school without worrying about traffic.
b She said that it would be good if I came to tea sometime / that I must/should come to tea sometime.
c She said that I had to remember to recycle the rubbish.
d She said that I mustn't smoke in the restaurant.
e She said that companies which pollute rivers must be fined.
f She said that if she had been mayor, she would have made public transport free.
g She said that if the children picked up the rubbish regularly, she would pay them.

4 Students should read the notes in the box above before they begin this exercise.

Suggested answers
a Tina suggested going to Crete this year for their/our holiday.
b Fred declared that he would always love Daphne. / Fred declared his undying love for Daphne.
c Colin decided to take the job.
d My mother sighed and forgave me for breaking it.
e The old man objected to the window being opened.
f Rose claimed that I had her book in my school bag.
g My brother insisted on going out.
h Lucy refused to go by train.

5 This exercise shows how using an adverb can enliven a reported sentence.

Suggested answers
a Tina tentatively suggested …
b Fred declared passionately that …
c Colin reluctantly decided …
d My mother sighed resignedly …
e The old man peevishly objected …
f Rose confidently claimed …
g My brother stubbornly insisted …
h Lucy categorically refused …

◎ Extension activity

Put the following verbs and adverbs on the board and ask students to make more sentences. More than one match is possible.

whisper	highly
announce	pompously
sneer	secretly
groan	loudly
boast	indignantly
scream	complacently
denied	derisively
recommend	angrily

Suggested answers
secretly whispered
pompously announced
angrily screamed
indignantly denied
sneered derisively
boasted complacently
highly recommended
groaned loudly

6 Students need to write in direct speech for this exercise, not reported speech.

Possible answers
a 'You'll pay for that broken jar!' the shopkeeper exclaimed angrily.
b 'Well, you've blocked that exit very nicely with your car, sir,' the police officer said sarcastically.
c 'No, Patricia, a colon, not a dash,' the teacher stated pedantically.
d 'Now, where are my glasses?' my grandfather muttered absent-mindedly.
e 'I think I'll go shopping this afternoon,' Theresa said decisively.
f 'What did you say your name was?' the doctor murmured reassuringly.
g 'Then don't let your children near my house,' my neighbour retorted rudely.
h 'Well now, I'll have to think about a pay rise,' his boss said cautiously.

7 This text is about how man first began to study nature. It could be set for homework.

Answers
1 as 2 having 3 turned/gave 4 way/style 5 up
6 not 7 sake 8 common 9 hardly/scarcely/barely
NOT rarely 10 such 11 more/better 12 without/
lacking 13 because/since 14 it 15 keep

8 Students should spend 10–15 minutes on this task. It could be prepared at home and presented to the class in the next lesson.

13.3 SB pages 114–115

Reading into Writing: Giving opinions

Lesson plan	
Introduction	5–15 minutes
Vocabulary	10–10 minutes
Reading two texts	20–20 minutes
Writing	25–45 minutes
SV	Set 3 for homework; ask students to finish 6 at home.
LV	See Extension activity for 1.

1 The illustration is of a blue whale, an Ascension frigate bird, a gorilla, an American bison and a giant panda. The bison is the only one which is no longer endangered, thanks to a special breeding programme carried out in the USA.

 Extension activity

Students could use the Internet and library to find and write up about other animals which are endangered and what is being done to help them. They could then present their findings to the rest of the class or write a report.

2 These words are useful when writing and talking about the environment.

Answers
a prey b to prey (on) c predatory d demographic
e sustainability f sustainable/unsustainable
g domesticate h coniferous i diversity/diversification
j diversification/diversity k diverse l evolve
m evolutionary n inevitability

3 Students often have difficulty with prepositions which follow these nouns so they should keep a note of new ones in their vocabulary notebooks.

Answers
a of b to/towards c into d of e of
f in g of h in/to i on j to

4 Ask students to read each text and decide on the key points.

Suggested answer
Text 1
• Large animals are very important to the ecology of their habitat.
• Helping an animal to survive will, generally, have far-reaching effects on other animals and lead to greater recognition of dangers to the planet.

Text 2
• It is not worth trying to save certain types of animal.
• Trying to decide which animal to protect is often not practical, as the nature of the Earth's eco-system is so complex.

5 In pairs, students should discuss ideas to use in the opinion part of the essay. There are some ideas to start them off in the box.

6 Refer students to the Exam spot and the Useful language box. Students should try to make use of the sentence openers that are suggested.

Suggested answer

The two texts contrast differing views of what to do about nature conservation. According to the first passage, which gives the example of the tiger, large species are of fundamental importance to the ecology of their habitat. Helping a species such as this to survive will, for the most part, have far-reaching effects on other species and lead to greater recognition of dangers to the planet.

Personally, I believe this argument to be correct. Even though it would appear that we are concentrating too many of our efforts on one 'flagship' species, as a rule, these species are at the top of the food chain and thus are vitally important for the survival of other species. Without them, the balance of nature would be in jeopardy.

The second text puts forward two contrasting ideas. One is that it is not worth trying to save certain types of animal. In the case of the panda, for example, its decline and eventual disappearance seems to be inevitable. The other line of argument is that assessments of this nature are not practical, given the elaborate nature of the Earth's ecology.

I believe that, if we accept the premise that the natural world as we know it today will disappear entirely and that we should do nothing to counter it, then we are also accepting an impoverished future for our own species. For this reason, I cannot agree with one of the ideas put forward in the second text. I do, however, feel that, with respect to certain species, for example the polar bear, perhaps too much effort has been spent highlighting its problems at the expense of smaller, equally endangered animals. In conclusion, I would say that everything should be done to help all species, as this can only help the planet.

(299 words)

Exam folder 7

SB pages 116–117

Paper 1 Part 5
Multiple-choice text

This text is an extract from an article in which two books are reviewed.

Students often worry too much about vocabulary they do not know, instead of trying to guess the meaning from the context. Sometimes it is difficult to guess the meaning, but it is always worth a try. Candidates are not allowed to take a dictionary into the examination. Refer students to the Exam advice.

Answers

1 C *Here is an uplifting array of thrift, vetch, yarrow and dozens more that toss and chatter, apparently immune to the salty south-westerlies.*

2 A *Only the dreariest Linnaean sergeant-major could want to dragoon all these into arum maculatum.*

3 D *Their champion is the naturalist Richard Mabey, whose* Defence of Weeds *must be the most eye-opening book I have read.*

4 C *Exotics arrive from round the globe, spilling from cargos on to roads and railway lines.*

5 B *Wild flowers have evolved a class system of their own: effete respect is shown to Raven's country cousins while war is declared on Mabey's 'vegetable guerrillas that have overcome the dereliction of the industrial age'.*

6 D *Despite the damage they do to other flora, that splendid weed, the daffodil, is planted out 'wild' by councils ... When a friend of mine drove round ... hurling poppy seeds from his car and delighting in the subsequent harvest of red, he found a year later that it had fallen foul of ministry herbicide.*

Get fit, live longer!

14.1

Exam skills	Reading and Use of English Paper 1 Part 7
Vocabulary	Register
	Phrases with *live*

14.2

Grammar	Articles review, prepositions
Exam skills	Reading and Use of English Paper 1 Part 4
Vocabulary	Phrases with nouns and no article
	Prepositions
	Word formation

14.3

Exam skills	Listening Paper 3 Part 3
Pronunciation	Noun/verb/adjective stress
Exam skills	Speaking Paper 4 Part 2

Workbook contents

1	Listening Paper 3 Part 4
2	Listening follow-up
3	Grammar – passive forms
4, 5	Vocabulary
6	Use of English Paper 1 Part 4
7	Use of English Paper 1 Part 3

14.1 SB pages 118–119

Lesson plan

Introduction	10–20 minutes
Reading	40–50 minutes
Phrase spot	10–20 minutes

SV	Keep the discussion in 1 brief; set some of the sentences in 4 for homework.
LV	See Extension activity after Phrase spot.

Speaking

1   The photos show a girl doing Pilates and people working out on exercise bikes in front of TV screens. Ask the class about the amount of exercise and the kind of exercise they do in a week. They should form groups to discuss the statements a–g.

Suggested answers

a   false – Depends on what your daily routine is. If you work on a building site then you probably don't need so much as someone who sits at a desk all day.

b   false – You need to keep active to keep your bones and muscles healthy.

c   true – They're carbohydrates, good sources of energy.

d   true – It will be digested much more easily than a large evening meal.

e   false – It is just one form of exercise. It is best in combination with other types of exercise.

f   false – The only known way of living longer is to live on a very low calorie diet.

g   false – Although having a personal trainer may make you more motivated.

Reading

2   Ask the class to read through all the texts before trying to answer the questions.

Answers

1   B (lines 14–17)
2   D (lines 16–18)
3   A (lines 16–18)
4   C (lines 12–15)
5   A (lines 7–9)
6   D (line 8)
7   B (lines 8–9)
8   D (lines 14–17)
9   C (lines 9–12)
10 A (lines 11–13)

3   The class should discuss the texts in pairs or groups.

Possible answer
I think I would much prefer to have a personal trainer who could tailor exercise to my particular needs. Knowing that someone would be coming to my house at a certain time every week would really motivate me to carry on exercising. I have tried Pilates and found it very difficult and some of the other types of exercise mentioned don't seem very effective.

4 This exercise gives practice in emphasis. Having a wide vocabulary, which can be used appropriately, will mean that students gain higher marks in Paper 2 Writing.

Answers
a harangued **b** resolved **c** swear **d** scrounge
e craved **f** was seething **g** yank **h** unearthed
i flouted

 Phrase spot

Check that students are keeping phrases and idioms in some sort of ordered way in their vocabulary notebooks.

Answers
a lived it up
b learn to live with
c lived up to our expectations
d live down
e lived through
f lived by his wits

 Extension activity

To round off the lesson ask students, in pairs, to talk about the following questions.
- Would you like to live forever? Why? / Why not?
- Is there anything you can do to help yourself live a very long life?
- What implications are there for society if people live longer than average?

14.2 SB pages 120–121

Articles review

Lesson plan

Grammar	40–40 minutes
Vocabulary	20–30 minutes
Use of English	0–20 minutes

SV Set 7 for homework.
LV See Extension activity for 4.

1 This exercise should throw up any problems students have with articles. Articles are a constant problem and students should regularly revise their knowledge of them. Refer students to the Grammar folder on page 185 of the Student's Book for greater clarification.

Answers
1 Indonesia, Berlin, Europe, Oxford University
2 European, university, one-day ticket, household, union, hotel
3 **a i** Ken's job is as a personal trainer. Article needed before jobs.
   b Both are correct. *The* gym – we all know which one.
   A gym – the first time it's been mentioned or one of many.
   c i
   d Both are correct. You use an article when you are referring to something in particular, no article if it is more general.
   e ii With nationality words of this type you need an article.
   f Both could be correct. Generally you don't use an article with meals. The exception is for public events, e.g. *the rugby club dinner*.
   g ii *I play violin* is American usage. British usage is an article before an instrument.
   h i No article with sports.
   i i *I want a drink of water* is more usual. *I want one drink of water* emphasises how many. You can say *I want one more drink of water*.
   j i You always use *the* with *weather* unless you are using an attributive adjective, e.g. *We won't go out if the weather's bad*. BUT *Fishing boats don't go out in bad weather*.
   k ii We use the possessive rather than an article for parts of the body unless they are referred to generally in a medical context.
   l Both are correct. No article if you are talking about the purpose for which the bed exists, i.e. to sleep in. You use *the* if you are talking about the piece of furniture. Similarly you use an article with *prison/hospital/school* if you are just referring to the building, but no article if you are referring to the building's purpose.

2 Ask students to read through the article quickly to find out what it is about. Remind them that there may be more than one answer, depending on meaning.

Answers
1 The **2** the **3** the/– **4** the **5** the **6** the
7 the **8** the/– **9** – **10** a **11** a **12** – **13** –
14 a **15** a/the/– **16** the **17** – **18** the **19** the
20 – **21** the **22** –

3 Students may know these idioms but perhaps weren't aware that they can be grouped together as nouns which don't take an article when they are part of an idiom. This may help them to remember them. The meaning of the idioms is given in brackets.

Possible answers

a All the orders were given by word of mouth to avoid leaving written evidence which might be later discovered. (by speaking only)

b The child lay face downwards in the sand and screamed. (on its stomach)

c Man first set foot on the island in the nineteenth century. (landed)

d My mother took me aside and suggested we have a heart to heart about my new boyfriend. (a good chat)

e They walked down the street hand in hand. (holding hands)

f Phil and I strolled arm in arm along the beach. (with arms linked)

g Traffic is nose to tail every morning on the road into the city centre. (bumper to bumper)

h Liz came face to face with Roger at the party. (met unexpectedly someone she didn't want to meet)

i His family lived from hand to mouth while he was growing up because his father was unemployed. (they were very poor)

j All our pottery is made by hand. (not by machine)

k The MP fought tooth and nail to get the bill through Parliament. (to fight very hard)

l I'm finding it increasingly difficult to see eye to eye with my boss. (to agree with)

Vocabulary

 Corpus spot

Students often have problems with prepositions.

Answers
a in b to c at d to/at e about/of
f at/near g to h of i on/against/for
j on k on l for m on

4 This exercise gives practice in using prepositions accurately. You could also point out how some words in English – prepositions, pronouns, conjunctions, articles and auxiliary verbs – have two pronunciations: one is used when they are stressed, and the other when they are not. Prepositions are stressed when they come at the end of a question. For example:

What did he apply for? *strong* for /fɔːʳ/

He applied for a grant. *weak* for /fəʳ/

Point out that when using a verb with a dependent preposition, the preposition will normally go at the end when a question is formed.

Possible answers

a Who did he rely on? He relied on his parents.

b What does she take pride in? She takes pride in her appearance.

c What are they looking forward to? They are looking forward to their holiday.

d What are they prohibited from? They are prohibited from smoking in the classroom.

e Who does the group consist of? It consists of three teachers and six students.

f What did he interfere in? He interfered in my plans for the party.

g What do you admire her for? I admire her for her strong opinions.

h Who did she apologise to? She apologised to my brother. What did she apologise for? She apologised for being rude.

i What are they accused of? They are accused of arson.

j What do you believe in? I believe in truth and justice.

 Extension activity

Encourage students to find ten other verbs which take prepositions for homework and to test each other on them.

5 This exercise links word formation with the text in 14.1. Students need to be able to say exactly what part of speech a word is. The main forms are listed. There may be one or two which are not in this list.

Suggested answers
agreeable (adjective) – disagreeable, agree, disagree, agreement, agreeably
imaginary (adjective) – imagine, imagination, unimaginable, unimaginably, image, imaginable
expectations (plural noun) – expect, unexpected, expected, unexpectedly, expectant
reality (noun) – real, realise, realism, unreality, unreal, realistic, realistically, unrealistically, surreal, surrealism
enthusiasm (noun) – enthusiastic, enthusiastically, unenthusiastic, unenthusiastically, enthuse
measure (verb) – immeasurable, measurement, measurable, measureless, measured
dismissive (adjective) – dismiss, dismissal, dismissively
clearly (adverb) – clear, clarity, clarify, unclear, unclearly
transform (verb) – transformer, transformation, transformed, untransformed
introductory (adjective) – introduce, introduction
excuses (noun) – excusable, inexcusable

6

Answers
a unexpected b dismissed c enthusiastic
d imagination e inexcusable/disagreeable
f clarity

7 Word formation is often tested in Paper 1 Part 4.

14.3 SB pages 122–123

Listening and Speaking

Lesson plan	
Introduction	5–10 minutes
Listening	25–40 minutes
Pronunciation	10–20 minutes
Speaking	20–20 minutes

SV	Keep the discussion in 1 brief; set 4 for homework.
LV	See Photocopiable recording script activity for 2.

The photos show:
salt, tomatoes, meat / a chicken, eggs, a sausage, coffee, cheese, a burger, orange juice, a mobile phone, deodorant

1 Explain that a health scare is when the public is made aware of a possible health hazard. However, more often than not, there is no good basis for the story.

2 **2 02** Ask the class to read through the questions and then play the recording twice.

Recording script

Alice: Health scares – don't they make you sick! Or do they challenge your complacency? Every few days a new story appears in the newspaper about, first of all, butter is bad for you, then butter is good for you. Salt is bad for us, salt is good for us. You just have to pick up a cup of coffee and you're engaged in a health debate. With me today to discuss this issue is Professor Robert Atkins. Robert, what do you think about all this?

Robert: Personally, I'd rather have ten false health scares and one of them prove to be serious – then it leads to action, than the cynical sense that somehow all this is just a media confection. That's what I really object to.

Alice: Mm, but how often do health scares come true?

Robert: There are random events in which microbes do emerge. They can be extraordinarily lethal and these account for massive epidemics that have occurred

in the past in human history and I think we would be arrogant in the extreme to think that such things may not occur again in the future.

Alice: You're thinking of bubonic plague, of course. But nowadays it seems is the best of times and the worst of times if you want to be healthy. This is a paradox, because, on the one hand, we live in a relatively healthy society. Our longevity is unprecedented. By historical standards communicable lethal disease is exceptionally controlled. Yet we seem to be getting better, but feeling worse. Why, if we're so healthy, are we so easily spooked?

Robert: If you were living two or three hundred years ago, you were in the hands of God or Fate and if you were struck down by a mortal disease you thought you'd been sinful, but you also had your beliefs to console you – you'd go to paradise or heaven or whatever. Nowadays, we have tremendously high expectations about long healthy life continuing and some of us no longer have an expectation of an afterlife. It's partly a matter of a crisis of rising expectations.

Alice: Um, so our health anxiety is like a big eater's gluttony or a rich man's miserliness. Health excites expectations of perfection. It's also an anxiety spread by commercial concerns, isn't it?

Robert: Indeed. The margarine industry, for example, is actually now a very powerful instrument in pushing the line that butter is bad for you and actually there's a strong industrial lobby that has a stake in making sure that we are all anxious and worried about our health.

Alice: And they're not the only players. If health scares sell pills they also sell papers. And what about the research community which keeps the health scare industry supplied with stories?

Robert: Health is always in the news. Sometimes it's the doctors themselves who are maybe responsible. In every branch of life there are people who like a touch of publicity and enjoy the turbulence. Others are often so convinced by their findings that they ignore the critical views of other doctors and have this urge to promulgate their ideas when it may not be appropriate to do so. If I wanted to avoid heart disease, I'd be taking aspirins, reducing my weight, I would probably frequent my local gym a bit more. I would eat this, that and the other and so on. Then there might be another disease I might get. What do I do then?

Alice: Mm, how much difference would it make to you if you made all those changes? Should you just discount what you read and hear?

Robert: Who knows? Some health scares can actually seriously damage your health – they lead to stress, deprive us of the comfort of eating chocolate and clog up doctors' waiting rooms. There is clearly an information overload and unfortunately, <u>when the real thing comes along, people might have difficulty distinguishing it from all the background noise.</u>

Alice: And of course it's difficult to disprove something once a claim has been made, however fallacious that risk is. Thank you, Professor Robert Atkins.

Photocopiable recording script activity (P)→page 148

Read through the recording script and underline the words which mean the following:

a   smugness
b   chance
c   dangerous
d   a contradiction
e   frightened
f   make you feel better
g   eating too much
h   spread/communicate
i   congest

> **Answers**
> a   complacency
> b   random
> c   lethal
> d   a paradox
> e   spooked
> f   console
> g   gluttony
> h   promulgate
> i   clog up

Pronunciation

3   **2** 🔲 The general rule is that when a word with variable stress is used as a verb, the stress is on the last part of the word; when it is used as a noun, then the stress is on the first part of the word.

Alice and Robert say: ob**ject**   fre**quent**   dis**count**

This is because these three words are being used as verbs in the listening extract.

4

> **Possible answers**
> Not all the words here follow the general rule given in 3, e.g. *alternate*. The stressed syllable is shown in capitals.
> I freQUENted the same places as Hemingway did in the 50s.
> He's a FREquent visitor to the club.
> The ENtrance to the hall is via the side door.
> She was enTRANcing in the part of Ophelia.
> I was inCENsed to find my car had been vandalised.
> I can't stand the smell of INcense.
> Your visa is inVALid, I'm afraid.
> Her aunt has been an INvalid for over ten years.
> Is everyone PREsent?
> I bought a PREsent for my father.
> Can I preSENT Mr Delgado to you?
> Students receive a DIScount on entry prices.
> Don't disCOUNT everything she says just because she's a child.
> The stall was covered in local PROduce.
> The factory proDUCes 5,000 components every year.
> I can see you on alTERnate mornings only.
> You will have to ALternate with Fred over who uses the room.

5   This section gives more practice in Paper 4 Part 2. Students should remember not just to describe the photos but to talk about the lifestyles of the people and make comments or give opinions on them. Make sure you time this activity so they get used to being concise and not spending too much time thinking.

The photos are of a group of teenagers slouched on a sofa eating pizza and watching TV and a teenage girl running outside.

6   This can be given for homework if time is short. Students should think about using appropriate vocabulary in their presentation. They might like to go through the unit underlining vocabulary connected with health and fitness, and then try to incorporate it into their talk.

Writing folder 7

SB pages 124–125

Part 2 Letter

1   Ask students to read the exam task carefully and underline key information.

2   Remind students of the importance of writing in a consistently appropriate register (formal, informal or unmarked) and tone (polite, persuasive, etc.). Ask them to go through the draft, underlining the parts to be edited. This could be done in pairs, or students could work on their own and then compare their ideas.

  Elicit possible improvements. The answer could be rewritten as optional extra homework.

Improved answer
Dear Sir or Madam
  Following the **rather negative** article on this college's current sports provision, we **would like you to reconsider your views** and print an apology – **the lion's share of your article is inaccurate**. We **would also like to seek your support** regarding a funding application – please see below.
  Your article claims that a lack of adequate facilities is **affecting the performance of** our basketball and swimming teams, yet both have represented the college at the highest levels of competition and **excelled themselves** over the years. Indeed, your newspaper featured the recent success of the basketball team in an article published in May. **This would appear to contradict your claim.**
  At the same time, there is some truth in your suggestion that the main sports hall requires some work, especially **the substandard flooring and inadequate lighting, which occasionally makes it hard to play at one's best.** In connection with this, **it has come to our notice that** funding is available nationally, which our college would be in a good position to apply for. We **estimate that this** grant would enable us to undertake the repairs alluded to above, and also allow for an extension of the present changing facilities, whereby separate 'wet' and 'dry' areas could be introduced, to service the pool and hall respectively.
  What **would be your opinion on this**? Would you be willing to run an article in support of our grant application? It would be in the public interest, given that members of the public have daily access to our sports facilities.
  We look forward to hearing from you in due course.
Yours faithfully,
(273 words)

3   Elicit answers. If time is short, suggest students do this for homework, using a dictionary to check meaning where necessary.

Answers
a A b A c B d A e C f B g A h C i A j C

4   Set the task for homework, reminding students to use an appropriate register and tone.

Sample answer
To the editor,
I am writing in response to the invitation to readers that featured in the last issue of your magazine. What I am currently most concerned about with regard to the environment is the shipping of hazardous waste around the world, which is sometimes referred to as 'toxic colonialism'.
  This practice seems to have grown alarmingly in recent years. The apparent reason for this is that environmental laws on waste disposal have been tightened up in the more developed countries, whereas the governments of many poorer developing countries are willing to accept hazardous material as a source of revenue. In reality, these 'host' countries may not be able to process or store toxic waste safely and there have been several cases of contamination on farms and other areas of land in Africa, for example.
  Not only does this state of affairs threaten the health of ordinary people in the developing world but it also poses a serious threat to marine life while any toxic cargo is in transit. If a ship carrying radioactive waste were to run aground or be damaged in some way while on the high seas, the leakage of lethal material could pollute a huge expanse of ocean and cause widespread loss of wildlife.
  To my mind, an international campaign to stop this unnecessary movement of harmful substances should be set in motion immediately. Governments worldwide should give priority to this environmental issue. Countries belonging to the G 20 group of nations could back the establishment of a global investigation into the actual amount of transportation that is going on and would ideally sanction major investment in safe methods of disposal in the countries of origin.
  We must take the initiative now to protect our planet. I urge your readers to join me in seeking an immediate end to toxic colonialism.
Yours faithfully,
(308 words)

15 The daily grind

15.1
Exam skills	Listening Paper 3 Part 3
Vocabulary	Collocations
	Neologisms

15.2
Grammar	Purpose and reason clauses
Exam skills	Reading and Use of English Paper 1 Part 2
Style extra	Gender-specific words

15.3
Exam skills	Reading into Writing: Contrasting ideas – Paper 2 Part 1

Workbook contents
1	Reading Paper 1 Part 6
2, 3	Vocabulary
4, 5, 6	Grammar – purpose and reason clauses
7	Use of English Paper 1 Part 1

15.1 SB pages 126–127

Lesson plan
Introduction	5–15 minutes
Listening	30–30 minutes
Vocabulary	20–35 minutes
Idiom spot	5–20 minutes

SV	Keep discussion in 1 brief; set Idiom spot for homework.
LV	See Photocopiable recording script activity in 3 and Extension activity for Idiom spot.

1 Elicit students' reactions to the contrasting jobs in the pictures, which show a blacksmith working in his forge and office workers in a call centre. Ask them which type of job is more likely to have changed and why – the office workers' jobs will have changed more due to modern technology. In contrast, a blacksmith crafts metal artefacts by hand and the skills needed will not have changed much in hundreds of years.

Suggest students discuss their views on the questions in pairs or small groups.

Possible answers
It depends – I'd like to stay in the same field, but I'm likely to have to move abroad to gain more responsibility.

Probably because the job market is so competitive – it's safer to stick with what you know.

It's crucial, as experienced people know so much more about how things work in an organisation.

I don't expect to stay with the same company, though I believe there will always be opportunities in my field.

Perhaps the workplace will become even more automated and computerised, with more mundane jobs being done by robots.

Listening

2 **2·03** Before they listen, ask students to read through the questions and check anything they are unsure of. Remind them that they will have one minute in the exam to do this. Play the recording twice, as in the exam.

Answers
1 B 2 B 3 D 4 C 5 A

Recording script
Interviewer: Diane Webber, you've switched careers more than once during your own working life, and you now run a highly regarded employment agency for media high-fliers, where, above all, you advise your clients, both companies and applicants, to be fully flexible. You seem to see this as a fundamental principle, if your agency slogan – 'Keeping your options open' – is anything to go by. Is that a fair assessment of how you operate?

Diane Webber: Absolutely. I know that not so very long ago we used to see jobs for life as the norm, with unquestioning company loyalty, and a golden handshake at the end of it all – which, nine times out of ten, probably wasn't in actual fact deserved – but things are very different now. And yes, there does seem to be something positive in all this, despite the obvious question mark over security. Successful players in the current job market cut their teeth in one firm, and are willing to step sideways more than once to gain fresh experience. Unlike their predecessors, they may only progress up the rungs when they land their third or fourth job, or even later in their career. This increased movement brings benefits, not just for them, but for the companies they work for, too.

Interviewer: In spite of the instability? Surely it's important to have some continuity?

Diane Webber: Well actually, it's a mixed blessing. Individuals can get terribly stale if they stick in one place for too long, especially if they report to managers who fail to challenge them. That implies a hierarchy riddled with complacency and under-achievement, which can no longer be tolerated in today's fast-moving, dog-eat-dog world. Also, much of today's work consists of fixed-term projects, done in teams, and if one or two members drop out along the way, it really doesn't matter, provided that the team remains an entity. The one exception to this is the team leaders themselves, who are not only the driving force, but the guardians of the project, who hold important historical detail in their heads, so yes, continuity is important there. But even then it's a clearly defined cycle. We're frequently approached by highly-experienced team leaders who, having completed one project, decide they can't face even the slightest whiff of repetition and so come to us seeking fresh challenges.

Interviewer: And they manage to find work?

Diane Webber: Oh, they're snapped up! Because generally speaking, a project-based job can easily demonstrate a track record, it's there in the successful completion of the project.

Interviewer: And these people would have no problem getting references from the employers they're essentially walking out on? I would have thought that that could be an issue …

Diane Webber: Employers don't view it like that at all. Their mindset is different now, as I said earlier, and companies actually take steps to foster a more dynamic environment, as they feel this yields better productivity, though the jury's still out on this, in my view. Nevertheless, with a flow of people, there's a quantum leap in terms of the ideas generated, not to mention the chance of new ways of problem-solving imported from elsewhere. These effects are tangible and they're often very attractive because they're perceived as lean and efficient, instant solutions, even if they generally turn out to be only quick fixes which later have to be reversed.

Interviewer: Ah, but isn't that the nub of it all, that this shifting and fragmented approach leads to poor decisions? Of course, the perpetrators are never taken to task, as they've already made a quick exit and are knocking on your door for another job!

Diane Webber: That's a bit unfair! For one thing, there've always been bad decisions. No company can rely on its personnel to make the right choices one hundred per cent of the time – even with the help of highly-paid outside consultants, staff will continue to get it wrong from time to time. However, I'd argue that it's the mediocre employees, who just want to keep their heads down, who are far more likely to cause problems than the risk-takers, who, don't forget, are only as employable as their last success.

Interviewer: Ruthless …

Diane Webber: Pragmatic!

Interviewer: Which brings us neatly back to your slogan, doesn't it? Keeping your options open. How far do you encourage people to go in this?

Diane Webber: With new opportunities opening up all the time, the sky's the limit really. It's certainly never too late to contemplate a move, and so the maxim has to be, don't rule *anything* in or out.

Interviewer: We'll end on that positive note. Diane Webber, thank you.

Diane Webber: It's been a pleasure.

3 **2 03** Play the recording again for students to check their answers, pausing after each question. Then elicit explanations of expressions a–m.

Photocopiable recording script activity P → page 149

Hand out copies of the recording script and give students a few minutes to underline the expressions. They can then explain the meaning with reference to the surrounding context.

Answers
a financial reward for long service
b get experience
c climb the career ladder
d good and bad
e fiercely competitive
f a tiny bit of
g recruited immediately
h evidence of previous success
i way of thinking
j people haven't decided
k huge improvement
l apparently simple and instant solutions (which don't succeed)
m avoid trouble by behaving in a quiet way

Vocabulary

4   Elicit explanations of the expressions in a–h. Students don't always need to paraphrase the adjectives used.

Answers
a   something quick to eat
b   the quickest but most competitive route to success (original meaning: the outside overtaking lane of a motorway)
c   (earn) money fast
d   the quickest line in e.g. airport check-in
e   a quick move of the head in acknowledgement
f   a public announcement to say that something isn't true, given quickly to prevent media interest
g   answering/reacting quickly
h   brief sleep, usually during daytime

5   Elicit answers. If there is time, ask students to suggest example sentences using the other three nouns.

Answers
a   growth   b   pace   c   signs   d   process   e   decline   f   lane

Idiom spot

Explain to students that many new expressions are entering the language, particularly in the areas of business and journalism. Ask them to work through 1–6, deciding which expressions from exercise 3 (a–m) should be used.

Answers
1   the jury's still out   2   a quantum leap
3   the slightest whiff of   4   quick fixes   5   track record
6   a mixed blessing

Students should then do the exercise below, forming the collocations and using them in sentences a–f.

Answers
a   red ink   b   green shoots   c   blue chip
d   white goods   e   golden hello   f   white knight

Extension activity

Ask students to write example sentences containing the remaining expressions from a–m.

15.2 SB pages 128–129

Clauses 1

Lesson plan	
Grammar	40–60 minutes
Style extra	20–30 minutes

SV   Set 4 for homework.
LV   See Extension activities for 4 and Style extra.

1   Check understanding of 'intern' – a student or other young person who works in a company for a short period in order to gain experience, generally earning little or no money. The picture is of Keri Hudson. Ask students to read the article and then discuss the question in pairs. Elicit opinions.

Possible answer
The judge's ruling makes sense in this case. If an intern is working long hours and genuinely contributing to the company, a fair wage should be paid. On the other hand, if an intern has no experience whatsoever and is merely there to learn from the company, then I don't believe they necessarily need to be paid for the work they do.

2   Refer students to the Grammar folder on page 185 in the Student's Book if necessary, asking them to read the paragraphs on purpose clauses and reason clauses. Note that according to the *Cambridge English Corpus*, *lest* appears to be more commonly used than the phrase *for fear that*. Both are fairly formal in use.

Suggested answers
in order to – so as to
for fear that – lest
Both phrases introduce a purpose clause.

3   Elicit suggestions on gender differences at work and then ask students to read the article.

Suggested answer
Although there are both male and female secretaries in an office environment, the men see themselves as more important, often spending time on the phone networking.

4

Answers
1   so   2   what   3   no   4   order   5   on   6   while/whilst/ though/although/if   7   their   8   rather

Extension activity

Elicit suggestions on other jobs that could be stepping stones.

> **Possible answers**
> Sales rep working on commission (stepping stone to Sales manager)
> Copy writer (stepping stone to Publicity manager)
> Administrative assistant (stepping stone to Office manager)

5 Suggest students work through a–h in pairs.

> **Answers**
> **a** lest / for fear that **b** so as not to / in order not to
> **c** in order to / so as to **d** in case **e** so that
> **f** so as not to / in order not to **g** in case **h** lest / for fear that

6 Ask students to finish the statements and then compare their answers in pairs.

> **Possible answers**
> **a** I would like to work abroad at some point, in order to broaden my experience.
> **b** When I'm older, I won't stay in the same job for more than two years, so as not to get stale.
> **c** I want to continue my English studies, in order to get a better job.
> **d** It would be useful for me to have my own website, so that I could promote my products.
> **e** I want to find work that I can do from home, in order to be able to spend more time with the children.

 Corpus spot

> **Answers**
> **a** in case **b** even if **c** in the same way as
> **d** (comma not full stop) such as **e** so as not to
> **f** In conclusion

 Style extra

Ask students to work in pairs to group the words and decide on their register and any usage restrictions – formal/informal use and other information on usage is given in brackets below.

> **Answers**
> **Nouns**
> **used of men**
> bounder (old-fashioned), charmer (slightly derogatory), geek (informal), lout, Neanderthal (informal and derogatory), nerd, patriarch (formal), thug

> **used of women**
> bag (informal and offensive), bimbo (informal and offensive), duchess (old-fashioned), vamp (old-fashioned)
> **used of both**
> actor, chairman (many people prefer to say chair or chairperson as a gender-neutral choice), chav (informal and offensive), freshman (US – the British equivalent is fresher), mate (informal), partner, sibling, spouse (formal), whizz kid
> **Adjectives**
> **used of men**
> chivalrous, effeminate
> **used of both**
> bullish, doting (but see Possible answers below), laddish, lanky (but usually of men and boys), prickly (but see Possible answers below), wimpy

Ask students to write their example sentences, using any suitable noun. These sentences could be done for homework if time is short.

In the possible answers below, the examples containing the eight adjectives are taken from the *Cambridge English Corpus* – the type of source is given in brackets. Additional usage notes reflect the corpus evidence.

> **Possible answers**
> I think you're the most chivalrous man I've ever met. (popular novel)
> Beckham is such a doting dad that he's had Brooklyn's name tattooed on his back. (tabloid newspaper – referring to the footballer David Beckham)
> Note: although the adjective can be used of men and women, there are notably more examples of 'doting dad' and 'doting father'.
>
> A pale, delicate, effeminate boy, who might have been taken for my master's brother ... (novel: *Wuthering Heights* by Emily Brontë)
> Note: most corpus lines are from literary sources and the use appears to be slightly old-fashioned.
>
> As Jon and I are the newest of new men, this insinuation of laddish sexism cuts very deeply. (student newspaper website)
> Note: the example contrasts a laddish attitude with the now slightly old-fashioned expression 'new man' (a man who is sensitive and caring, and takes responsibility for childcare and traditionally female chores).
>
> The lanky centre forward found himself rushing towards a head-on collision with the goalkeeper. (sports report)
> Note: there are many similar examples in the corpus relating to sports players.

He has a reputation as an efficient and decisive if somewhat prickly manager. (broadsheet newspaper) Note: the *Cambridge English Corpus* indicates that the adjective is more often used of men than women. The adjective is also used to describe things that cause anger or annoyance, e.g. *a prickly issue/matter/subject.*

Beautiful men are a bit vain and wimpy. (tabloid newspaper)

◉ Extension activity

Investigate the area of gender-specific and gender-neutral adjectives further. You could run an advanced search in the English Vocabulary Profile to find suitable adjectives at C2 and then access a corpus or a monolingual dictionary to find typical examples of their use. A couple of other adjectives you might choose to focus on are: *formidable (opponent/wife/woman)* and *pushy (mother/mum/salesman).*

15.3 SB pages 130–131
Reading into Writing: Contrasting ideas

Lesson plan

Introduction	10–20 minutes
Reading two texts	20–20 minutes
Writing	30–50 minutes

SV	Keep discussion in 1 brief. Set 6 and 9 for homework.
LV	Ask students to draft their essays in class.

1 Elicit qualities for each person and then allow students to discuss other leadership characteristics, possibly based on famous people (past and present), e.g. politicians, world leaders, high-profile business people.

Suggested answers
a decisiveness, intuition, vision
b assertiveness, determination, fairness
c decisiveness, specialist knowledge, stamina

Other characteristics:
ambition, ability to articulate ideas, being a good public speaker, charisma

2 Ask students to read both texts on their own and then discuss their views.

Suggested answer
For me, the Affiliative Style described in Text 1 is likely to be the more effective as it values staff, consequently promoting harmony and company loyalty. Conversely, the leadership style in Text 2 is bound to lose employees through its demotivating approach.

3 Stress the need for reformulation, explaining that students will lose marks if they 'lift' words and phrases from the two texts in the exam.

Answers
a proponents   b bonds   c reaping the benefits of
d quandary   e rise to the occasion   f morale
g initiative h the big picture

4

Answers
The three verbs for downward movement or decline are *drop, evaporate* and *dwindle.* Other possible verbs are:
drops – plummets
evaporate – fade
dwindles – diminishes

The verb that describes an upward trend is *rises.* Possible verbs to replace it are *soars/blossoms.*

5

Answers
Be that as it may   Conversely   Despite this
Even so   In contrast   Nonetheless
On the other hand   Whereas

6

Answers
1 more   2 said (contrastive)   3 being   4 the same
5 Notwithstanding / Having said (contrastive)

7

Possible answers
(Yellow highlighting) The 'Affiliative Style' of leadership treats employees as individuals and they therefore become very committed to the company, whereas the 'Pacesetting Style' doesn't engender any such allegiance and employees don't recognise their role within the organisation at large.

(Blue highlighting) Under the 'Pacesetting Style', employees can easily become demotivated as their targets are unrealistic. Conversely, the 'Affiliative Style' ensures that morale is kept high and the company is likely to get more out of its employees because of this.

(Pink highlighting) Affiliative leaders allow employees far greater independence and have faith that they will get the job done in the best way possible. Pacesetters, on the other hand, are reluctant to delegate responsibility and discourage individual creativity.

(Green highlighting) It seems to be the case that individuals who underperform within the 'Pacesetter Style' of leadership are rapidly detected and measures are taken to either increase their productivity or to get rid of them. In contrast, underachievement may not be addressed within the 'Affiliative Style'.

8   Draw a grid on the board with two columns for the two styles of leadership. Elicit students' views on each idea in turn and write pluses and minuses in these two columns.

9   If students draft their essays in class, suggest they work in pairs and do some peer evaluation.

Sample answer

Leadership styles within companies often vary enormously. The texts provide two contrasting examples – the 'Affiliative Style' and the 'Pacesetting Style'. The former is probably the more appropriate, though it is not without its flaws. Let us consider both approaches here.

The Affiliative Style of leadership treats employees as individuals and they therefore become very committed to the company, whereas the Pacesetting Style doesn't engender any such allegiance and employees don't recognise their role within the organisation. This could be wasteful in terms of human resources.

Under the Pacesetting Style, employees can easily become demotivated as their targets are unrealistic. Conversely, the Affiliative Style ensures that morale is kept high and the company should get more out of its employees because of this.

Affiliative leaders allow employees far greater independence and have faith that they will get the job done in the best way possible. Pacesetters, on the other hand, are reluctant to delegate responsibility and discourage individual creativity. Personally, I would find it impossible to work under such a 'repressive' regime.

It seems to be the case that individuals who underperform within the Pacesetter Style of leadership are rapidly detected and measures are taken to either increase their productivity or to get rid of them. In contrast, underachievement may not be addressed within the Affiliative Style. Even so, this might not adversely affect the company performance at large, since the majority of employees would be 'achievers'.

In reality, the optimum leadership style may well be a blend of these approaches, since it cannot be denied that objectives have to be set by the leader and met by the workforce. However, if a company is to succeed in the longer term, it has to rely on its employees. The investment in people shown by the affiliative leader undoubtedly contributes to the greater good and should ensure that the company prospers, unless outside circumstances prevent this.
(314 words)

Exam folder 8

SB pages 132–133

Paper 3 Part 2
Sentence completion

1   Ask students to read through the advice carefully. They should then look at the questions and try to predict what the answer will be. Time spent looking carefully at the question paper is never wasted and they have 45 seconds to do this. It is important to read ahead when listening so that if something is missed, there is no sense of disorientation. There is no need to panic, as the piece will be heard twice.

2   **2 04** Play this track, which is the beginning of John Farrant's monologue. Students need to decide which words are grammatically correct and could complete the sentence.

Answer
1   respectful

Recording script
You will hear a man called John Farrant talking about his job, working for a car hire company. For Question 1, listen to the first part of the recording as far as '... a plastic wallet'. Then, with a partner, decide which is the word you heard which fits in the space.

Good morning. My name is John Farrant and I have the job of reservations manager at a large, international car hire company based in London. Dealing with the public can be a tricky business. You get to meet all types from the arrogant and rude to the downright abusive. We aren't expected to reply in kind, of course, or come over all ingratiating and deferential either. It's down to us to be <u>respectful</u> and remember the customer is always right. Sometimes it can be difficult, especially with a real joker. For example, when taking a booking, we have to ask certain questions, one of which is: 'Do you possess a clean driving licence?' To which one man snapped at me, 'Of course I do. I keep it in a plastic wallet!

3 Refer students to the recording script so that they can underline the descriptive adjectives.

Answer
They will hear 'rude' and 'deferential', but only 'respectful' is correct. The words 'arrogant' and 'ingratiating' do not fit grammatically.

4   **2 05** Play the continuation of the monologue and ask students to complete the task.

Answers
2 refresher course   3 roundabouts   4 long-term rental(s)   5 (thick) mud   6 test drive   7 handbrake 8 (best) interest(s)   9 hand controls

Recording script

Now listen to the rest of the recording and, for Questions 2 to 9, complete the sentences with a word or short phrase.

John Farrant: Sometimes we can hardly believe some of the customers aren't pulling our legs. We once had an elderly gentleman ring up about a car to go to Paris the following morning. We went through the questions and he said he was 69, and it turned out that, although he'd passed his driving test, he hadn't driven for years. He said, 'Is there any way you could give me a refresher course over the phone?' We suggested he let his friend drive.

Travel doesn't always bring out the adventurer in people, though. We had an American tourist ask for a car to drive to Scotland, and who said: 'How many circles are there between London and Scotland?' After some questioning, I realised he meant roundabouts. There are hardly any in the USA – they prefer traffic lights and he'd only ever driven on motorways here before. He only wanted me to work out a route for him!

Now, most people assume that car hire companies make their money from renting out posh, expensive cars like Mercedes and BMWs. This isn't the case – it's the long-term rentals which bring in the money. But of course, it does depend where you go with the car and if you make your intentions clear at the time.

We had one English client book a car for a month. So far, so good. Four weeks later I received a call from him in Spain, saying he was just about to drop off the car. I said, 'Sorry, sir, where are you?' He said, 'Barcelona.' I asked if he'd told the reservations clerk he intended to go abroad with the car, and he said no, really unconcerned. Presumably he didn't realise, or maybe even care, that he hadn't been covered by insurance. I spoke to the supplier afterwards. He said when they got the car back it didn't have any dents or scratches on it but it was so thick with mud it took two days for them to valet it.

Then, we had one gentleman who had a medical condition that meant that he was on drugs that made him semi-drowsy, but he had a certificate from his doctor saying that he could drive. I got a call from the depot manager saying, 'I'm not giving him a car. He can hardly stand up.' We decided he should give the customer a test drive round the block. This guy pulled out of the depot and there was a car coming towards them. He didn't even see it. The depot manager didn't even have time to sound the horn, he had to pull on the handbrake. He said he'd never been so scared in his life.

Other people refuse to believe you're genuinely concerned about safeguarding their best interests. I remember it once took me 15 minutes to persuade a customer that it really wasn't worth hiring a small car, with low power, to go over the Alps. He'd just get stuck and it would ruin his holiday. He simply refused to accept that this type of car wouldn't be up to the job. What d'you do?

We can solve most problems though. We had one gentleman who wanted to go to Oxford. Everything was fine until he suddenly said, 'By the way, I've only got one leg.' I had to call in a few favours, but one of my suppliers managed to get me a car with hand controls. So, although it may not be straightforward, I enjoy my job on the whole – I guess it's the challenge – every day is different after all!

16 Hidden nuances

16.1 SB pages 134–135

Lesson plan

Introduction	10–20 minutes
Reading	50–70 minutes

SV Keep discussion in 1 brief.
LV Allow students more time for 1; see Extension activity for 3.

Reading

1 Allow students a few minutes to discuss their views and then elicit answers.

Possible answers
A short story has few pages and so there is little space to develop characters or plot. The writing must be succinct and 'lean'.
In a novel it is easier to use flashback and other time reference devices. There is much more scope to include long descriptions and/or subplots.

2 Ask students to read the text and then elicit the significance of the title – Elizabeth's behaviour and that of her parents shows nothing new or different from previous generations. It is predictable.

Background information
Laurie Colwin wrote five novels and three collections of short stories before she died in 1992. This story appears in her second collection, *The Lone Pilgrim*, a book that includes many stories to do with early experiences of adult life.

3 Now ask students to read the text more carefully and choose the correct answers.

Answers
1 C 2 B 3 B 4 A 5 D 6 C

 Extension activity

Ask students to justify their answers, making detailed reference to the text (see detailed explanation below).

Detailed explanation:
1 The answer (C) is in the words 'was extraordinarily pretty, and such children are never called difficult'. A is wrong, as the text only refers to one child who was older, Nelson Rodker. B is not suggested: the use of 'original' does not imply great intelligence. D is ruled out as there is no evidence of 'painstaking preparation' and only one relationship is referred to (her parents hoped Nelson and Elizabeth might marry).
2 The answer (B) lies in the final sentence of the second paragraph. There is no evidence that she had a 'sense of duty' (A), in fact the reverse is true. C is ruled out as it was Elizabeth who hated the Rodkers, not the other way round. Although it is true that Elizabeth did hide her true feelings ('she learned to turn a cheerful face'), there is no evidence to suggest she disliked doing this (D).
3 The answer (B) is rooted in 'none of her friends wanted to entertain at home'. A is ruled out because the careers weren't always successful ('blacklisted movie producers'). There is no evidence to support C; Holly was the only friend who came home and Elizabeth's mother approved of her, so she would have been unlikely to feel uncomfortable. D is not suggested by the text.
4 The answer (A) lies in the words 'manure was not on her mother's mind' and 'she was much relieved' – presumably her mother had been imagining an illicit relationship with a man at the stables. There is no evidence that Elizabeth's mother begrudged spending the money on the jodhpurs (B). C, though plausible, is not true: her parents 'who felt riding once a week was quite enough' were mildly interested and the mother did arrange the purchase of the jodhpurs. D is likely, but not stated in the text.

5 The answer (D) lies in the final sentence of the fifth paragraph. A is insufficiently rooted in the text: although it implies her parents believed in moderation in reading, we do not know how she was brought up. B is wrong, as Elizabeth's appearance didn't change (only her behaviour at college did). C is wrong as it was other students who 'went wild', while Elizabeth spent time alone in her room.

6 The answer (C) lies in the words 'wanted to enjoy it finally on her own terms' and 'refusing to take a cent of their money'. A is wrong, as she used the bracelet 'as collateral' to borrow money – that is, she didn't sell it but named it as an asset that could be set against the loan if she defaulted on her payments. B is not stated, even if implied by the fact that the daughters of her parents' friends were getting engaged. D is wrong as Elizabeth had always loved New York.

4 Ask students to discuss this global question in pairs.

Answer
The answer is D. A and C are not supported by the reality in the text. B is wrong, as both Nelson and Elizabeth had a good education and in her case, the text shows us it led to other things.
Relevant sentences in the text that support D:
At college, Elizabeth had her first taste of freedom.
Had they known what sort of adult Elizabeth had become, great would have been their dismay.
Elizabeth further puzzled them by refusing to take a cent of their money, although her mother knew the truth: what you dole out to the young binds them to you. To have Elizabeth owing nothing was disconcerting to say the least.

5

Answers
a Elizabeth's mother forced herself to sound positive.
b Elizabeth pretended to be happy, when really she loathed the Rodkers and her parents.
c Beautiful daughters like Elizabeth are over-protected.
d It might have adversely affected Elizabeth's social life.
e Elizabeth's parents regarded 'adult behavior' as important.

6 This vocabulary work can be set for homework.

Suggested answers
Nelson is conventional, spineless and apathetic.
Opposites for the other words:
articulate / inarticulate
brazen / modest
callous / compassionate
fickle / steadfast
flawed / impeccable
garrulous/ taciturn
trustworthy / treacherous
unflappable / panicky

16.2 SB pages 136–137

Clauses 2

Lesson plan	
Introduction	10–30 minutes
Use of English	15–15 minutes
Style extra	20–25 minutes
Corpus spot	15–15 minutes
Use of English	0–15 minutes

SV Omit 2 and set 4 for homework.
LV See Extension activity for 2.

1 Elicit students' reactions to the poems. Ask if they see anything odd about the second one (the poem is made up; the poet's name, if put together as one word, is the name of a make of beer, which echoes the content of the final line).

Background information
Spike Milligan (1918–2002) is perhaps best known for his collaboration with Harry Secombe and Peter Sellers in the BBC radio comedy series *The Goons*, which has influenced many other comedians' work. Gary Snyder (born 1930) is an American poet who was part of the 'Beat Generation' and a friend of the writer Jack Kerouac. Snyder has won the Pulitzer Prize for Poetry and has also translated literature from ancient Chinese and modern Japanese.

2 Allow students enough time to discuss their views on the three questions. Then elicit ideas.

Suggested answer
Poetry can be translated, but demands additional skills on the part of the translator. It is sometimes impossible to preserve the original rhyme or rhythm. For this reason, a translator should be able to 'take liberties' that the translator of a novel wouldn't contemplate. The first poem contains some idiomatic language (switch off your face, put your love into neutral) that might be difficult to translate within the same rhythm. The first two poems have tightly defined rhythm and some lines rhyme, so perhaps the free verse of Gary Snyder would be easier to translate. On the other hand, some of its nuances are personal to the poet and might be difficult to understand fully and/or get across in another language.

◎ Extension activity

Students choose one of the poems to translate. It is probably easier for them to work in groups, discussing the text and consulting dictionaries as necessary.

3 The picture is of Eugenio Montale. Ask students to work through the word formation task in pairs.

Answers
1 analysis   2 scholars   3 mistrusted/untrustworthy
4 supposedly   5 imperial   6 imprisons   7 Familiar
8 enigmatic

 Style extra

Elicit the five occurrences of *as* (two are in the same example).

Answers
as the poet Robert Frost once claimed
As a result
Familiar *as/though* I was with
As remote *as*
The change in word order adds emphasis to the fact that it is unlikely.

Refer students to the Grammar folder on page 186 after they have written their sentences and answered the questions (c and d do not contain concessive clauses).

Suggested answers
a Greatly acclaimed though this novel is, I find it rather disappointing.
b As entertaining as the play is, it is lightweight in comparison with his earlier works.
c As well as being a writer, Romano was a painter.
d As Robert Frost said, 'A poem begins in delight and ends in wisdom.'
e Gripping though the storyline of the novel undoubtedly is, its characters lack development.
f Much as I have tried to get into the book, it remains impenetrable.

 Corpus spot

Suggested answers
a In spite of / Despite the nice atmosphere ...
  OR Although the atmosphere is nice ...
b ... despite the fact that ...
  OR despite my knowing only ...
c Although it is not easy ...
d Despite what she felt ...
e Although one could see ...
f In spite of that / Despite that ...
g Even though I was wrong ...
h ... in spite of writing ...

4

Answers
1 even if its/the rhyme is/gets lost OR even if he/she loses the rhyme
2 my hand at (writing) short stories, poetry is
3 enjoy/like poetry readings, I sometimes take exception to
4 as/though the biographer's progress was / had been initially
5 strike it lucky with/by creating a bestseller, although/though/but/whereas/yet
6 for fear (that) / out of fear (that) it would/should/might/could

16.3 SB pages 138–139
Listening and Speaking

Lesson plan	
Introduction	5–10 minutes
Listening	15–25 minutes
Pronunciation	20–20 minutes
Speaking	20–35 minutes

SV	Keep discussion in 1 brief; omit 8 and 9, asking students to record their final talks for homework.
LV	See Photocopiable recording script activity for 3.

1 Ask students to identify the different genres shown:
   • *Don't Sweat The Aubergine* – cookery/food writing
   • *The Flanders Panel* – crime/detective fiction
   • *A Bigger Message: Conversations with David Hockney* – art/biography
   • *Matter* – science fiction
   • *Mozambique Mysteries* – travel writing

   Ask students to discuss the questions in pairs and then elicit answers.

Possible answer
The ingredients in a good book depend on the genre – a good novel might have an intriguing plot, a cast of well-developed characters and be expertly crafted. A good biography, on the other hand, would be informative and accurate, with well-researched details and human interest.

A book that is hard to put down usually has a fast-moving plot or suspense of some kind, whereby the reader feels compelled to continue to the end without pausing.

2 **2 06** Play the extracts, which are fairly short, and elicit the books and genres mentioned. Play them a second time if necessary, to allow students to summarise the qualities mentioned by each speaker.

The Dumas Club (detective story)
Congo Journey (travel writing)
Qualities:
The Dumas Club: subtle plot (two strands, apparently interlinked), compelling, makes the reader come up with links and suppositions
Congo Journey: more than straight description, brilliant insights into a remote region, meticulous detail on wildlife, superb use of dialogue, funny, moving

Recording script
Speaker 1: If I had to single out one book from the many I read last year, it would be *The Dumas Club*, by Arturo Pérez-Reverte – that's in translation from the original Spanish. Although I read the opening couple of chapters quite slowly, I soon got completely immersed in the subtleties of the plot, so much so that I quite literally could not put the book down until I had finished it. Some books have this compelling effect on me, and not just detective stories like this one. What is so skilful about the way *The Dumas Club* has been constructed is that there are two strands to the plot, and as a reader, you assume these are interwoven and all the time you're engaging with the text on this basis, making links and suppositions of your own. Well, without giving anything away, there is a masterful twist, which makes this an exceptional book.
Speaker 2: I read loads of travel writing, partly because I have a penchant for travelling myself. That said, I do expect a lot more than straight description and first-hand observation from a truly great travel book. Redmond O'Hanlon's masterpiece *Congo Journey* does not disappoint! Will Self – the author – named it as one of his books of the year and said he felt like starting it again the minute he'd finished it, which is praise indeed! I'll certainly re-read it at some point. It's got brilliant insights into what is a really remote region of our planet. There's meticulous detail on its wildlife and superb use of dialogue … brings the whole thing to life. And then much more besides – it's funny, moving – so you're reading it on many different levels. Above all, though, you marvel at his sheer guts in enduring such a difficult and dangerous journey. Epic stuff.

3 **2 06** Play the recording again or use the Photocopiable recording script to find the answers to a–h.

Photocopiable recording script activity **page 150**

a immersed **b** compelling **c** assume **d** suppositions
e masterpiece **f** insights **g** meticulous **h** guts

Pronunciation

4 **2 07** The word *subtleties* has a silent 'b'. Ask students to discuss the words in pairs and try saying them aloud before underlining the silent consonants. Play the recording for them to check their answers. Silent consonants are underlined in the recording script.

Recording script

<u>k</u>nowledge	cou<u>p</u>	dou<u>b</u>t
<u>w</u>retched	inde<u>b</u>ted	<u>m</u>nemonic
rus<u>t</u>le	ex<u>h</u>ilarating	condem<u>n</u>
r<u>h</u>ythm	denouement	apropo<u>s</u>
<u>h</u>eir	<u>p</u>seudonym	penchan<u>t</u>

5 Ask students to complete the word puzzle, shown below. The silent consonant is 'b'.

1	a	p	r	o	p	o	s				
2					c	o	u	p			
3	m	n	e	m	o	n	i	c			
4					p	e	n	c	h	a	n	t
5					p	s	e	u	d	o	n	y	m
6		d	e	n	o	u	e	m	e	n	t
7			i	n	d	e	b	t	e	d

6 Ask students to make brief notes on each of the prompts and then look at sentences a–e. Remind students that they need not cover all the prompts in the exam.

a technological alternatives OR practical advantages
b technological alternatives
c practical advantages
d educational issues
e practical advantages OR technological alternatives

7 Suggest students plan their talks individually, working through the checklist. If they are unable to record their talks (on a computer, phone, etc.), ask them to take it in turns, one listening to the other. Students then analyse their talks (or their partners'), referring to the checklist.

8 Put students into groups of three and explain that they will now each deliver the final version of their talk. Student C takes the role of the interlocutor and timekeeper, stopping the talk after two minutes and asking the follow-up questions.

9 These questions are now standard for Part 3 and allow the original candidate to comment on the other student's brief response.

Writing folder 8

SB pages 140–141

Part 2 Set text question: Review

1   Suggest students underline the key parts of the question as they read the task.

Background information
Matthew Kneale (born 1960) is best known for his novel *English Passengers*, published in 2000, which won the Whitbread Book of the Year and was also shortlisted for the Booker Prize for Fiction. He began writing while teaching in Japan and currently lives in Italy. His other novels include *Sweet Thames* (1992) and *When We Were Romans* (2007). He has also written a collection of short stories entitled *Small Crimes in an Age of Abundance* (2005).

2   Ask students to read the review, ignoring the missing sentence openers. They can then work in pairs, deciding where the openers fit.

Answers
1 G   2 F   3 B   4 D   5 A   6 C

3   Elicit answers from students. The sentences can also be done orally or set for homework (as part of 5), if time is short.

Answers
b C   c B   d E   e C   f B
g E   h B   i E   j B   k E
Possible sentences
By and large, the author is successful in his portrayal of female characters.
In much the same way, memories of the past are included as flashbacks.
As it turns out, Prentice could not have witnessed the event.
Within a matter of hours, her condition had worsened and she died the following day.
By the same token, nobody should have been working that day.
On balance, this is an ambitious first novel, which promises much for this talented young writer's future.

4   Ask students to spend a few minutes writing possible collocations and then compare their answers in pairs. Suggest they keep the collocations for use in their homework in 5.

Possible answers
utterly impressive characterisation
zealously detailed chronicle
painstakingly accurate depiction
utterly enigmatic hero
hauntingly moving images
intensely compelling narrative
ingeniously woven plot
subtly realistic portrayal
annoyingly pompous protagonist
exquisitely intricate storyline

5   Ask students to write the review for homework, following the advice given.

Units 13–16 Revision

Lesson plan	
Use of English	40–45 minutes
Writing	20–25 minutes
SV	Set 4 for homework.
LV	Elicit students' reactions to the texts in 1 and 3.

The aim of this revision unit is to focus on the language covered in Units 13–16, as well as extending the work done on the letter in Writing folder 7. Specific exam practice is provided for Paper 1 Parts 1, 3 and 4. This Use of English section could be done as a timed test of 40 minutes. Alternatively, the whole unit could be set for homework.

Use of English

1   The picture shows the WORLDMAP software in action. Once students have completed the task, elicit their reactions to the WORLDMAP program for monitoring biodiversity. How is it helpful? Who would be likely to use it?

Answers
1 endangered 2 rarity 3 analyses 4 rectangular
5 likelihood 6 patchiness 7 complementary
8 maximise/ize

2

Answers
1   the outset the man | (had) denied
2   never saw eye to eye | when it
3   as I sympathise with / am sympathetic to/towards | the line
4   as it may | seem (to you)
5   is setting/placing / sets/places | great/much store on
6   came as (something of) | a surprise (to us)

3

Answers
1 B 2 C 3 C 4 A 5 D 6 D 7 A 8 B

Writing

4   Ask students to read the letter. Point out that it is written as a joke – the date is 1 April. Suggest students discuss how to improve the letter in pairs. The rewrite could be set for homework.

Background information
On April Fool's Day, people in Britain play tricks on their friends and work colleagues. Newspapers often carry 'spoof' articles – ones that aren't true. The joke has to be done before midday.

Sample answer
To the Managing Director   1 April
    As conscientious members of the IT department, we would like to propose a few amendments to our working conditions. You are aware of our expertise in dealing with computing problems company-wide. Indeed, we think it is fair to say that we are indispensable. To guarantee a rapid response, we have always been willing to work long hours whenever necessary. However, we are not prepared to continue working in this way unless you can put something extra on the table. We would like to suggest the following:
    Firstly, it is unreasonable to expect us to travel in on public transport, given that we start very early and stay late. Could we perhaps suggest that the company invests in some stretch limousines (five should be adequate), to cover door-to-door transport. This would clearly lead to better productivity and goodwill.
    Secondly, we are rather disappointed with the restaurant downstairs and suggest that it would be more convenient if we had our own chef and facility on this floor. We feel an extended lunch break would be only reasonable, as we work so late into the evenings.
    Thirdly, we regret to tell you that the salaries paid by this company are derisory. It would be appropriate for you to offer us a little more at this point, particularly given our track record.
    Could you possibly give us some form of response before midday?
With thanks,
Frank McGeek
IT Department
(241 words)

Crossword

This includes some of the idioms, phrasal verbs and other vocabulary from Units 13–16.

Topic Happiness and well-being

17.1

Exam skills	Listening Paper 3 Part 4
	Reading and Use of English Paper 1 Part 1
Vocabulary	Idioms, metaphor

17.2

Grammar	Comparison
Vocabulary	Synonyms
Exam skills	Reading and Use of English Paper 1 Part 2
	Reading and Use of English Paper 1 Part 4

17.3

Exam skills	Reading into Writing: Full Task 1 – Paper 2 Part 1
Vocabulary	Idioms to do with hardship

Workbook contents

1	Reading Paper 1 Part 7
2, 3	Grammar – comparison
4, 5, 6	Vocabulary
7	Use of English Paper 1 Part 1

17.1 SB pages 144–145

Lesson plan

Introduction	5–10 minutes
Listening	25–35 minutes
Vocabulary	30–30 minutes
Use of English	10–25 minutes

SV Set 7 for homework.
LV See Photocopiable recording script activity for 3.

1 The pictures show, from left to right:
- a girl reading a book in a meadow
- two teenage girls at a funfair
- a father holding his newborn baby
- a mountaineer who has just reached the summit

Elicit the meaning of each quote and then ask students to share their own views on the nature of happiness. Suggest they keep their discussion to general beliefs rather than giving examples from their lives (this comes up in 8 at the end of the lesson).

Sources of quotes (in order of presentation in Student's Book): Thomas Jefferson, Anatole France, Marcus Aurelius, Democritus, Robert Kennedy

Listening

2 Check understanding and elicit the three meaning groups.

Answers
bliss, elation, euphoria, rapture
contagious, infectious, invasive, virulent
ephemeral, fleeting, momentary, transient

3 **2.08** Before playing the recording, give students 45 seconds (the time they will have in the exam) to look at the task. Play the extract twice to replicate exam conditions and then elicit answers.

Answers
1 H 2 E 3 B 4 F 5 C 6 B 7 H 8 A 9 D 10 G

Recording script
Speaker 1
Well, I suppose I would visualise certain snapshots in my life, fleeting moments when I was on cloud nine – the birth of my second child or, more recently, a forest walk on a beautiful morning with the birds singing their hearts out – at times like these, you sort of step outside yourself and think, yes, this is as good as it gets. So it's not about having material possessions or a huge income, though if you have any worries on that front it surely rules out the chance of happiness. It's more to do with personal satisfaction and inner peace.

Speaker 2
For me it's not necessarily a transient feeling. I can recall whole periods of my life when things were basically going right, especially in my career, and I think a positive experience like that works as a catalyst. I suppose I can't have been in the same state of ecstasy from dawn till dusk, but looking back, perhaps through rose-tinted spectacles, it certainly feels that way. But if I had to pick just one event, it would be the elation I felt aged nine on receiving a silver trophy at my first judo contest, something beyond my wildest dreams.

Speaker 3
In my book, it's all to do with shared positive vibes, like infectious laughter rippling through a close family group. Being in a loving relationship is key, as this provides stability. And happiness can be found in small things – the security of a comfortable sofa, curled up with a good book while the wind's howling outside – that's something I remember from my childhood. It may be an old cliché, but it's true, you can't buy it, not at any price.

Speaker 4

Sometimes I've felt <u>a surge of joy</u> in the midst of a perilous situation, and <u>one moment I'll always treasure occurred in the Andes with two fellow-climbers, handling a tricky descent in appalling weather conditions</u>. I hadn't known them that well when we set out, but in that situation, you put yourself on the line and <u>make the impossible happen through mutual trust and cooperation.</u> Others might claim well-being is a mental thing, but that's not what really counts. <u>If you're feeling under the weather, you won't experience emotional highs, so it's vital to stay in shape. Well, that's my view, anyway.</u>

Speaker 5

<u>Locations have always been important to me – they seem to contribute so much to a person's mood.</u> A few years ago, I was studying marine activity on a coral reef, part of a close-knit research team on an otherwise unpopulated and <u>stunningly beautiful island.</u> There was one particular day when I'd done three dives, the last at night, and although I was exhausted, I couldn't turn in. So I went back to the beach alone. I lay on the ghostly white sand, gazing at the canopy of stars above me, and <u>saw the most awesome meteor shower – an absolute first for me. It doesn't always take much to tip the balance in favour of happiness, does it?</u>

Photocopiable recording script activity **→ page 151**

Hand out copies of the recording script so that students can underline the wording that provides the answers. They could also refer to the recording script in the next exercise on idioms, rather than listening to the recording again.

Idiom spot

Elicit answers, following either method above.

Answers
a be extremely happy
b with a positive view of the past that is unrealistic
c better than anything you could imagine or hope for
d in my opinion
e commit yourself, stand up for what you believe in
f feel ill
g sway (an argument) in one direction

Suggested answers
1 In the roomful of people, Jack was the only one to put himself on the line and challenge the speaker.
2 Fiona sees her teenage years through rose-tinted spectacles.
3 In my book, children should show respect for their elders.
4 The fact that the sun was shining tipped the balance and they took the day off.

Style extra

Explain to students that judicious use of metaphor in Paper 2 Writing (and Paper 4 Speaking, if the tasks are suitable) will impress the examiner.

4 Elicit possible collocates.

Suggested answers
bruised egos
contagious criticism
fatal dose of scepticism, flaw in the argument
feverish state of activity
healthy bank balance, criticism, dose of scepticism, turnout of voters
jaundiced criticism, sense of humour
sick sense of humour, bank balance
sore loser

5 Explain that metaphors may be easier to learn by topic. A useful book on this area of language learning is *Meanings and Metaphors: Activities to practise figurative language* by Gillian Lazar (Cambridge University Press).

Answers
a growth/plants   b water/liquid   c fire
d bad weather/storms   e light   f cooking

6 Students could decide phrases in pairs and then take turns to come up with the sentences. Remind them not to mix their metaphors (see second answer).

Possible answers
The recent wave of violent protests against globalisation has caused many injuries.
A whirlwind of activity sweeps through our house just before we go away on holiday. (Note: *feverish* has been deleted, as this would be a 'mixed' metaphor.)

7 This can be set for homework if time is short.

Background information
Gerald Durrell, younger brother of the writer Lawrence Durrell, grew up on the Greek island of Corfu, which is where his interest in the natural world began.

Answers
1 B   2 C   3 C   4 D   5 A   6 B   7 C   8 D

8 Elicit the examples of similes and metaphor. Ask students to discuss their memorable moments in pairs. They could write these up afterwards.

Answers
Similes   as gently and clingingly as pollen
glossy and colourful as a child's transfer
Metaphor   the dark skin of night would peel off
barred with gold

17.2 SB pages 146–147

Comparison

Lesson plan

Introduction	10–10 minutes
Use of English	15–15 minutes
Grammar	25–25 minutes
Vocabulary	10–20 minutes
Use of English	0–20 minutes

SV Set 6 and 7 for homework.
LV See Extension activity after 5.

1 The picture shows a marble bust of the ancient Greek philosopher Epicurus. Ask whether students know about him already. Refer to the lists and explain that the word 'natural' in the three headings means that it is understandable for a human being to want such things. Elicit students' views on whether the lists hold true as they are – or whether things need to be added in each column.

2 Ask students to work through the cloze test and then compare answers.

Answers
1 odds **2** What **3** Few **4** least **5** whose
6 far/further **7** on **8** Such/These

3 Statements a–h exemplify other comparative structures. Refer students to the Grammar folder on page 186 after they have discussed the statements in pairs.

Possible answers
a I'm actually happier now than I was then.
b I agree – it's often more enjoyable to eat good food at home in good company.
c I disagree!
d Obviously the most important thing to anyone is to be in good health.
e It depends – sometimes it is easier to hear the songs at home, though it is definitely more exciting to be there on the spot.
f I disagree – it is far better to watch than play, especially during the winter.
g It is a remedy, but the best one is to meet someone else who you care for.
h I'd have to agree with this one – it's not nearly as comfortable being out in a snowstorm as being inside by the fire.

4 Elicit what is happening in examples a and b – the two things mentioned are interrelated and a change in the first influences the second (if the party is held later, more people will come; if it were to be held earlier, fewer people would come).

   Ask students to complete sentences c–h, dividing the class in half and asking them to complete three sentences each if time is short.

Possible answers
c The more possessions you own, the less satisfied you are.
d The wider the gap between rich and poor, the greater the inequality of opportunity is for the next generation.
e The longer you go on buying sweets, the less easy it will be to give them up.
f The later you tell him about the problem, the worse it'll be for you.
g The higher you jump, the harder you fall.
h The more anxious the parents are, the less contented the baby will be.

Vocabulary

5 Remind students that many English words have multiple meanings. The English Vocabulary Profile uses guidewords like these to signpost different meanings in entries. Ask students to match the guidewords for the different meanings of 'happy' to sentences a–d. Then refer students to the dictionary definitions and elicit which meanings of 'happy' are closest to the two synonyms.

Answers
a WILLING **b** NOT WORRIED **c** LUCKY **d** PLEASED
fortunate = LUCKY
ecstatic = PLEASED

 Extension activity

Ask students to decide what the happiest moment in their lives has been, but not to reveal this. Students then form small groups. One student in the group is questioned by the others, who try to establish what that happiest moment was. The student being questioned can only answer 'yes' or 'no'.

Questions that could be asked include: *Were you with someone else? Were you at home? Did this happen when you were very young?*

6 This exercise could be set for homework.

Possible answers
PLEASED cheerful, content, merry
LUCKY opportune, propitious, timely
WILLING amenable, inclined, prepared

7   This exercise could also be set for homework.

Answers
1   set her sights on | visiting / a visit to
2   changed his tune / sang a different tune | when he
3   keep a straight face | in OR keep a straight face | because/as/since it was
4   on cloud nine | at winning/gaining/getting first OR on cloud nine | when she won/got/gained first OR on cloud nine | having won/got/gained first
5   nowhere near | as much
6   sooner Ralph moves out the better | so

17.3 SB pages 148–149
Reading into Writing:
Full Task 1

Lesson plan

Introduction	10–20 minutes
Reading two texts	20–20 minutes
Writing	20–40 minutes
Idiom spot	10–10 minutes

SV   Keep discussion in 1 brief.
LV   See Extension activity in 4. Students rewrite the essay in class.

1   Elicit students' definitions of 'quality of life': the general well-being of individuals in society. The pictures show:

• a healthy-looking woman riding a horse
• a desirable house in the sun
• a family walking along a beach.

2   Refer students to the factors listed and check understanding of each one.

3   Give students five minutes to read the exam task, including the two texts.

4   Refer students to the Exam spot and remind them of the importance of expressing ideas from the texts in their own words. Working through the sample answer will make them more aware of the issue and the need to reformulate words and phrases. See rewritten answer below for suggested changes, which are given in italics.

Answer
The 'lifted' words and phrases in the rest of the answer on page 149 are as follows:
Second paragraph: *health and well-being, climate, job satisfaction, aspects, political freedom*
Third paragraph: *healthy, supported by friends and family*

Suggested reformulation
Both texts deal with the concept of 'quality of life' and consider which factors within this umbrella term are the most important in reality. In both cases, *healthiness* is seen as *a crucial attribute,* since *it dictates whether someone can hold down a job* and *therefore influences other 'quality of life' indicators.*

The first text gives an overview of the factors that go to make up a person's quality of life, mentioning *their state of health and general happiness,* social involvement, work, the political status quo and the local *weather conditions.* Not only does it underline the fact that without good health, *being able to work and having* an active and fulfilling role in *society* are impossible, but also, it argues that some *things* cannot be changed *by the individual – how their country is governed* and *any consequent limits on their rights,* for example.

The second text focuses on the annual phenomenon of quality-of-life indexes and, while viewing them as informative, questions the value of their having such prominence in the media. For most of us, it is academic which city in the world has the best quality of life, as we have no real opportunity to uproot our existence and rush to start a new life there. Nor is it necessary, argues the writer, as a good quality of life is still possible, provided that the individual is *physically fit* and *enjoys some stability in relationships.*

While this may be true up to a point, it is nevertheless going to be far more difficult for people trapped in poverty to gain a quality of life equal to that of people at the other end of the wealth spectrum – especially in our materialist society, where possessions seem to count for so much and we are constantly encouraged to wish for more.
(301 words)

 Idiom spot

The idiom *make ends meet* means manage on very little money. Ask students to match the idioms to the cartoons and then elicit their meanings.

Answers
a   feel the pinch   b   tighten your belt
c   keep your head above water   d   cut corners

cut corners – save time, money or effort by not following the usual procedure
down and out – without hope and usually without a job or place to live
keep your head above water – struggle to survive, usually under pressure
feel the pinch – have less money than previously and suffer as a result
in the red – overdrawn at the bank
on a shoestring – with very little money
tighten your belt – economise
a rough ride – a time when you experience a lot of problems

Exam folder 9

Paper 3 Part 1
Multiple-choice questions

1   **2 09** It should be pointed out that in the examination there are three different extracts. Here, there are only two because of lack of space. Refer students to the Exam advice. You will hear each extract twice.

Answers
1 A   2 B   3 C   4 A

Recording script

Part 1

You will hear two different extracts. For questions 1–4, choose the answer (A, B or C) which fits best according to what you hear. There are two questions for each extract.

Extract One

Man: Now, from what I can tell from this current album, apparently the singer Lisa Gray is on cloud nine. It's interesting isn't it – the alternative artist who, in her long singing career, has always refused to conform to mainstream notions of musical genres, but who has just made a commercial album which looks set to be a hit. Why the about-face, do you think?

Woman: It looks as if she has now found a kind of fulfilment, after years of swimming against the tide – possibly because of her marriage. After hits like *Needing You* and *Crying Out*, Gray seemed hardly likely to make an album celebrating happiness in love. But, with her new album, that is exactly what she has done and it'll get her a lot of new fans.

Man: Well, she certainly seems to have got over her aversion to pop and with this new album she has definitely proved that she can do it.

Extract Two

Critic: The American artist Dorota Kowalska claims to view her homeland with affection, but the fact that she left the USA and has lived in Europe since 2007 suggests that what might be *Always Fun in the USA* – the title of her latest book of photographs – isn't necessarily something she herself subscribes to. Her images depict largely working-class Americans amusing themselves in ways that only a nation hopelessly committed to the pursuit of pleasure could devise. *Aquapark* gives a bird's-eye view of trippers aimlessly drifting along the concrete waterways on their huge rubber rings. As with most of the characters in Kowalska's eccentric collection, their quest for enjoyment looks naive or perhaps, at worst, even vulgar and trashy. The documentary style in which the photographs show the people contrives derisively to offer the recreational habits of these individuals for our amusement, rather than suggesting a sentimental reaction to such eccentricity.

Paper 3 Part 3
Multiple-choice questions

2 **2** 🔟 Refer students to the Exam advice. This is a complete Part 3 question. You will hear the recording twice.

Answers
1 D 2 A 3 D 4 C 5 A

Recording script

You will hear two people, Darren and Helena, talking about Darren's new career. For questions 1–5, choose the answer (A, B, C or D) which fits best according to what you hear.

You now have one minute in which to look at Part 3.

Helena: So, Darren, I hear that you've got a new job working in the voluntary sector. It must have been a bit of a wrench, wasn't it, giving up your high-powered banking job in the City, with those huge annual bonuses and long City lunches? Most people we know thought it was a passing phase, <u>but I always thought you were a bit of a square peg in a round hole, so I've always half expected it.</u> So I guess armed with your degree and a tidy sum put by, you thought you could change careers just like that? But why did it take you two years to make the move?

Darren: I didn't know what I wanted to do; I only knew what I didn't. I was really stuck in a rut until someone I worked with got fed up with me and told me to 'go and do voluntary work or something'. So I decided to take some time off and volunteer for a charity. I reckoned that if I guaranteed them six months, during that time I would be bound to find a proper job, you know a paid one! It wasn't quite as easy as I thought, though. I decided to apply to 12 well-known charities, ranging from overseas aid to homelessness. I put in my applications, <u>but I guess my lack of real conviction and experience was pretty obvious, and they saw straight through me.</u> They didn't even bother to reply.

Helena: <u>Quite right. I don't know why you'd think they would. They need big hitters just like in banking, not people who don't know what they want</u> – I can't imagine why people think that charities should be charitable when it comes to employing people.

Darren: <u>Well, I can see that now obviously.</u> Anyway, I got a lucky break. A friend of a friend had a contact with one of the charities I had applied to. She gave me a name, Anna Rogers, and within days Anna had come back with a proposal. Now, I'm a history graduate and I'd spent two years on a trading floor in the City, so most of her spiel on government research papers went straight over my head, but I did manage to make out that she wanted me to find out about schemes that prevented or alleviated homelessness. <u>I jumped at the chance and handed in my notice at work straightaway.</u> My colleagues told me they'd thought I'd never really do it – they had no idea how desperate I was.

Helena: So how did it go?

Darren: Well, I actually found it a bit on the quiet side, but that was OK. I could hear the tapping of keyboards and conversations on the phone. Even the people were different – they spoke in whole sentences, without the 'yeah, yeah, right, right, offer this, bid that, done' tempo I was used to. I was expecting a collection of meek do-gooders, and I was surprised to find they were OK, and <u>I just got on with things.</u> They were a nice bunch and were only mildly curious as to why I had given up a well-paid job. The biggest surprise, however, was me. I never expected to enjoy it so much.

Helena: So, what about the future?

Darren: Well, that project took five months to complete. That done, I had no real desire to leave and volunteered for another couple of months, writing bits and pieces, even stuffing envelopes. It was novel to be working 14-hour days without moaning for what I once regarded as a pittance. I don't think the City is an easy life. Mind you, this isn't a breeze either – there are still targets here. Equally, <u>the City just wasn't right for me, while this is.</u> I feel pretty stupid that it took me so long to figure that out. I'm just glad I got there in the end and one day I can work on a bigger project where I can start to make a difference to people's lives.

Now you will hear Part 3 again.

18 On freedom

18.1

Exam skills	Reading and Use of English Paper 1 Part 6
Vocabulary	Synonyms

18.2

Listening	Non-exam listening
Grammar	Review of modals
Exam skills	Reading and Use of English Paper 1 Part 4
	Reading and Use of English Paper 1 Part 3

18.3

Exam skills	Speaking Paper 4 Part 2
	Reading and Use of English Paper 1 Part 1
Pronunciation	Stress and intonation

Workbook contents

1	Listening Paper 3 Part 1
2, 3, 4	Vocabulary
5	Grammar – modal verbs
6	Use of English Paper 1 Part 1
7	Use of English Paper 1 Part 2
8	Use of English Paper 1 Part 3

18.1 SB pages 152–153

Lesson plan

Introduction	10–10 minutes
Reading	40–60 minutes
Vocabulary	10–20 minutes

SV   Set 5 for homework.
LV   See Extension activity for 3.

1   Elicit what students already know about the United Nations and the Universal Declaration of Human Rights. Then ask them to evaluate whether the four statements are adhered to all over the world today.

Reading

2   The picture shows the tearing down of the Berlin Wall in 1989, which signalled the end of the 'Cold War' and led to the re-unification of Germany.

Ask students to carry out the gapped text task, following the advice given in Exam folder 5 (see Student's Book page 83). Remind them in particular to underline key words and phrases in both the base text and the paragraphs.

Answers
1 E   2 H   3 B   4 F   5 D   6 A   7 G

3   Allow students to discuss their views in small groups and then summarise ideas on the board.

Possible answer
In general, I believe the future for human rights looks less bleak than it did twenty or thirty years ago. Thanks to the Internet and social media, individuals can find out quickly what is going on around them, and most repressive governments in the world wield less power than they used to because of this 'openness'. Indeed, some regimes have been toppled because they were unable to prevent their citizens from having access to worldwide media coverage. However, it should not be forgotten that human rights abuse still goes on in some parts of the world. And at the same time, increasing globalisation means that we are in danger of losing our cultural identity, which could affect individual freedom too.

◎ Extension activity

As a follow-up to the discussion, run a formal debate on the statement below. Ask two students to volunteer to give a brief talk (1–2 minutes), one for and one against the statement. Allow the rest of the class to choose their viewpoint and then reorganise the room, with those 'for' on one side and those 'against' on the other. After everyone has had a chance to speak, ask students to vote whether they are still for or against the statement.
'Increased globalisation will lead to less freedom for the individual.'

4   Allow students time to find the words and phrases, which are all in the text on page 152. Elicit answers.

Answers
a in limbo   b a rather faltering endeavour
c a loosening of the reins   d a (soft) sideshow
e dealing a blow to   f remit

5

18.2 SB pages 154–155

Modals review

Lesson plan	
Introduction	10–10 minutes
Listening	20–20 minutes
Grammar	15–30 minutes
Use of English	15–30 minutes

SV Set 4 for homework.
LV See Photocopiable recording script activity for 2.

1 The pictures are taken from two animal welfare campaigns run by PETA and Lush.

Possible answer
We share our planet with animals, but it cannot be denied that human beings are the dominant species. So should animals have the same rights as us? It is a complex issue because of our perceived needs. Many people across the world depend on animals for their livelihoods, and domesticated animals provide sustenance for their families. However, the provision of food is one thing, whereas abusing animals in other unnecessary ways is quite another. For me it is unacceptable to cause an animal suffering in the pursuit of a new cosmetics line or even in the development of potentially life-saving drugs. We humans should treat animals with the respect and compassion they deserve.

2 **2** 🔟 Play the recording and elicit whether the speaker is for or against animal testing (he is against). Then play it a second time so that students can make notes.

Recording script
Two-and-a-half million animals are used in Australian medical research every year, half a million in Victoria alone. They justify the obscene waste of life like this: animals must be used in order to trial new drugs and treatments safely. But a growing number of doctors and scientists have challenged this line, saying that in fact,

animal research is counterproductive. It could in fact be damaging to human health. This is because animals are not like us – their bodies are different, they suffer from different diseases and obviously their reactions to drugs are also different. So animals cannot be used to find cures for humans.

Why does animal testing continue? Answer: it's a huge industry. There are many, many vested interests in animal research, from the big pharmaceutical companies themselves to the manufacturers of the cages that these poor dumb animals end up in. Then, apart from those obvious commercial interests, there are the many scientists who have chosen to base their careers on animal experiments. They would lose their jobs tomorrow if animal testing was stopped, wouldn't they?

Basically, animal research is the ultimate quick fix. In general, it requires many years to monitor the progression of a human disease. Obviously laboratory animals, with their shorter lifespans, tend to decline more rapidly. This means that research projects can be wrapped up quickly. Papers presented, trials successfully concluded, bam, new drugs hit the market. It can't be scientifically sound. But what should have been done – full-scale controlled monitoring within a human population – is ruled out as uneconomic. The hard truth is that just about every medical advance has come about either independently from, or despite, animal research. You shouldn't believe everything you hear, right?

Photocopiable recording script activity 🅿️ ➔ page 152

Hand out copies of the recording script and ask students to underline all sentences containing modal verbs, then discuss how the modal verb is being used in each one.

Answers
1 … animals must be used in order to trial new drugs and treatments safely (obligation)
2 It could in fact be damaging to human health. (speculation)
3 So animals cannot be used to find cures for humans. (impossibility)
4 They would lose their jobs tomorrow if animal testing was stopped, wouldn't they? (conditional)
5 This means that research projects can be wrapped up quickly. (ability)
6 It can't be scientifically sound. (deduction)
7 But what should have been done – full-scale controlled monitoring within a human population – is ruled out as uneconomic. (unfulfilled obligation)
8 You shouldn't believe everything you hear, right? (advice)

Corpus spot

Elicit the corrections needed. Refer students to the section in the Grammar folder on Student's Book pages 186–187.

Answers
a can be kept … must have
b must/should be changed
c ought to have been / should have been
d correct
e can't have been
f wouldn't have bought
g could live
h wouldn't

3 Suggest students work in pairs, or elicit the answers from the whole class.

Answers
a shouldn't have   b might have   c must have
d needn't   e don't have to   f shouldn't
g Ought   h Would

4 These key word transformations can be set for homework if necessary.

Answers
1 to have put in | more
2 have been less humane | prior to the establishment
3 put themselves / their job | on the line
4 have let us know (about) / let us in on | Lisa's
5 the record straight | about how / about the fact that
6 raise any objection(s) | to my/me

5

Background information
The text comes from the book The *New Existentialism* by Colin Wilson, a British philosopher whose most famous book *The Outsider* was written when he was only 24.

Answers
1 insignificant   2 evolutionary   3 interminable
4 submissively   5 empower   6 resourcefulness
7 footing   8 natural

18.3 SB pages 156–157

Listening and Speaking

Lesson plan	
Introduction	5–5 minutes
Listening	20–20 minutes
Pronunciation	10–10 minutes
Speaking	25–40 minutes
Use of English	0–15 minutes

SV   Set 6 for homework.
LV   See Extension activity for 5.

1 Ask students to identify what is happening in the pictures, which show:

- children working in a carpet factory
- someone making a speech at Speaker's Corner in Hyde Park, London
- a demonstration being broken up violently by the police.

Suggested answers
Picture A shows a factory where child labour is being used to produce goods. You might call it a sweatshop and it is preventing these girls from gaining a full education.

Picture B shows a man talking to a crowd of onlookers and he is dressed quite unconventionally! He is probably able to say whatever he wants to in public, but the right to free speech isn't universal and some political regimes would have that man arrested on the spot.

Picture C shows some kind of civil disobedience, perhaps a protest about something, so I suppose it is illustrating the right to demonstrate in public – there is some form of riot control taking place, though, so maybe this illustrates the lack of such freedom.

2 2🔢 Ask students to look at the pictures as they listen to the first part of the recording. See if students notice how the man keeps interrupting the woman and doesn't allow her to give her own opinions. He also challenges what she says quite aggressively, which is rather unfair in an interview situation.

Recording script

Interlocutor: Now, in this part of the test you're going to do something together. Here are some pictures on the theme of freedom. First, I'd like you to look at pictures A and C and talk together about what might have happened just after these photos were taken. You have about a minute for this, so don't worry if I interrupt you.

Man: Er … shall I start?

Woman: Sure, go ahead.

Man: Well, I'll choose the easier of the two. So, if we consider what C shows, it's some kind of demonstration which may have started off peacefully but has obviously turned sour. Er, the police are in there, there'll obviously be lots of arrests, and maybe worse, physical abuse of some kind …

Woman: The … there's a doctor or someone with a medical training there, the armband has a red cross, it doesn't look good …

Man: Yes, yes. The police might take away banners, too, that's what often happens in situations like this. Anyway, what about picture A?

Woman: Well, I'm sure the owners of the factory weren't too happy with the photographer, so perhaps they tried to confiscate the film.

Man: Mm, but we're looking at the photo, so what you suggest can't be true!

Woman: I didn't say they succeeded. Yes, obviously the photographer …

Man: Um, perhaps it was taken in secret? That's what that kind of investigative journalist often does.

Woman: Uh-huh.

Interlocutor: Thank you.

3 **2 13** Play the second part and then elicit which additional aspects of freedom the candidates decide to include (education and animal rights).

Recording script

Interlocutor: Now, I'd like you to look at all three pictures. I'd like you to imagine that they are all going to be used in a book about freedom. Talk together about the aspects of freedom that are shown. Then suggest two other aspects of freedom that you feel should be included in the book. You have about three minutes to talk about this.

Woman: Well, we've already identified political freedom and the rights of children, haven't we? Looking at picture B, I suppose it's illustrating the rights of the individual, isn't it?

Man: Mm, yes. It's taken in Hyde Park in London, the place is called Speaker's Corner and every Sunday …

Woman: I didn't know that. Anyway, the man is holding forth to the crowd about something, so it's all about free speech. He's rather unusually dressed, he's got a mortar board on his head like teachers used to wear, and look, he's wearing a real dog's collar! That's underlining the message of personal liberty – in a liberal society, you can wear what you want.

Man: Yes, that's an important point – you don't have that freedom of choice everywhere. Well, we have to suggest other aspects of freedom to include in this book … um …

Woman: Um, speaking purely for myself, I'd want to include something on education. It's a basic human right. I suppose it's linked to those girls in the factory, they're being deprived of what they should be doing at that age, going to school and learning. If they can't read and write, they'll be trapped for the rest of their lives.

Man: Mm, that's true. But how would you select a photo to show this type of freedom? If you just show a class of schoolchildren, it wouldn't make the point, education's something we take for granted.

Woman: Right, well fortunately, we don't have to worry about which photo is actually chosen, but I do think the book should focus on education.

Man: Oh yes, yes, I, I agree. And then, something else? Mm, freedom of the press maybe? That's part of political freedom, but also the book could focus on how the paparazzi chase after famous people, you'd get a good photo of that!

Woman: I'm not sure that's strictly about freedom, though. And it seems rather flippant, after we've been considering basic human rights like education and freedom of speech. What about including animal rights? It's an important element – we're not the only species on the planet, after all.

Man: But now I'm beginning to wonder what the focus of this book is. I mean, you can't just call it 'Freedom' and put everything in it – there would have to be some limits?

Woman: I don't see why. It would be very interesting. Perhaps a bit long.

Man: Just a little! Er, well, OK, we'll include animal rights. But in my humble opinion, the book will become very unwieldy, an editor's nightmare.

Woman: Maybe …

Interlocutor: Thank you.

Pronunciation

4   **2** Refer students to the Exam spot and then ask them to listen to utterances a–f, which have been recorded separately. They should repeat what the speaker says, paying particular attention to their stress and intonation.

5   Ask students to read the task and spend just a few seconds thinking about their ideas.

Students should carry out the task in pairs, speaking for three minutes.

◉ Extension activity
Record each pair of students carrying out the task and allow them to review their performance afterwards.

---

6   The picture shows people protesting peacefully in Cairo during the 'Arab Spring' of 2012.

Answers
1 B   2 C   3 A   4 B   5 D   6 C   7 D   8 A

Writing folder 9

SB pages 158–159

Part 2 Article

1   Before looking at the task, ask students to look back at the advice given in Writing folder 5 on page 91.

Answers
The article will appear in an academic journal and be read by academics, so it must be formal, serious and impersonal in style.

2   Ask students to work individually and then compare what they have noticed.

Answers
All content is relevant to the task.

Inconsistencies in style:

use of an informal phrasal verb and chatty tone in title: *Hang on to your rights!* – certain phrasal verbs are appropriate in academic writing, for example *weigh up* in paragraph 1. However, students need to be careful when using phrasal verbs as informal ones stand out and contribute to a negative effect on the examiner (e.g. *help [us] out*).
several instances of *I think ...* – an article for an academic audience should avoid use of the first person and adopt an impersonal style.

Inappropriate informal use (students rewrite these parts in exercise 4):

really that great (paragraph 1)
the big plus; kids (paragraph 2)
the downside of ; 24/7 (paragraph 3)
the Internet gives us the ability to control our lives, right? (paragraph 4)
help us out (paragraph 5)
the big snag (paragraph 6)

3   Check that students understand the meaning of 'slips' – very minor, unintentional mistakes. To achieve a Band 3 or above for Language in *Cambridge English: Proficiency*, students have to show a high level of accuracy. For further information on marking, see the C2 assessment scale (Language) on page 24 of this Teacher's Book.

Ask students to tick the boxes that apply and then elicit their answers.

Answers
Boxes that apply:
Complex ideas are communicated convincingly.
Text is a well-organised, coherent whole.
Errors only occur in less common words and may be slips.
Choice of vocabulary generally shows sophistication and precision.

4

Rewritten answer

(Stylistic changes and spelling corrections in italics)

SOCIAL MEDIA: THE IMPLICATIONS FOR PERSONAL LIBERTY

The prevalence of mobile communication devices together with the widespread use of social networking and the Internet have altered our way of life fundamentally. This article weighs up their impact on individual freedom and assesses whether the outcomes are *unequivocally advantageous.*

Arguably, the main asset of Smartphones and tablets is that friends and family are always contactable. Parents need not be concerned for the *welfare* of their teenage children, as they can keep track of them. This may be beneficial to the older generation, but I think it imposes unfair limits on the liberty of their *offspring.*

One drawback of mobile devices from the working adult's standpoint is that they can be reached *at all times* and the distinction between work and home life becomes blurred. This again places constraints upon the individual, who has fewer opportunities to shut out the stress of everyday life. At the same time, *it is undeniable that* the Internet gives us the ability to control our lives. From booking a holiday to selecting a new home, everything can be done direct, without any middleman restricting what is on offer. So that is an example of greater freedom – the freedom of choice.

As for social networking, the chance to share ideas and communicate more effectively means that nobody need feel alone in the modern world. Furthermore, the role played by social media in disseminating information under less tolerant political regimes shows how networking sites can be used *for the greater good,* contributing to *profound* social change.

However, *the adverse impact of* all this is an inevitable erosion of privacy. People seem happy to display their innermost thoughts and aspirations in a way that would have been unheard of in the previous century, but at what cost? It is impossible to turn the clock back, yet it must be acknowledged that through social media, restrictions have been placed on individual freedom, which society at large may come to regret. (323 words)

5   Ask students to work in pairs, each taking three paragraphs (a–d occur in paragraphs 1–3). Check answers to a–h and then elicit any other words that students know in each word family. Consult the English Vocabulary Profile for further word family information (see 6 below).

Answers

a prevalence	d constraints	g aspirations
b contactable	e tolerant	h restrictions
c beneficial	f erosion	

6   Remind students of the benefits of recording new vocabulary in word families.

Answers

a tolerant	c intolerable	e intolerant
b intolerance	d tolerance	

7   Ask students to follow the Exam advice when they write their article for homework. If time permits, brainstorm some ideas in class that students can add to the mind map on page 159.

Sample answer

THE POSITION OF THE INDIVIDUAL WITHIN CONTEMPORARY SOCIETY

How much freedom do we have in modern society? In some ways, we enjoy far more freedom than previous generations, but in other ways, we most definitely do not. This article considers both aspects of this question.

Nowadays, the individual has a strong entitlement to protection under the law, especially in relation to gender and race. Equal rights of this kind seem fundamental to personal freedom. Men and women should earn the same rates of pay for the same job, whatever their age and people of different ethnic backgrounds should be able to attend the school of their choice.

However, at the same time it cannot be denied that some constraints must be placed on the individual if a society is to function properly and these limits are generally enshrined in law. Model citizens recognise that they must abide by the law, in order to protect the weak and vulnerable members of their society, whereas lawless states lack the proper safeguards for these individuals.

In a civilised society, tolerance of others allows free speech and religious freedom. It is vital for individuals to be able to state their beliefs and political views without fear of reprisal. Similarly, everyone should be able to dress as they wish, rather than being attacked for their appearance.

However, there are many limits to personal freedom, not least due to the huge amount of data that exists about us online these days, from our shopping habits to our relationships. Furthermore, in many modern societies, children have less freedom to play unsupervised than in the past and CCTV cameras are everywhere. This undoubtedly affects everybody's freedom in one way, though it undeniably protects us at the same time.

In contemporary society we all carry the notion that we are 'free' but in reality, this isn't always the case. Although 21st-century citizens would probably not want to return to a pre-digital age, the constraints imposed on them are inevitably greater nowadays, largely thanks to the ubiquity of technology. (331 words)

19 The unexplained

Topic Strange places and happenings

19.1

Exam skills	Listening Paper 3 Part 2
	Reading and Use of English
	Paper 1 Part 1
Vocabulary	Adjectives describing personality
Style extra	Onomatopoeia

19.2

Grammar focus	Word order and adverbs
	Adverb or adjective?
Exam skills	Reading and Use of English Paper 1
	Part 2

19.3

Exam skills	Reading into Writing: Full Task 2 –
	Paper 2 Part 1
Vocabulary	Word formation

Workbook contents

1	Reading Paper 1 Part 5
2, 3	Vocabulary
4	Grammar – word order and adverbs
5	Use of English Paper 1 Part 4

19.1 SB pages 160–161

Lesson plan

Introduction	5–10 minutes
Vocabulary	10–10 minutes
Listening	25–30 minutes
Style extra	20–20 minutes
Use of English	0–20 minutes
SV	Omit 4 and set 5 for homework.
LV	See Extension activity for 5.

Speaking

1 The photo is from the *Twilight* series of films.

Ask the class to discuss the questions in pairs or groups.

Vocabulary

2 The adjectives refer to personality. Encourage the class to use an English–English dictionary to find the odd one out. Students can use any of the words they feel best describes someone who believes in ghosts.

Answers

a sceptical The other words all have the idea of 'easy to mislead or deceive'. *Sceptical* means 'doesn't believe things easily'.
b derisive The other words all mean 'easy to deceive'. *Derisive* means 'not worth taking seriously'.
c apathetic The others all have an active meaning. *Apathetic* is passive.
d sensible The other words have the meaning of being aware of things. *Sensible* means 'having common sense – knowing what to do'.
e humble The other words all mean wanting to find out about something. *Humble* means modest.
f upright This is a positive word – the others are all negative.
g eccentric The other words mean 'forceful'. *Eccentric* means 'unconventional'.
h pragmatic The other words mean 'clever' or 'skilful'. *Pragmatic* means 'practical in decision making'.
i impulsive The other words mean 'careful' or 'sensitive'. *Impulsive* means 'hasty'.

Suggested answer
Someone who believes in ghosts is probably gullible, naïve, credulous and susceptible.

Listening

3 **2 15** Ask students to read through the questions and try to predict the answers with a partner. The story you will hear is true. Play the recording twice.

Answers
1 chains 2 burial 3 crisis apparition 4 patch of mist
5 plumber 6 ladder 7 waist 8 shave 9 dagger

Recording script
Presenter: Good morning. Today on the programme I'm going to talk about one aspect of the supernatural – ghosts! Now, ghosts have always been with us and are as much of a mystery now as they were in the first century AD, when Athenodorus, a hard-up philosopher, rented a house in Athens which was cheap because of its eerie reputation and noisy neighbours. Sitting working late at night, Athenodorus heard the rattling of <u>chains</u> and, suddenly, the horrifying figure of an old man appeared before him. It beckoned to him and, although Athenodorus tried to ignore it and get on with his work, it refused to let him. So Athenodorus

followed the ghost into the garden, where it pointed to a spot on the ground and disappeared. Next day, a hole was dug at the place indicated by the ghost and a human skeleton was discovered. After the remains were given a proper <u>burial</u> and the house purified, the haunting ceased.

This was clearly a ghost with a purpose, but usually the reason for haunting is not clear. There have been a few modern cases where ghosts seemed to have a message, such as a '<u>crisis apparition</u>' of a person, seen by close friends and relatives at the time of his or her death, an event unknown to them until confirmation came later. However, in many ghost sightings, there seems to be no purpose and the ghost's identity remains unknown.

Some people are sceptical and do not believe in the existence of ghosts. It is indeed likely that some witnesses who claim to have seen ghosts out of doors have, in fact, mistaken <u>a patch of mist</u> for a human figure, especially if they have been alone and the place was eerie. Other people may have vivid imaginations and 'see' externally something that is really only in their mind.

One of the most vivid apparitions on record was that seen in 1953 by 18-year-old Harry Martindale. Now a retired gardener, but a <u>plumber</u> at the time of the sighting, Martindale was working in the Treasurer's House in York. One day he was at work in the cellar, when, to his astonishment and fright, he saw a Roman soldier step out of the wall. He instantly dropped his tools. What he did not know at the time was that he had put his <u>ladder</u> on the course of an old Roman road. He later described in detail what he had witnessed.

Harry: I heard a sound – the only way I can describe it is the sound of a musical note. At the same time, a figure came out of the wall. And the head of the figure was in line with my <u>waist</u>, and it had on a shining helmet. I was terrified. I got out of the way and scrambled into the corner. And from there, I got a bird's eye view of what it was. It was the head of a Roman soldier. He crossed the room and disappeared into a pillar. Then another soldier on horseback came by, followed by soldiers walking in pairs, side by side. You couldn't see through them. They were all about one metre five, in want of a <u>shave</u>! Nothing smart about them. They all had the same helmets on, with the plume coming out of the back, down the neck. They all carried a short sword on the right-hand side. I used to think that Roman soldiers carried a long sword, but this was similar to a <u>dagger</u>. And they went as quick as they came. When they were in the centre of the cellar, I could hear a murmuring – no speech, just a murmuring.

Presenter: When the museum curator found the terrified Harry collapsed at the top of the cellar steps, he immediately knew what had happened because he had seen the soldiers himself seven years before. And he knew Harry didn't know that the soldiers' legs were missing because they were walking on the course of the old Roman road, which was beneath the cellar floor.

4 Spend four or five minutes rounding up the listening with a class discussion on the subject.

 Style extra

The aim of this exercise is to introduce students to onomatopoeia. Using onomatopoeic words will help give life to their compositions.

Suggested answers
Chains were described as 'rattling' and the Roman soldiers as 'murmuring'.
creak – wooden floors
tinkle – a bell; broken glass
squelch – mud
rumble – thunder, train on track
crunch – gravel or crisp snow when walked on
slash – an angry person cutting cloth viciously with a knife
slap – waves on the beach, hand against face
slam – a door
click – door lock
hiss – steam, a snake
growl – angry dog, people
screech – parrot, brakes
drip – a tap
peal – bells, laughter
slither – snake moving smoothly, person sliding down or across something smooth

a creaked **b** squelched **c** slashed **d** slithered
e crunches **f** dripping **g** tinkled **h** hissed

Possible answer
I was lying in bed at home one night – all alone, except for my dog, as, for once, my family had gone out for the evening to a concert. It was a cold, rainy evening and the shutters had begun to bang against the side of the bedroom wall. I could hear the wind getting up and it howling down the chimney. Suddenly, I heard something tinkle, like glass breaking, then a crunch. I turned over, determined not to be spooked by this. Then, there was a creak. This is when I began to get worried, as I knew the third stair from the bottom always creaked. Betsy began to growl softly and then I knew that something was really wrong. I reached for my mobile phone.

5 Students should read through the text, which explains what a poltergeist is.

Answers
1 B is correct. A is when something is written in stone or metal; C is written in a meeting; D is for a course or in school.
2 A is correct because the text goes on to give the translation of the word.
3 C is correct. *Turned over* means 'put upside down'.
4 D is correct because it is the only verb here that is reflexive.
5 B is correct because it collocates with 'rules'.
6 A is correct because 'spontaneous' is the only one which can be used with an object.
7 A is correct because it gives the meaning of 'started'. B, C and D need the preposition 'from'.
8 D is correct because it has the idea of future ability.

 Extension activity

When students have finished with the reading text, ask them to close their Student's Books and then give them the text as a dictation. Read a small section out twice. At the end, read the text out once all the way through. This will help them to think about spelling.

19.2 SB pages 162–163
Word order and adverbs

Lesson plan	
Grammar	60–70 minutes
Use of English	0–20 minutes
SV	Set 4 for homework.
LV	See Extension activity for 1.

1 Refer students to the Grammar folder on pages 187–188 of the Student's Book. The examples given cover most of the basic word order rules. Some words can change order depending on what you want to emphasise.

Answers
a Yesterday I went home on foot. OR I went home on foot yesterday.
b Later she briskly walked up the hill to where, luckily, another coach was waiting.
c Last night I was hardly in the mood to go swimming. OR I was hardly in the mood to go swimming last night.
d Of course he is still lying. OR He is still lying, of course. OR (with the meaning of not moving) Of course he is lying still.

e In fact, Stephen spoke to me in a friendly way the other day. OR Stephen spoke to me in a friendly way the other day, in fact.
f Strangely enough, it rained heavily non-stop all day. OR It rained heavily non-stop all day, strangely enough.
g Apparently, people rarely hide things of value in the attic. OR People rarely hide things of value in the attic, apparently.
h She performed the dance far too slowly.
i To be honest, I think you should get out of the house more often. OR I think you should get out of the house more often, to be honest.
j I saw the comet in the sky only yesterday. OR Only yesterday, I saw the comet in the sky.

 Extension activity

Students are often unaware that there are rules for the order of adjectives. Ask students to put these adjectives in the right order and explain the rules for adjectival word order. Obviously students should be discouraged from writing a long list of adjectives before a noun, but it is important to make sure that if they use two or three adjectives, they are in the right order.

a green deciduous large tree beautiful
some mouldy old boots football
the small bowl salad antique French wooden
a plastic square writing table

Answers
a beautiful, large, green, deciduous tree
some mouldy, old, football boots
the small, antique, French, wooden salad bowl
a square, plastic, writing table

The rules for adjective order are:
determiner, opinion, size, shape, colour, origin, material, purpose

2 Students will probably find this exercise quite difficult. If that is the case, give them the first couple of words to start them off. Check that their punctuation is correct.

Background information
Uluru (formerly known as Ayers Rock) is a huge red rock in SW Northern Territory, Australia, 450 km SW of Alice Springs. It rises from the desert to a height of 348 metres. It is the largest monolith in the world.

Answers

a   Another tells how after a terrible battle ...
b   One legend states that Uluru was originally a lake.
c   ... that has been sacred to the Aboriginal people for hundreds of years.
d   Many Aboriginal paintings tell important Earth stories.
e   ... the time when the world was created.
f   ... the Earth rose up in revolt at the bloodshed to form the great blood-coloured rock.
g   They believe that it was made by spirits in the 'Dreamtime' ...

The order is Example, c, g, e, d, b, a, f

 Corpus spot

a   He slumped into the nearby velvet armchair, **holding his briefcase tightly** in his hands.
b   **Looked at statistically**, however, the centre has attracted more people, spending more money than before.
c   **Being into contemporary rather than old-fashioned art** I don't find the good old Tate Britain a place I would visit too often.
d   correct
e   I have always wanted to remember **every movie I see and every book I read perfectly**.
f   It goes without saying that **you will seldom** OR **seldom will you** see a very shy person wearing a bright orange shirt.
g   Kerry is a very green county: you **can hardly** find a road where two cars pass each other.
h   Most of us are aware of the fact that **this solution is not always** economically viable.
i   Before he appeared on the music scene, **'Pop' music hardly existed**.
j   correct

3   Refer students to the notes about adverbs and adjectives. Explain the difference in meaning between the adverbs in each pair.

Answers
a hardly   b highly   c wrongly/rightly   d hard
e shortly   f wrong (also possibly wrongly or right)
g lately   h right   i short

4   This text gives background information on how to carry out a ghost hunt.

Answers
1 make   2 carry   3 of   4 on/forth   5 As/When/If
6 to   7 taken   8 any

19.3 SB pages 164–165

Reading into Writing: Full Task 2

Lesson plan	
Introduction	10–20 minutes
Reading two texts	20–20 minutes
Word formation	5–10 minutes
Writing	30–50 minutes

SV   Ask students to finish the rewriting task in 6 for homework.
LV   See Extension activity for 2.

1   The pictures are of Abraham Lincoln and John F. Kennedy, both American presidents. Ask the class to read the information, which mentions various coincidences in their lives. They should then discuss their reaction to them.

Possible answer
I think that these coincidences are really very interesting. However, it has been shown that what people think is 'a once in a million chance' of something happening has a good probability. Take, for example the coincidence of people having the same birthday in a small group. It is actually more common for up to three people to have the same birthday in a group of, say, twenty people, than you would think.

2   Ask students to discuss the expressions.

Answers
Talk of the devil! – said when you mention someone and they then appear

to have a guardian angel – said about the feeling that there is someone you can't see who protects you

It's a small world – said about a coincidence involving people known to both speakers

to have second sight – to be able to know what will happen in the future

female intuition – a feeling that women are supposed to have about something that might happen

a feeling of déjà vu – a feeling of being in a place you've visited before or of experiencing something that has happened before

a sixth sense – a feeling that you have that tells you something isn't quite right – rather like intuition but used by both sexes

Extension activity

There are many idioms in English connected with ghosts and the devil. Ask students how many they can find.

Here are some:

to give up the ghost – to stop working, e.g. *The car has given up the ghost.*

a ghost ship – one which is imaginary

a ghost town – one which is deserted

a ghost train – a frightening fairground ride

a devil of a job – a difficult job

to have a devil-may-care attitude – not to worry about anything

to play devil's advocate – to take the opposite position on a subject so that both sides of the argument can be considered

to be between the devil and the deep blue sea – to have to choose between two equally unattractive options

3 Ask students to read through each text carefully.

4 Ask students to look through the texts again in order to find the words and describe which part of speech they are.

Answers
speak out (phrasal verb) outspoken (adjective)
anonymity (noun) anonymous, anonymously
disturbing (adjective) disturb, disturbance, undisturbed, disturbed, disturbingly
conscious (adjective) unconscious, unconsciously, subconscious, consciousness
impression (noun) impress, impressive, unimpressive, impressively, impressionable
dismissed (past participle) dismiss, dismissive, dismissal

5

Answers
a outspoken b dismissive c anonymous
d disturbance e impressionable f subconscious

6 This is a full Writing Part 1 task. Students should read the question carefully and then read the attempt at an answer. They should discuss in pairs what improvements can be made to it.

Suggested areas for improvement
- The answer is too short – slightly over length answers are not penalised, but answers that are too short are.
- The answer uses abbreviations (etc., e.g.) rather than words (and so on, for example).
- For each text, only one point is mentioned but there are always two.
- There is a lack of paraphrase (i.e. the student has copied what is in the texts) – e.g. ring up, embarrassed.
- The language used is very simple – more complexity is needed.
- There is no adequate conclusion and the student seems to have ended in the middle of a paragraph.

Refer students to the advice in Writing folder 3 before they write an improved answer.

Suggested improved answer
The two texts discuss the arguments supporting and refuting the idea of coincidence, whether they are evidence of the paranormal or can be explained on a purely rational level. Text 1 puts forward the idea that people react to coincidence in one of two ways. At worst, they are extremely uncomfortable at the thought of being stigmatised as an idiot, or, at best, they are troubled by a worrying occurrence.

Personally, I see myself in the latter category. I heartily agree with the writer that it is important to find out the truth behind a worrying occurrence or coincidence. I think that most people have experienced a feeling of déjà vu and it can be unnerving, especially if they see themselves as quite sensible, level-headed types. It's hard to know where these feelings spring from, but I tend to think they are past memories of possibly a similar place or occurrence coming to the fore.

Text 2 mentions that people are first of all alerted through their senses to something not being 'quite right'. These feelings are generally thought to be ludicrous, especially given that time has shown that science can explain things which were previously thought to be mysterious.

I'm in two minds about how much science can explain. While I am by no means a gullible person, I still believe there may be room for the unexplained. I have never actually narrowly avoided a plane crash, but I do know people who have escaped serious injury through pure chance. Many coincidences can be easily explained away and the scientific theory of probability has gone a long way to disabusing people of how often some coincidences happen. However, I still believe that there are some things which are not easily explained.
(292 words)

Exam folder 10

SB pages 166–167

Paper 4 Speaking

In the examination there will be two or three students and two examiners. For the purpose of this test, students should be in pairs or threes and take it in turns to play the part of the examiner.

Make sure that the timing is correct: Part 1 – two minutes (three minutes for groups of three), Part 2 – four minutes (six minutes for groups of three) and Part 3 lasts for 10 minutes (15 minutes for groups of three). There can be anything from one to seven pictures/visuals in the examination. Here there are five photographs.

The photographs for Part 2 are as follows:

A   a small car

B   a desktop computer

C   a book

D   a clock

E   a refrigerator

20 A sense of humour

Topic Humour

20.1

Exam skills	Reading and Use of English Paper 1 Part 5

20.2

Grammar	Uses of *have, get* and *go*
Vocabulary	Expressions with *go*
Exam skills	Reading and Use of English Paper 1 Parts 2 and 4

20.3

Exam skills	Listening Paper 3 Part 3
Pronunciation	Loan words
Exam skills	Speaking Paper 4 Part 3

Workbook contents

1	Listening Paper 3 Part 2
2	Grammar – *have* and *get*
3, 4, 5, 6	Vocabulary
7	Use of English Paper 1 Part 4

20.1 SB pages 168–169

Lesson plan	
Introduction	10–15 minutes
Reading	50–75 minutes
SV	Keep the discussion in 1 brief; set 4 for homework and omit 5.
LV	See Extension activity for 5.

Take some cartoons into class and pass them around to find out students' reactions.

Speaking

1 Ask students to say what they feel about the different types of comedy/humour. If necessary, explain what they are.

slapstick – silly behaviour like moving a chair when someone is about to sit down – similar to Charlie Chaplin humour

political satire – cartoons in the newspaper or comedy TV programmes on political topics

stand-up – where a comedian is alone on stage telling jokes to the audience

farce – a (sometimes irritating) type of comedy where the audience is aware that the actors are confused about a situation – often within a family

black comedy – making fun of something you shouldn't – like death or murder

Reading

2 Tell students something about Bill Bryson (see below). Ask them to scan the text to find out what impression he gives.

Possible answer
He gives the impression of someone who is fairly happy to be back in his own country, but with reservations. He is enjoying playing with new toys.

Background information
Bill Bryson was born in Des Moines, Iowa in 1951. From 1977, he lived for many years in England with his English wife and family. He then moved back to the States, but has returned to live in England again with his family. His best-selling books include *The Lost Continent* (about America), *Mother Tongue* (about the English language), *Neither Here nor There* (about travelling in Europe), *Notes from a Small Island* (about Great Britain) and *Down Under* (about Australia).

3 Allow students time to read the text again and answer the questions.

Answers
1 **D** is correct because he talks about her enjoying simple pleasures like iced water and she thinks the waitress is just being nice to *her*, not everybody she meets. **A** is wrong because although he mentions food he doesn't say anything about it. **B** is wrong because she does get things for nothing, but nothing suggests that she might not be happy if she didn't. **C** is wrong because he says she is 'slavishly uncritical'.
2 **A** is correct because he thinks a National Health Service is more important. **B** is wrong because he doesn't mention money. **C** is wrong because he doesn't criticise the way things are done. **D** is wrong because he doesn't imply that it is a waste of time, just rather pointless.
3 **A** is correct because it does everything it is supposed to do. **B** is wrong because he doesn't mention anything about free time. **C** is wrong because there is no comparison made between what he thought it would be like and what it is like. **D** is wrong because there is a bit of a fuss when you put in chopsticks and coffee grounds.

4 **C** is correct because he talks about only attempting this when his wife is out of the house. **A** is wrong because he isn't irritated so much as horrified. **B** is wrong because he isn't mending the machine for his wife, but because he himself has been playing with it. **D** is wrong because, although he tries a wider variety of garbage, he doesn't say it should take it.

5 **A** is correct because they make children feel intimidated. **B** is wrong because the incidents do not actually happen. **C** is wrong because there is no competition. **D** is wrong because there is no mention of real arguments.

6 **B** is correct because effusive means enthusiastic. **A** is wrong because he isn't critical of his home. **C** is wrong because nostalgic means thinking fondly about the past and he is talking about the present. **D** is wrong because he isn't angry about anything.

4   Some of these phrases are put in for humorous effect.

> **Answers**
> **a** I don't want to start being too serious here
> **b** a volcano-like eruption
> **c** presumably now dead and a skeleton
> **d** some young dynamic father
> **e** other good things about American household life that are taken for granted
> **f** I'll let you know what happens

5   Round off the lesson with a class discussion on the extract.

⦿ Extension activity

This might be a good point to revise plurals in English. The plural of *grocery* is *groceries* and *restaurant* is *restaurants*. However, there are many irregular plurals in English. Write the following words on the board and ask students to form the plural.

bus	criterion	roof	appendix
cargo	basis	monkey	concerto
mouse	tooth	potato	bureau
fungus	thief	sheep	phenomenon

> **Answers**
>
> | | | | |
> |---|---|---|---|
> | buses | criteria | roofs | appendices |
> | cargoes | bases | monkeys | concerti/concertos |
> | mice | teeth | potatoes | bureaux |
> | fungi | thieves | sheep | phenomena |

20.2 SB pages 170–171

Uses of *have*, *get* and *go*

> **Lesson plan**
> Grammar   60–70 minutes
> Use of English   0–20 minutes
>
> **SV**   Set 3 and/or 5 for homework.
> **LV**   See Extension activity for the Corpus spot.

1   Refer students to the cartoon and explain the joke if they aren't sure.

> **Answer**
> The words *tow* and *toe* have the same pronunciation – it's a play on words.
> *To give someone a tow* means to tow their car for them, i.e. pull it using a rope or chain.
> A *toe* is what you have on your foot. A chiropodist is someone who looks after feet.
> The first driver doesn't want to mend the vehicle himself.

2   Students should be familiar with the construction *have/get something done*, so this should be revision.

> **Answers**
> **a** have   **b** get   **c** got   **d** had   **e** has/gets   **f** get

3   This exercise can be done for homework if time is short.

> **Answers**
> **a** down with   **b** in for   **c** on   **d** over/through
> **e** for   **f** out   **g** off   **h** with   **i** without   **j** off
>
> be spent on = go on
> ebb = go out
> fetch = go for
> enter (a competition) = go in for
> become ill with = go down with
> explode = go off
> match = go with
> go sour = go off
> examine = go over/through
> manage without = go without

4   Expressions with *go* are often tested in Paper 1 Part 4.

> **Answers**
> 1   promotion | has gone to Penny Stone's
> 2   went / kept going over | and over (again) in his
> 3   went on | record as saying
> 4   was (ever) allowed to | go to waste OR (ever) went | to waste
> 5   didn't (always) go off | at a tangent
> 6   make a go of | her business in spite

Corpus spot

This exercise is error correction. The sentences contain a variety of different common student errors. Refer students to the appropriate Grammar folder if they need further help. Also see the Extension activity below.

Answers
a <u>As it was</u> a wet evening, I stayed at home.
b We would like to know <u>everything that</u> has happened.
c He <u>is already</u> here.
d Only by listening intently, <u>will you hear</u> it singing.
e It would be easier to decide if my son <u>were/was</u> here.
f I have <u>passed</u> my exam this summer.
g It's worth <u>being</u> alive on such a lovely day.
h My family consists <u>of</u> six people.
i That is a mistake I <u>often make</u>.
j Your hair <u>badly needs</u> cutting.
k I suggest <u>doing</u> it immediately.
l This team is the <u>better</u> of the two.
m correct
n My <u>information isn't</u> up to date.
o I <u>have been wanting / have wanted</u> to meet you for a long time.
p I congratulate you <u>on having got / on getting</u> married.
q I wish it <u>would stop</u> raining.
r You can eat as soon as <u>dinner is</u> ready.
s It's a <u>five-mile</u> journey.
t A man came into the compartment to <u>check</u> the tickets.

 Extension activity

Check students' answers carefully and then go back to revise the areas that they still have difficulties with.

5 This exercise can be done for homework if time is short.

Answers
1 order 2 before 3 terms 4 no
5 nowhere 6 turned/came 7 All 8 more/other

6 This discussion is a round-up for this part of the unit. It might be a good idea to set the topic for homework so students have more time to think of an incident. Either they could talk about it or they could write a short paragraph describing the incident for homework.

20.3 SB pages 172–173

Listening and Speaking

Lesson plan	
Introduction	10–20 minutes
Listening	20–20 minutes
Pronunciation	15–15 minutes
Speaking	15–35 minutes

SV   Keep the discussion in 1 brief.
LV   See Extension activity for 5.

1 Ask students to define what they think 'eccentric' means. They should then read the text on an eccentric and comment on it.

2 **2 16** Ask students to read through the questions. Play the recording twice.

Answers
1 B 2 A 3 D 4 C 5 C

Recording script
Terry: Dr Morris, thanks for lending me that book on eccentricity. I really enjoyed it – especially that bit about Oscar Wilde taking a lobster on a lead for walks and that American-Indian guy who spends his life walking backwards. Oh, and, of course, we all know nowadays from new research that this sort of behaviour has nothing in common with what used to be called lunacy. But <u>it was a bit of an eye-opener that eccentrics are renowned for their longevity.</u> The book reckons that eccentrics don't repress their inner nature and therefore suffer less stress!
Dr Morris: That's right, Terry. They are happier as a result and their immune systems work more efficiently. Anyway, what I've always believed is that human behaviour ranges from absolute conformity, at the normal end of the spectrum, to utterly bizarre non-conformity at the opposite end. Though <u>exactly how much deviation from the norm it takes to qualify as a true eccentric is a bit of a vexed point.</u>
Terry: So, actually we are all eccentrics to a greater or lesser extent?
Dr Morris: That seems to be right. The question of what is normality is pretty personal. We have all had the experience of talking with a friend who tells us that he has just met someone with the most bizarre or risqué habit – only to hear described something which we ourselves routinely do or might wish to do.
Terry: I enjoyed the chapter on innovation in the book. Eccentrics seem to be able to see problems from new and unexpected angles and they can then make imaginative leaps. So, does the man in the street always react negatively to eccentricity?

Dr Morris: Well, <u>we all love eccentrics and yet we are profoundly ambivalent about them.</u> Our collective imagination is piqued by the bizarre behaviour of someone like, for example, Howard Hughes, once the richest man in the world, who lived the last days of his life like a mystical hermit. Eccentrics have thrown off the constraints of normal life to let themselves do exactly as they please – and anyone who doesn't like it can get on with it.

Terry: The book said only about one person in every 5–10,000 is a classic full-time eccentric and most exhibit traits from an early age. They seem to share five traits: being non-conforming; creative; strongly motivated by curiosity; idealistic, and obsessed by one or more hobbyhorses. <u>Non-conformity seems to be the principal characteristic.</u>

Dr Morris: <u>True,</u> though hobbyhorses also feature highly. There was an eighteenth-century aristocrat with a love of animals called Jack Myers. One time havoc broke loose at one of his dinner parties, when he appeared in full hunting costume, mounted on his bear. In the ensuing panic, while his friends jumped out of windows or clambered behind chairs, Myers called out 'Tally-ho' and spurred his mount, which turned impatient and ate part of his leg.

Terry: Amazing! I think I'll have to go into this in more detail now.

Dr Morris: You should. I came across some new findings recently that <u>participants in a study of eccentrics were more likely to endorse what for a better expression we call 'magical thinking' – dreams that portend the future, déjà vu, things like that.</u> They tend to focus their attention on their inner universe at the expense of social or even self-care needs.

Terry: Could you lend me that research, do you think?

3 **2** Students may come across some of the many words English has borrowed from other languages. The ones mentioned here are the most common.

Answers and recording script

in lieu of	instead of
ad infinitum	to infinity / without end
ad nauseam	continually so as to bore someone
par excellence	pre-eminently
quid pro quo	something in return
faux pas	a mistake
prima facie	at first sight
niche	recess in a wall, a suitable place, sector
risqué	racy – usually jokes
protégé	someone you have under your wing / a follower
fracas	disturbance
cul-de-sac	street open at one end only
clique	small group of people not welcoming to outsiders
nom de plume	pseudonym used when writing
bête noire	something you dislike
tête à tête	friendly, confiding conversation
hoi polloi	the ordinary people
coup de grâce	finishing stroke

4 This exercise can be done for homework if time is short.

a faux pas **b** in lieu **c** nom de plume **d** risqué **e** tête à tête **f** ad nauseam / ad infinitum **g** cul-de-sac **h** bête noire

5 Ask students to read the information in their books. Check that they realise that hesitating, if it is in English, is acceptable, as long as it isn't for too long! Refer them to the expressions at the bottom of the page. Time them as they speak. They have two minutes each on their subject.

Extension activity

Ask students to work in pairs. Each student should prepare one of the following tasks. They will then have to speak to and be questioned by their partner on their particular task. They shouldn't use notes when they speak.

Task A

What qualities make an ideal:

- friend?
- husband/wife?
- president?

Task B

What is your ideal job?

- pay
- conditions
- qualifications

Writing folder 10

Part 2 Articles and Letters

1   Suggest students discuss the tasks in pairs. Elicit their answers about functions and then ask them to consider the style and tone.

Answers
Functions
A   factual description; speculation; narrative
B   factual description; opinion
C   opinion; comparison; speculation
D   evaluation; opinion
E   description; opinion; evaluation

Style and tone
A   should be light-hearted, as this is requested.
B   should be fairly serious.
C   (letter) should be formal; could be fairly light (anecdotal) or more serious.
D   could be either, depending on the set book.
E   (letter) should be formal and polite.

2   Explain that this activity is to remind students of some of the vocabulary they have learned during the course, which might be relevant to these tasks.

Suggested answers
A   adventure, exhilarating, expansion, far-flung, historic, likelihood, multiplicity, unknown, venture
B   emissions, expansion, global warming, impinge, intolerable, judicious, multiplicity, perspective, tendency, trend, wipe out
C   birthrate, bread-winner, code, domesticity, historic, intolerable, likelihood, morals, patriarch, rules, stress, trend, unemployment
D   code, denouement, exhilarating, judicious, morals, perspective, plot, rules, tendency, trend, unmistakable
E   context, denouement, judicious, plot, unmistakable

3   Stress to students that they will not have time in the exam to write a rough copy first. They should make a paragraph plan and then start writing their answer.

4   Allow students to choose one of the tasks on page 174 for homework, following the instructions on timing and reading all the advice given.

Units 17–20 Revision

SB pages 176–177

Lesson plan	
Use of English	25–40 minutes
Writing	30–40 minutes
SV	Set 4 for homework.
LV	Elicit students' reactions to the text in 1.

The aim of this revision unit is to focus on the language covered in Units 17–20 and to provide support for the Part 2 Articles and letters (see Writing folder 10). Specific exam practice is provided on Use of English Paper 1 Parts 1, 2 and 4. These tasks could be done as a timed test of 30 minutes. Alternatively, the whole unit could be set for homework.

Use of English

1

Answers
1 A   2 A   3 D   4 B   5 B   6 A   7 C   8 A

2

Answers
1 mustn't/shouldn't/can't allow the rumours to carry | on OR mustn't/shouldn't/can't let the rumours carry | on
2 needn't have helped | us do/with
3 come when/whenever he likes | as far as I'm
4 to preserve/protect her anonymity, | I had the press
5 her sore throat / having a sore throat, Eliza | excelled (herself)
6 other than / less than / but a full apology | would be acceptable

3

Answers
1 with   2 for   3 being/remaining   4 their   5 whether
6 at   7 its   8 needs/has/ought

Vocabulary

4

Answers
a click   b peal   c growled   d trusting   e derisive
f head   g waste   h tangent   i faux pas   j fracas

Writing

5

Sample answer
A strange being stood stock still in the middle of the road. There was mist swirling around and it was impossible to make out who or what it was, but I swear I could see horns on its head and a pair of evil, red eyes. As I rammed on the brakes, the radio crackled and went dead. I sat there for a moment, staring in the gloom, trying to work out what was ahead. Then, steeling myself, I sounded the car horn repeatedly and drove towards the ghastly creature, which thankfully bounded off across the moorland as I approached.
(100 words)

Crossword

This includes some of the idioms, phrasal verbs and other vocabulary from Units 17–20.

Photocopiable recording scripts

Unit 1, 1.1 Exercise 3

Speaker 1

I've had a really fantastic year. It all started last November, when I was dragged along to a party by a friend. I was in a terrible mood, I remember, and nearly didn't go. Anyway, I was wearing an outfit I'd made myself – in soft black leather and antique lace, quite an unusual combination! Kelly Johns, the presenter of a big daytime TV show, was there and my little number caught her eye. We got chatting and she asked whether I could come up with something original for her to wear on the show. I jumped at the opportunity. That was a real turning point for me and I was soon able to quit my day job and concentrate on the clothes side full time. Through Kelly's show, I've had lots of orders. I've just finished an exclusive range for a top designer and I've even taken on an assistant to help me. Just think if I'd stayed at home that night!

Speaker 2

People often ask me how I got to be where I am today, with sell-out concerts in big stadiums around the world, thinking that I've spent years playing in local clubs, but the truth is, I'm literally an overnight sensation! I don't mean that arrogantly. It was just one lucky break, all down to being in the right place at the right time. There I was, an absolute nobody, hanging around backstage with Arrowhead, when their lead guitarist tripped over a pile of speakers and broke his arm, five minutes before they were due on. I'd been telling them about my awesome guitar style, so naturally, they all turned to me and said 'Kid, help us out here …' and I did. The place was packed and I can still feel my hands shaking as I played that very first solo. It went OK though, and the rest is … history.

Speaker 3

I was in Milan visiting friends, trying to cheer myself up after a dismal few months – my long-term boyfriend and I had broken up, plus I'd left a job without another to go to. My money was running out and I was planning to leave a few days later. Anyway, my friends suggested that I should take a look at Verona before going back home and told me what time train I could get from Milan. Well, for some reason, I ended up on a slow train going south, without realising my mistake – both trains had left at the same time. I fell asleep in the compartment and woke just as the train arrived in Bologna! I had a wander round and fell in love with the place, and knew it was where I wanted to be. Everything just fell into place – I found a teaching job, took a room in a beautiful flat and settled in immediately. I lived there for six years and I go back regularly.

Speaker 4

It's funny how you can hit a run of bad luck: one moment, things are moving along quite normally in your life and then, bam, something comes out of the blue and knocks you sideways and then, wham, something else. I'm OK now, but I've had a difficult couple of years. My problem was quite simply that I'd been living beyond my means for a long time and some debts finally caught up with me. Even then, I thought I'd be OK; I arranged to pay them off little by little from my salary, monthly, you know. But then, the place where I was working cut back on its workforce, and they let me go. Well, that was it, I suppose I panicked, I wasn't thinking straight, you know. So I just packed a bag, got on a coach and left town for London, where my life went downhill fast. I got in with a bad crowd, and one thing led to another. It's a miracle my brother ever tracked me down, but he's got me back and sorted, with a roof over my head and a new job on the cards.

Speaker 5

It could be a story in *True Romance*, but it really happened just like this. Almost twenty years ago to the day, I was waiting for a bus after another mind-numbingly awful day at work, no bus in sight, of course. I was in a rut, my job was going nowhere. Anyway, there I was, staring gloomily at my reflection in a puddle, feeling utterly sorry for myself and thinking: is this really all there is to life? Then I saw two things in that puddle, one imperceptibly after the other. The first was no surprise, huge splashes of rain, as the heavens opened yet again, but then, this enormous red umbrella, appearing behind my head as if by magic! A gorgeous gravelly voice to my left said did I mind, it was big enough for two and he didn't want my hair to get wet. Very fortunately, it was another fifteen minutes before the bus finally turned up and hooray, it didn't stop raining! His name was Terence, though he's been Terry to me ever since – and Dad to our three wonderful children.

Unit 3, 3.1 Exercise 2

Sue: Good morning. Now, the huge growth of interest in environmental issues has led to a careful re-examination of all kinds of traditional lore. With me today, I have Peter Watkins. He's written a best-selling book *The History of Weather Folklore*, which explains country sayings and the role of animals and birds in forecasting the weather. Sayings my granny used to come out with like, *Birds flying low, expect rain and a blow*, which I've always felt rather sceptical about.

Peter: Well, Sue, the way in which animals and birds can apparently predict changes in the weather before we can has always fascinated people and, for that matter, still does. If it didn't, the sayings wouldn't still be in current use, and of course, nowadays the weather is anxiously studied because of climate change.

Sue: But is there any truth in these old sayings? Given that there are so many, apparently 500 at the last count, and they've been around a while, presumably they should be fairly accurate?

Peter: Mm, well generally, there's a better chance of their being right for short-term weather forecasting rather than long-term. Of course, the most interesting natural weather forecasters are the birds, which is why there are so many sayings relating to them. Birds depend on the right weather conditions for flying and, in particular, birds that fly very high, like swifts and swallows, stand very little chance of survival if they get caught in a bad storm. They are also insect feeders and when the weather is fine the insects are high and the birds will follow them. Insects have good reason to dive for cover if rain is imminent as they are covered with water-repellent hairs. It actually doesn't take much for them to get completely soaked, so they respond quite rapidly if there's a drop in temperature or a rise in humidity.

Sue: Oh, so there's an element of truth in that one. Now, I used to live off the coast of Scotland and they had a saying on the islands about a bird called the red-throated diver. They used to call this bird the rain goose, and the saying went pretty much like this: *If the rain goose flies to the hill, you can put your boat where you will, but if she flies to the sea, you must draw your boat and flee*. I must say that I used to be rather puzzled by this saying, as I didn't understand why it would fly out to sea when the weather was getting worse. Anyway, one time when I was out in a boat the wind started to get up. We tuned into the radio and it said a gale was due from the north. We saw the geese everywhere flying around and heading out to sea. So despite common sense telling you otherwise, the saying of the local people seemed to be true.

Peter: Yes, and we still don't know the reasons for its strange behaviour. But you know, not all weather lore is about misery. Some birds can predict when things are about to brighten up. Certain geese set off for their breeding grounds in Iceland when the weather is fine – you just have to wait and watch and then plan your harvesting or house painting!

Sue: Not very practical! However, if there is some truth behind these weather sayings, do they ever have any practical use?

Peter: Obviously, weather lore had a very important application in the farmer's world. Farming and weather are intrinsically linked and the ability to predict, or at least think you could predict, was very important to them, although of course, they weren't the only ones with a vested interest in weather forecasting. One of the things about human beings is that we do not like to feel that things are happening with no purpose whatsoever. Weather lore makes a connection between something that is happening and something that is going to happen – we need to feel we're not simply the victims of chance and circumstance. Although it's very difficult to put dates on these sayings, many of them probably go back thousands of years. Some of them work and some of them don't, and some of them don't even make sense. Many actually negate each other.

Sue: Quite. So, how reliable are sayings which predict the year ahead, if we can't even rely on ones predicting the weather the next day?

Peter: Mm, well, I find it very difficult to believe that you can tell the rest of the winter from the way birds are flying or how your cat behaves in the autumn. By putting our own interpretations on how nature works we can get it completely wrong. For our ancestors the weather was a life and death situation – not just an inconvenience – and I think that had they had anything more reliable, they wouldn't have had to base their predictions on this kind of thing. They were really clutching at straws when they observed animal and bird behaviour and linked it to the weather, but they really had no other choice.

Sue: My thanks to Peter Watkins. Next week we'll …

Objective Proficiency Second Edition by Annette Capel and Wendy Sharp

Unit 4, 4.1 Exercise 2

Unlike many modern families, mine still holds to the tradition of large family meals at times of celebration or crisis. I use the word 'large' of both the group and the amount of food on offer. The pattern is always the same: endless phone calls weeks ahead of the occasion to mobilise distant cousins and elderly aunts; on the eve of the event, the preparation of excessive amounts of food by the host family member, which never fails to be stress-inducing for all concerned; and then, on the day itself, we slip into our well-established roles, devouring all that is set before us and expressing the joy and contentment that convention demands. Once the wine has started to flow, the praise of succulent dishes gives way to another, more sinister part of the ritual: snide comments on family members not present, the surfacing of ancient grudges and petty family rivalries. This in turn leads to the more general but equally predictable debates on politics and the world at large. Manners always prevent us from actual bodily assault, but the verbal gloves are certainly off at this late stage in the proceedings. As the insults start to fly, the host hurries away to prepare coffee, hunting out chocolates and jugs of ice-cold water, in a valiant attempt to restore calm. Ritual behaviour dictates that all hostilities cease at this point and so, finally, peace prevails. After his second cup of coffee, handing down a final blessing to the assembled group, the most senior member takes his leave, signalling that it is time for others to do the same. Another memorable family occasion draws to a close.

Objective Proficiency Second Edition by Annette Capel and Wendy Sharp

PHOTOCOPIABLE RECORDING SCRIPTS

Unit 5, 5.1 Exercise 3

Paula: Good morning. On the programme today we have Mike James, a familiar face on television as the champion of consumers' rights. Mike, you've been doing *Pricewise* a long time now, is it something you set out to do?

Mike: Far from it Paula. It all began in 2002, when I was a reporter on a nightly news programme. They wanted a consumer slot, so I took it on. It wasn't until nearly ten years later that it became a programme in its own right. Now, we regularly get more than ten million viewers.

Paula: Where do the stories you look into come from?

Mike: Well, from you, the public. We get thousands of letters, phone calls and emails that tell us about poor service, ridiculous small print, malpractice and the need for information. We actually read all the correspondence and we follow up some stories immediately but most are filed for future use on our database.

Paula: What happens when you get a particularly juicy story?

Mike: We check it out thoroughly of course, and then we contact everyone involved, write the script and arrange filming. Sometimes we use actors and sometimes real people. Of course, it's essential that our lawyers check the script over. It's all done to very tight deadlines.

Paula: Do any particular stories stand out in your memory?

Mike: Oh, yes, many. There was one about an advert which promised to give you a title for anything up to £1,000. So, Bob and Trace became Lord Robert and Lady Tracy de Vere. You also get a piece of land but that only measures 20cm by 20cm. One of our researchers handed over the cash and tried to find out if being a lord would help him out in London.

Paula: And did it?

Mike: He went to Harrods, the department store, and they were very nice to him, but then they're nice to everyone. He then tried to book a table in a trendy restaurant and he got one – but not in a prime position next to the window – but by the kitchen door! So, really, it won't do you a lot of good being a lord nowadays.

Paula: Any other interesting stories?

Mike: Well, we did a programme not long ago about shopping on the Internet. The big supermarkets will deliver to your door if you order online, as you know.

Paula: Yes, it's a great idea, but I've not actually tried it out.

Mike: Well, it does usually work well. However, we did find that some customers hadn't received quite what they'd ordered. One poor man had asked for apples and got hairspray! The supermarket was very apologetic when we pointed out these problems and sent the customer some shopping vouchers.

Paula: Do you think consumers are more ready to complain these days?

Mike: Oh, yes. Research has been done that shows that attitudes have changed remarkably in the last forty years. Take a well-known brand of trainer. You could understand if they leaked, but actually these particular ones squeaked. Now, as they cost upwards of a hundred pounds, people weren't prepared to put up with this, but when they returned them to the shop, the shop didn't want to know.

Paula: So they wrote to you for help.

Mike: Yes. We bought a pair of the trainers and sent them to be inspected by an expert who said that some of the glue inside the shoe had come unstuck. We contacted the manufacturer with evidence of the problem and they were more than happy to back down and refund the money paid by the purchasers.

Paula: Another success then.

Mike: Yes, it's funny how quickly manufacturers and retailers react when they think they might attract bad publicity.

Paula: Indeed! It just shows what a good job you're doing. Now next week …

Unit 8, 8.3 Exercise 2

Interviewer: OK, well there are three people sitting in the studio with me now – Sally, Meg and Kevin – who are about to embark on a rather unusual 'lifeplan' as they call it, something that will bring about a change of gear for all three of them. By way of introduction, we need to go through some recent history, and I'm going to start with you, Sally, because it's your discontent about where you're living now that has played a large part in all this. Sally, tell us where you and Meg call home at the moment.

Sally: It's a tiny village in the Welsh hills, which no one will have heard of. Last November we quit London and headed for the border. Mum and Dad decided to go their separate ways, you see – I think Mum took this literally, she wanted to get as far away as possible from Dad at the time.

Meg: It wasn't quite like that, but yes, the divorce had a lot to do with needing to get out of the city and start again.

Interviewer: So out of the blue you chose a remote Welsh village?

Meg: Not quite, I had good friends there …

Sally: Who have since left.

Meg: Yes, but, well, anyway, as Sally will tell you, it hasn't quite worked out for her, though for me at the beginning, winding down was a godsend, it gave me the chance to rethink my life and decide on priorities.

Interviewer: Mm, so, Sally, why has it been less than perfect for you?

Sally: I'm 15 now and I left really good friends behind me, some I'd known my whole life. Plus, I've had to learn Welsh to even function at school and that's been hard. And as you can imagine, there isn't exactly a lot to do where we are – most people of my age just hang around the village green or go to each others' houses. It's not that great. Fortunately, I've been staying some weekends at my Dad's place – so I can meet up with some of my old friends, go to clubs, you know.

Interviewer: Mmm … so the country idyll, not such good news for you, but for you, Meg, you're content with your life there?

Meg: Yes and no-o. I have to confess that once the honeymoon period was over (a rather unfortunate term in my case) well, you know after a while I woke up and realised that this wasn't right for me either. It's hard to pin down exactly why – I don't suffer from boredom, and I still get a rush out of the sheer beauty and calm that surrounds us, but I … I feel that I'm missing out too, that I should be working, socialising more, going to exhibitions, all those things I used to take for granted, but which are totally out of the frame at the moment.

Interviewer: And that's where Kevin comes in …

Kevin: One lucky break all round …

Sally: Well, it's pretty flukey. Basically Mum and I sat down one night and agreed we had to get back somehow … but we realised that there was no way we could expect to move back to London as easily as we'd left.

Meg: Selling the cottage wouldn't be easy, and nor would finding somewhere in our price range in London.

Sally: Mum had this real brainwave. She decided to look for anyone who might be interested in changing places, house swaps, that sort of thing.

Kevin: And thanks to the power of the Internet, they tracked me down.

Interviewer: And everything's fallen into place. But what's in it for you, Kevin? You've already told me you have a large flat in a very desirable part of London, a good job, …

Kevin: What I've got is a nice flat I hardly ever see, a high-profile, high-stress job in share-dealing, no girlfriend, 'cos she dumped me a month ago, so life's not exactly a bed of roses. But I've been very successful and can afford to negotiate my future. Well, I want to get out for a while but not burn my boats completely, so Meg's proposal is perfect.

Interviewer: And how is this lifeplan going to unfold now?

Meg: In a nutshell, we've agreed to change places for three months initially, swapping everything – we leave the car, the furniture, the tins of soup in the kitchen …

Kevin: Not the clothes though!

Meg: If we're all happy, then we'll extend to a year, which will give Sally and I a wonderful base in London and Kevin some peace and quiet to realise his dream.

Interviewer: Which is?

Kevin: I've got an idea for the next bestseller, a racy paperback on city slickers.

Interviewer: Ah, plenty of first-hand experience to draw on – sounds promising! And Sally, you'll get back your social life, but isn't it potentially disruptive, to your schooling and so on?

Sally: We're going to be moving at the start of a new school year, so there's a natural break anyway. And if things don't pan out, I can always move in with Dad.

Meg: But I think we're all quietly confident that it *will* work out.

Kevin: Yeah, 'cos it's what we all want deep down. And if I make it as a writer, well it might end up a permanent arrangement, you know, six months on, six off, the best of both worlds.

Interviewer: Well, they say *the grass is always greener*, but you seem to have things pretty much sorted out. Meg, Sally, Kevin, the very best of luck.

All: Thank you.

Objective Proficiency Second Edition by Annette Capel and Wendy Sharp

PHOTOCOPIABLE RECORDING SCRIPTS

Unit 9, 9.1 Exercise 5

Speaker 1

When I left school, I was taken on by an environmental charity. I turned up in a suit, but instead of being stuck behind a desk, I was out on the streets, fundraising. My boss at that time was a bit of a rebel. She had quite a funky hairdo and tended to wear ethnic stuff she'd picked up on her travels. I guess she came across as something of a hippie. We got on really well and I thought I'd opt for the same kind of outfits – I can't remember anyone saying anything to make me do that but, to be honest, I think the others at work saw me more as one of them. But I do remember my mother not recognising me when she saw me in the street!

Speaker 2

I play in a metal band called Zandroid. I have a dragon tattoo on my face and wear a leather jacket with a dragon on it. It does mean that people can spot me immediately and I'm constantly getting asked for autographs when I'm out which is great! It makes me feel loved by the fans I guess! I had the tattoo done properly by this guy who I really respect and it wasn't cheap, I can tell you. It was funny how my look came about – I was on the train to a music festival and I picked up one of those free papers. There was a whole thing about dragons in it. I was hooked on the idea in a flash.

Speaker 3

The dress code at my school is fairly formal so I have to wear smart clothes, but I go for tops and trousers rather than suits and high heels. I wouldn't want to raise too many eyebrows among the other staff members so no jeans. Not that the school is super posh or anything, but very casual clothes wouldn't go down too well. What I wear is great really because I have to spend quite a bit of time delving into cupboards. I tend to go for high-end clothes which aren't skin tight – ones that move with me. And they should last – if they were cheap, they'd soon come apart.

Speaker 4

When I left university, I had long hair and wore old jeans. Job interviews were coming up and I didn't want to get up any interviewer's nose and lose out on a good job. There was this job advertised which seemed perfect as a designer at this factory making cars, so I got myself a suit and tie and landed the job. I realised later that I'd got hold of the wrong end of the stick as no one was the least bit bothered, but there you go, better safe than sorry. Anyway, one thing I've found is that suits are good as there's only a minimum outlay and now we have dress-down Friday I can still wear my jeans then.

Speaker 5

I'm Indian, but I live in the US, doing research in a university. For years, I've worn western clothes, mainly skirts and blouses. I'd always steered clear of the sari as it seemed to me to be not quite right for the workplace, although some other colleagues wear them. Something changed for me last year when I went back to India to see my relatives. The women in saris looked so elegant and I realised that the only person who was stopping me wear one was myself. Now, when I put on my sari, I feel pride in my heritage and realise that what I wear is not going to come between me and promotion or being accepted by others.

Objective Proficiency Second Edition by Annette Capel and Wendy Sharp

Unit 11, 11.1 Exercise 3

Interviewer: Last week, Steve came into the studio to prove to us that life still has some happy endings. Here's his story … So, Steve, your relationship with Abby has been through some ups and downs but is definitely on a high now?

Steve: That's right, and we're finally tying the knot next month. Just over five years ago, I met this bubbly little lady – Abby. We went out, shared some laughs, and pretty soon, I knew she was the one for me.

Interviewer: And was it love at first sight for her too?

Steve: She was happy enough to spend lots of time with me, but treated me more like a big brother, if anything – she even told me about another guy she was hoping to get together with. At which point, realising I would get nowhere romantically, I decided I'd better cast my net elsewhere. I met a nice girl called Samantha, very down-to-earth – the opposite of Abby – and we started seeing each other once in a while. We had well-paid jobs and money to burn. After a good holiday in Spain, we decided to move in together. I think we both understood that it wasn't true love, but we rubbed along fairly well. Unfortunately, quite soon after that, Abby made up her mind that I was Mr Right after all, and made this very plain to me, though not to Samantha.

Interviewer: How did you take this bolt from the blue?

Steve: It was baffling. I actually wondered whether she was joking, she used to do that, but I knew deep down she wouldn't pull that trick any more. I rationalised it as her whipping up a fleeting fantasy – she had time on her hands, as she'd been fired from her job and was on her own a lot – her then current boyfriend worked long hours.

Interviewer: And there were displays of obvious jealousy, weren't there?

Steve: Yeah, we'd be at the same pubs and there would be anguished looks from Abby across the room, deep sighs if she was ever standing next to me at the bar, that sort of thing – I misread the situation for ages – she's always had a streak of theatricality.

Interviewer: What was your reaction once you realised it was genuine?

Steve: Well, it dawned on me that I was calling the tune now; if I wanted it, Abby and I would have a life together – otherwise, things would stay the same. It wasn't straightforward, there was Samantha to consider. She'd always been very supportive and loyal. For a while, I couldn't decide what to do. To fend off the problem, I threw myself into my job.

Interviewer: And did colleagues at work pick up on anything different about you?

Steve: Very much so – I'd never been that keen and efficient before! Although my daily routine was much the same, I was glad to get to work, because it distracted me – but I made sure I kept my private life out of our usual conversations. As time went on, there was growing pressure on me to do something – for all I knew, Abby might give up in disgust.

Interviewer: Then, one summer's day …

Steve: Yes, one beautiful morning last June, I couldn't keep up the pretence any longer. I sat Samantha down at the kitchen table and blurted everything out. She was terrific, far from holding back tears, she didn't even seem mildly phased by the revelation that I'd been carrying a torch for someone else and it was over. Just rolled up her sleeves and started sorting out my life for me: phoned my office to say that I was at death's door and wouldn't be coming in, then told me to get round to Abby's place pronto, preferably with a big bunch of flowers – she let me buy those myself.

Interviewer: And so Samantha walked out of your life and Abby walked in.

Steve: Yeah. Abby and I rented a cottage out in the country. Last summer was idyllic, and, well, it matched our mood. We got to know each other properly, spent every evening gazing into each other's eyes at sunset and … well, I'm sure you can picture the rest.

Interviewer: Absolute rapture, straight out of *True Romance* … how wonderfully slushy! So when did you finally pop the question, Steve?

Steve: I was at a big family wedding, one of my cousins, and Abby hadn't come, I think she had flu. Anyway everything seemed to fall into place at that event. I managed to sit down with my mother and talk about Abby – Mum'd been giving me the cold shoulder, as she'd really liked Samantha and, social norms being what they are, had seen her as a prospective daughter-in-law. Anyway, she came round after our heart-to-heart and I went off to offer a lift to my cousin's old schoolfriend, who lives in the States – I hadn't seen him for five years. Well, he looked me between the eyes and said, 'You've always loved Abby, so how come you're not married yet – get a grip, Steve.' So I did, leapt in the car without him, drove back and proposed. It's funny though, it had taken someone at one stage removed from my life to state the obvious.

Interviewer: Well, Steve, I wish you and Abby every happiness – you certainly deserve it.

Steve: Thank you.

Unit 12, 12.3 Exercise 3

Interlocutor: Now, in this part of the test you're each going to talk on your own for about two minutes. You need to listen while your partner is speaking because you'll be asked to comment afterwards.

So Jana, I'm going to give you a card with a question written on it and I'd like you to tell us what you think. There are also some ideas on the card for you to use if you like.

All right? Here is your card.

Jana: Well, I don't have a scientific background, but I think science is something that affects us all nowadays. You can't afford to ignore what's going on in advanced science. There's a lot of media interest right now in the latest developments in, say, genetics and DNA profiling. Er, I do think it's worrying how genetic testing can be used, actually. For example, if you have a genetic disorder of some kind, you may not be able to take out life insurance … or get a job even. But then, on the other hand, DNA analysis is helping to solve crimes, and that's good for society, so it's good and bad, I suppose.

The main problem centres around information. Most people don't know the facts and so naturally they're worried. So what is needed is more information in simple language for ordinary people to understand – and perhaps this needs to come from the government. Because I think the biggest worry of all is that the whole area of genetics is being driven by the business world. Much of the research going on today is backed by big companies – drugs co…, pharma… pharmaceutical companies and so on – and they're going to want something back from their investment. Which means that the research is not being done just as research, it's not pure, not independent. … I think too, that they're not controlling this research.

The public needs to be properly informed. There are potential benefits, yes, but we must be told what's happening and why. You know, things are being pushed ahead at such an alarming rate and … mm, I don't know, it seems to me, it's maybe not always going to be helpful for society.

Interlocutor: Thank you. Erik, what is your view on current career opportunities in science?

Erik: I'm actually in the final year of a biology degree so I can comment on that personally. We're always being told by our lecturers that more progress will be made in biology in the next five to ten years than has occurred in the last fifty. It's a fast-moving field. As Jana said, there are many new companies … biotech companies springing up, so yes, job prospects are good for someone like me, I think, plenty of different directions to go in. So it's not all doom and gloom, far from it.

Interlocutor: What do you think, Jana?

Jana: Well, Erik is speaking from experience! It's good to hear his positive take on things.

Interlocutor: Thank you.

Unit 14, 14.3 Exercise 2

Alice: Health scares – don't they make you sick! Or do they challenge your complacency? Every few days a new story appears in the newspaper about, first of all, butter is bad for you, then butter is good for you. Salt is bad for us, salt is good for us. You just have to pick up a cup of coffee and you're engaged in a health debate. With me today to discuss this issue is Professor Robert Atkins. Robert, what do you think about all this?

Robert: Personally, I'd rather have ten false health scares and one of them prove to be serious – then it leads to action, than the cynical sense that somehow all this is just a media confection. That's what I really object to.

Alice: Mm, but how often do health scares come true?

Robert: There are random events in which microbes do emerge. They can be extraordinarily lethal and these account for massive epidemics that have occurred in the past in human history and I think we would be arrogant in the extreme to think that such things may not occur again in the future.

Alice: You're thinking of bubonic plague, of course. But nowadays it seems is the best of times and the worst of times if you want to be healthy. This is a paradox, because, on the one hand, we live in a relatively healthy society. Our longevity is unprecedented. By historical standards communicable lethal disease is exceptionally controlled. Yet we seem to be getting better, but feeling worse. Why, if we're so healthy, are we so easily spooked?

Robert: If you were living two or three hundred years ago, you were in the hands of God or Fate and if you were struck down by a mortal disease you thought you'd been sinful, but you also had your beliefs to console you – you'd go to paradise or heaven or whatever. Nowadays, we have tremendously high expectations about long healthy life continuing and some of us no longer have an expectation of an afterlife. It's partly a matter of a crisis of rising expectations.

Alice: Um, so our health anxiety is like a big eater's gluttony or a rich man's miserliness. Health excites expectations of perfection. It's also an anxiety spread by commercial concerns, isn't it?

Robert: Indeed. The margarine industry, for example, is actually now a very powerful instrument in pushing the line that butter is bad for you and actually there's a strong industrial lobby that has a stake in making sure that we are all anxious and worried about our health.

Alice: And they're not the only players. If health scares sell pills they also sell papers. And what about the research community which keeps the health scare industry supplied with stories?

Robert: Health is always in the news. Sometimes it's the doctors themselves who are maybe responsible. In every branch of life there are people who like a touch of publicity and enjoy the turbulence. Others are often so convinced by their findings that they ignore the critical views of other doctors and have this urge to promulgate their ideas when it may not be appropriate to do so. If I wanted to avoid heart disease, I'd be taking aspirins, reducing my weight, I would probably frequent my local gym a bit more. I would eat this, that and the other and so on. Then there might be another disease I might get. What do I do then?

Alice: Mm, how much difference would it make to you if you made all those changes? Should you just discount what you read and hear?

Robert: Who knows? Some health scares can actually seriously damage your health – they lead to stress, deprive us of the comfort of eating chocolate and clog up doctors' waiting rooms. There is clearly an information overload and unfortunately, when the real thing comes along, people might have difficulty distinguishing it from all the background noise.

Alice: And of course it's difficult to disprove something once a claim has been made, however fallacious that risk is. Thank you, Professor Robert Atkins.

Unit 15, 15.1 Exercise 3

Interviewer: Diane Webber, you've switched careers more than once during your own working life, and you now run a highly regarded employment agency for media high-fliers, where, above all, you advise your clients, both companies and applicants, to be fully flexible. You seem to see this as a fundamental principle, if your agency slogan – 'Keeping your options open' – is anything to go by. Is that a fair assessment of how you operate?

Diane Webber: Absolutely. I know that not so very long ago we used to see jobs for life as the norm, with unquestioning company loyalty, and a golden handshake at the end of it all – which, nine times out of ten, probably wasn't in actual fact deserved – but things are very different now. And yes, there does seem to be something positive in all this, despite the obvious question mark over security. Successful players in the current job market cut their teeth in one firm, and are willing to step sideways more than once to gain fresh experience. Unlike their predecessors, they may only progress up the rungs when they land their third or fourth job, or even later in their career. This increased movement brings benefits, not just for them, but for the companies they work for, too.

Interviewer: In spite of the instability? Surely it's important to have some continuity?

Diane Webber: Well actually, it's a mixed blessing. Individuals can get terribly stale if they stick in one place for too long, especially if they report to managers who fail to challenge them. That implies a hierarchy riddled with complacency and under-achievement, which can no longer be tolerated in today's fast-moving, dog-eat-dog world. Also, much of today's work consists of fixed-term projects, done in teams, and if one or two members drop out along the way, it really doesn't matter, provided that the team remains an entity. The one exception to this is the team leaders themselves, who are not only the driving force, but the guardians of the project, who hold important historical detail in their heads, so yes, continuity is important there. But even then it's a clearly defined cycle. We're frequently approached by highly-experienced team leaders who, having completed one project, decide they can't face even the slightest whiff of repetition and so come to us seeking fresh challenges.

Interviewer: And they manage to find work?

Diane Webber: Oh, they're snapped up! Because generally speaking, a project-based job can easily demonstrate a track record, it's there in the successful completion of the project.

Interviewer: And these people would have no problem getting references from the employers they're essentially walking out on? I would have thought that that could be an issue …

Diane Webber: Employers don't view it like that at all. Their mindset is different now, as I said earlier, and companies actually take steps to foster a more dynamic environment, as they feel this yields better productivity, though the jury's still out on this, in my view. Nevertheless, with a flow of people, there's a quantum leap in terms of the ideas generated, not to mention the chance of new ways of problem-solving imported from elsewhere. These effects are tangible and they're often very attractive because they're perceived as lean and efficient, instant solutions, even if they generally turn out to be only quick fixes which later have to be reversed.

Interviewer: Ah, but isn't that the nub of it all, that this shifting and fragmented approach leads to poor decisions? Of course, the perpetrators are never taken to task, as they've already made a quick exit and are knocking on your door for another job!

Diane Webber: That's a bit unfair! For one thing, there've always been bad decisions. No company can rely on its personnel to make the right choices one hundred per cent of the time – even with the help of highly-paid outside consultants, staff will continue to get it wrong from time to time. However, I'd argue that it's the mediocre employees, who just want to keep their heads down, who are far more likely to cause problems than the risk-takers, who, don't forget, are only as employable as their last success.

Interviewer: Ruthless …

Diane Webber: Pragmatic!

Interviewer: Which brings us neatly back to your slogan, doesn't it? Keeping your options open. How far do you encourage people to go in this?

Diane Webber: With new opportunities opening up all the time, the sky's the limit really. It's certainly never too late to contemplate a move, and so the maxim has to be, don't rule *anything* in or out.

Interviewer: We'll end on that positive note. Diane Webber, thank you.

Diane Webber: It's been a pleasure.

Unit 16, 16.3 Exercise 3

Speaker 1: If I had to single out one book from the many I read last year, it would be *The Dumas Club*, by Arturo Pérez-Reverte – that's in translation from the original Spanish. Although I read the opening couple of chapters quite slowly, I soon got completely immersed in the subtleties of the plot, so much so that I quite literally could not put the book down until I had finished it. Some books have this compelling effect on me, and not just detective stories like this one. What is so skilful about the way *The Dumas Club* has been constructed is that there are two strands to the plot, and as a reader, you assume these are interwoven and all the time you're engaging with the text on this basis, making links and suppositions of your own. Well, without giving anything away, there is a masterful twist, which makes this an exceptional book.

Speaker 2: I read loads of travel writing, partly because I have a penchant for travelling myself. That said, I do expect a lot more than straight description and first-hand observation from a truly great travel book. Redmond O'Hanlon's masterpiece *Congo Journey* does not disappoint! Will Self – the author – named it as one of his books of the year and said he felt like starting it again the minute he'd finished it, which is praise indeed! I'll certainly re-read it at some point. It's got brilliant insights into what is a really remote region of our planet. There's meticulous detail on its wildlife and superb use of dialogue … brings the whole thing to life. And then much more besides – it's funny, moving – so you're reading it on many different levels. Above all, though, you marvel at his sheer guts in enduring such a difficult and dangerous journey. Epic stuff.

Unit 17, 17.1 Exercise 3

Speaker 1

Well, I suppose I would visualise certain snapshots in my life, fleeting moments when I was on cloud nine – the birth of my second child or, more recently, a forest walk on a beautiful morning with the birds singing their hearts out – at times like these, you sort of step outside yourself and think, yes, this is as good as it gets. So it's not about having material possessions or a huge income, though if you have any worries on that front it surely rules out the chance of happiness. It's more to do with personal satisfaction and inner peace.

Speaker 2

For me it's not necessarily a transient feeling. I can recall whole periods of my life when things were basically going right, especially in my career, and I think a positive experience like that works as a catalyst. I suppose I can't have been in the same state of ecstasy from dawn till dusk, but looking back, perhaps through rose-tinted spectacles, it certainly feels that way. But if I had to pick just one event, it would be the elation I felt aged nine on receiving a silver trophy at my first judo contest, something beyond my wildest dreams.

Speaker 3

In my book, it's all to do with shared positive vibes, like infectious laughter rippling through a close family group. Being in a loving relationship is key, as this provides stability. And happiness can be found in small things – the security of a comfortable sofa, curled up with a good book while the wind's howling outside – that's something I remember from my childhood. It may be an old cliché, but it's true, you can't buy it, not at any price.

Speaker 4

Sometimes I've felt a surge of joy in the midst of a perilous situation, and one moment I'll always treasure occurred in the Andes with two fellow-climbers, handling a tricky descent in appalling weather conditions. I hadn't known them that well when we set out, but in that situation, you put yourself on the line and make the impossible happen through mutual trust and cooperation. Others might claim well-being is a mental thing, but that's not what really counts. If you're feeling under the weather, you won't experience emotional highs, so it's vital to stay in shape. Well, that's my view, anyway.

Speaker 5

Locations have always been important to me – they seem to contribute so much to a person's mood. A few years ago, I was studying marine activity on a coral reef, part of a close-knit research team on an otherwise unpopulated and stunningly beautiful island. There was one particular day when I'd done three dives, the last at night, and although I was exhausted, I couldn't turn in. So I went back to the beach alone. I lay on the ghostly white sand, gazing at the canopy of stars above me, and saw the most awesome meteor shower – an absolute first for me. It doesn't always take much to tip the balance in favour of happiness, does it?

Objective Proficiency Second Edition by Annette Capel and Wendy Sharp

Unit 18, 18.2 Exercise 2

Two-and-a-half million animals are used in Australian medical research every year, half a million in Victoria alone. They justify the obscene waste of life like this: animals must be used in order to trial new drugs and treatments safely. But a growing number of doctors and scientists have challenged this line, saying that in fact, animal research is counterproductive. It could in fact be damaging to human health. This is because animals are not like us – their bodies are different, they suffer from different diseases and obviously their reactions to drugs are also different. So animals cannot be used to find cures for humans.

Why does animal testing continue? Answer: it's a huge industry. There are many, many vested interests in animal research, from the big pharmaceutical companies themselves to the manufacturers of the cages that these poor dumb animals end up in. Then, apart from those obvious commercial interests, there are the many scientists who have chosen to base their careers on animal experiments. They would lose their jobs tomorrow if animal testing was stopped, wouldn't they?

Basically, animal research is the ultimate quick fix. In general, it requires many years to monitor the progression of a human disease. Obviously laboratory animals, with their shorter lifespans, tend to decline more rapidly. This means that research projects can be wrapped up quickly. Papers presented, trials successfully concluded, bam, new drugs hit the market. It can't be scientifically sound. But what should have been done – full-scale controlled monitoring within a human population – is ruled out as uneconomic. The hard truth is that just about every medical advance has come about either independently from, or despite, animal research. You shouldn't believe everything you hear, right?

Sample answer sheets: Reading and Use of English

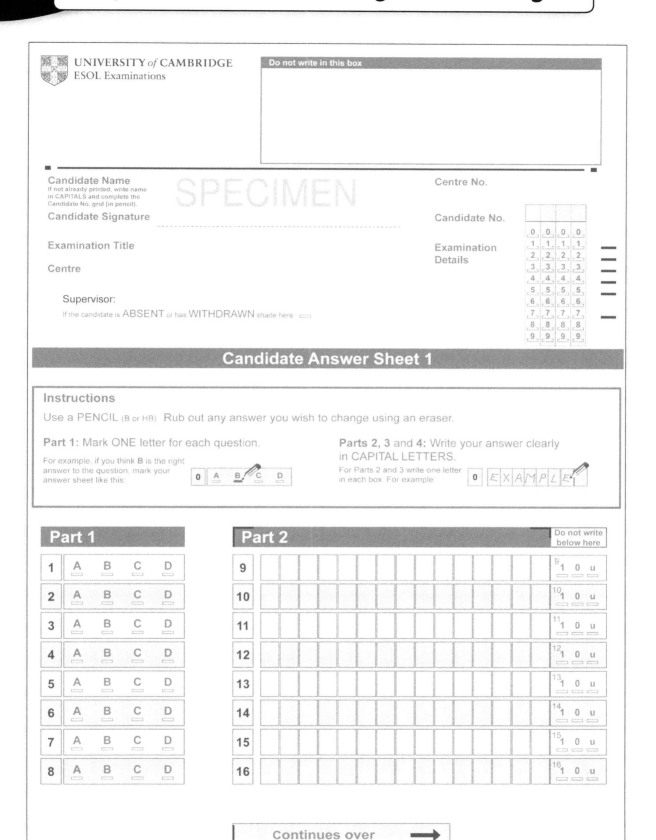

Sample answer sheets: Reading and Use of English

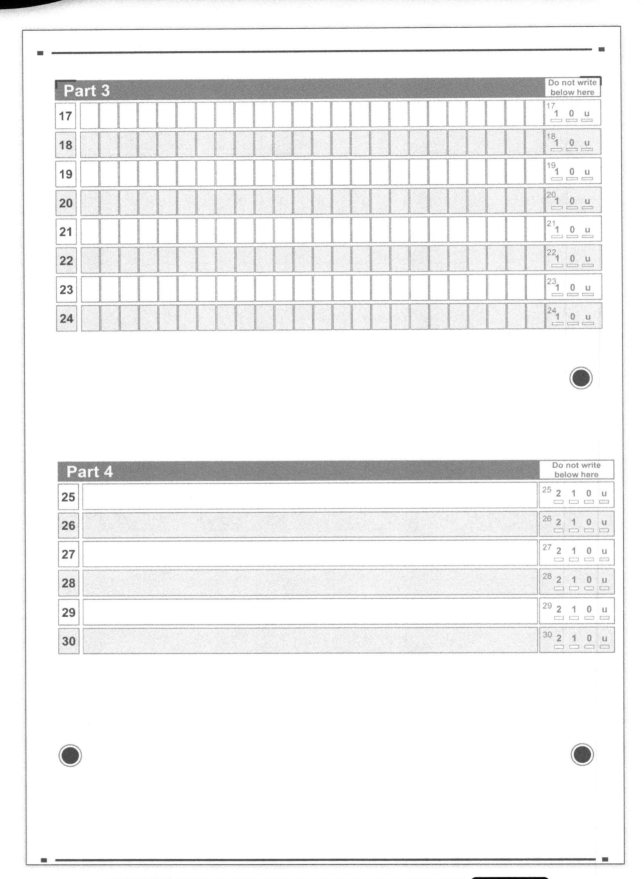

Part 3

Do not write below here

17		17 1 0 u
18		18 1 0 u
19		19 1 0 u
20		20 1 0 u
21		21 1 0 u
22		22 1 0 u
23		23 1 0 u
24		24 1 0 u

Part 4

Do not write below here

25		25 2 1 0 u
26		26 2 1 0 u
27		27 2 1 0 u
28		28 2 1 0 u
29		29 2 1 0 u
30		30 2 1 0 u

Sample answer sheets: Reading and Use of English

UNIVERSITY *of* CAMBRIDGE
ESOL Examinations

Do not write in this box

Candidate Name
If not already printed, write name
in CAPITALS and complete the
Candidate No. grid (in pencil).

SPECIMEN

Candidate Signature

Examination Title

Centre

Supervisor:

If the candidate is ABSENT or has WITHDRAWN shade here ▭

Centre No.

Candidate No.

Examination
Details

0	0	0	0
1	1	1	1
2	2	2	2
3	3	3	3
4	4	4	4
5	5	5	5
6	6	6	6
7	7	7	7
8	8	8	8
9	9	9	9

Candidate Answer Sheet 2

Instructions

Use a PENCIL (B or HB). Rub out any answer you wish to change using an eraser.

Parts 5, 6 and 7: Mark ONE letter for each question.   For example, if you think **B** is the right answer to the question, mark your answer sheet like this.

0 A B̶ C D

Part 5

31	A	B	C	D
32	A	B	C	D
33	A	B	C	D
34	A	B	C	D
35	A	B	C	D
36	A	B	C	D

Part 6

37	A	B	C	D	E	F	G	H
38	A	B	C	D	E	F	G	H
39	A	B	C	D	E	F	G	H
40	A	B	C	D	E	F	G	H
41	A	B	C	D	E	F	G	H
42	A	B	C	D	E	F	G	H
43	A	B	C	D	E	F	G	H

Part 7

44	A	B	C	D	E	F
45	A	B	C	D	E	F
46	A	B	C	D	E	F
47	A	B	C	D	E	F
48	A	B	C	D	E	F
49	A	B	C	D	E	F
50	A	B	C	D	E	F
51	A	B	C	D	E	F
52	A	B	C	D	E	F
53	A	B	C	D	E	F

Sample answer sheets: Listening

UNIVERSITY *of* CAMBRIDGE
ESOL Examinations

Do not write in this box

Candidate Name
If not already printed, write name
in CAPITALS and complete the
Candidate No. grid (in pencil).

Candidate Signature

Examination Title

Centre

Supervisor:
If the candidate is ABSENT or has WITHDRAWN shade here

Test version: A B C D E F J K L M N   Special arrangements: S H

SPECIMEN

Centre No.

Candidate No.

Examination
Details

0	0	0	0
1	1	1	1
2	2	2	2
3	3	3	3
4	4	4	4
5	5	5	5
6	6	6	6
7	7	7	7
8	8	8	8
9	9	9	9

Candidate Answer Sheet

Instructions

Use a PENCIL (B or HB).
Rub out any answer you wish to change using an eraser.

Parts 1, 3 and 4:
Mark ONE letter for each question.

For example, if you think **B** is the
right answer to the question, mark
your answer sheet like this:

Part 2:
Write your answer clearly in CAPITAL LETTERS.

Write one letter or number in each box.
If the answer has more than one word, leave one
box empty between words.

For example:

Turn this sheet over to start.

Sample answer sheets: Listening

Part 1

	A	B	C
1	⬚	⬚	⬚
2	⬚	⬚	⬚
3	⬚	⬚	⬚
4	⬚	⬚	⬚
5	⬚	⬚	⬚
6	⬚	⬚	⬚

Part 2 (Remember to write in CAPITAL LETTERS or numbers)

Do not write below here

7		7 1 0 u
8		8 1 0 u
9		9 1 0 u
10		10 1 0 u
11		11 1 0 u
12		12 1 0 u
13		13 1 0 u
14		14 1 0 u
15		15 1 0 u

Part 3

	A	B	C	D
16	⬚	⬚	⬚	⬚
17	⬚	⬚	⬚	⬚
18	⬚	⬚	⬚	⬚
19	⬚	⬚	⬚	⬚
20	⬚	⬚	⬚	⬚

Part 4

	A	B	C	D	E	F	G	H
21	⬚	⬚	⬚	⬚	⬚	⬚	⬚	⬚
22	⬚	⬚	⬚	⬚	⬚	⬚	⬚	⬚
23	⬚	⬚	⬚	⬚	⬚	⬚	⬚	⬚
24	⬚	⬚	⬚	⬚	⬚	⬚	⬚	⬚
25	⬚	⬚	⬚	⬚	⬚	⬚	⬚	⬚
26	⬚	⬚	⬚	⬚	⬚	⬚	⬚	⬚
27	⬚	⬚	⬚	⬚	⬚	⬚	⬚	⬚
28	⬚	⬚	⬚	⬚	⬚	⬚	⬚	⬚
29	⬚	⬚	⬚	⬚	⬚	⬚	⬚	⬚
30	⬚	⬚	⬚	⬚	⬚	⬚	⬚	⬚

Lightning Source UK Ltd.
Milton Keynes UK
UKHW032111110719
345979UK00003B/21/P